◇

SURVIVING THE SLAUGHTER

HIS

WOMEN IN AFRICA
AND THE DIASPORA

Series Editors

STANLIE JAMES
AILI MARI TRIPP

Surviving the Slaughter

The Ordeal of a Rwandan Refugee in Zaire

MARIE BÉATRICE UMUTESI

Foreword by
CATHARINE NEWBURY

Translated by
JULIA EMERSON

THE UNIVERSITY OF WISCONSIN PRESS

The University of Wisconsin Press
1930 Monroe Street, 3rd Floor
Madison, Wisconsin 53711-2059

www.wisc.edu/wisconsinpress/

3 Henrietta Street
London WC2E 8LU, England

Originally published in France as *Fuir ou Mourir au Zaïre,*
copyright © 2000 L'Harmattan
Translation copyright © 2004 The Board of Regents of the University of Wisconsin System

3   5   4   2

Printed in the United States of America

Library of Congress Cataloging-in-Publication Data
Umutesi, Marie Béatrice, 1959–
[Fuir ou Mourir au Zaïre. English]
Surviving the slaughter : the ordeal of a Rwandan refugee
in Zaire / Marie Béatrice Umutesi;
foreword by Catharine Newbury;
translated by Julia Emerson.
p.   cm. — (Women in Africa and the diaspora)
"Originally published in France as Fuir ou mourir au Zaïre" — T.p. verso.
ISBN 0-299-20490-1 (hardcover : alk. paper)
ISBN 0-299-20494-4 (pbk. : alk. paper)
1. Rwanda — History — Civil War, 1994. — Refugees.
2. Umutesi, Marie Béatrice, 1959–
3. Rwanda — History — Civil War, 1994 — Personal narratives.
4. Genocide — Rwanda.
5. Rwanda — Ethnic relations.
6. Refugees — Congo (Democratic Republic).
7. Rwandans — Congo (Democratic Republic).
I. Title.   II. Series.
DT450.435.U513   2004
305.9′06914′09675109049 — dc22   2004012634

◆

Dedicated to the memory of
ZUZU

Midway upon the journey of our life
I found myself within a forest dark
For the straightforward pathway had been lost
—Dante Alighieri

Contents

Foreword

In the mid-1990s, the tragedies of Central Africa haunted the world. Many works have been published about the Rwanda genocide of 1994, depicting the horror of these atrocious events and exploring why they occurred. We have also seen much soul-searching about the failures of the international community during the genocide. In these studies, however, certain voices were missing. As Béatrice Umutesi shows in this remarkable book, the crisis was not merely a single event—it was a multiplication of catastrophes. Though Umutesi is not an ordinary person, her account helps us understand what "ordinary" individuals lived through—fleeing the genocide in Rwanda, living in crowded refugee camps of eastern Zaire, and then trying to survive during the war of Laurent Kabila and the AFDL rebels in 1996 and 1997.

By describing and trying to interpret what happened during this painful period, the author aspires to rescue from oblivion the memory of the many who did not survive. Some may be tempted to characterize this testimony as emanating from someone who was implicated in the genocide perpetrated against the Tutsi, because the author is Hutu. But as this book makes abundantly clear, many people—irrespective of ethnic category—were caught up in the maelstrom; not all Hutu were *génocidaires*. Other observers will see in this a victim's story, representative of hundreds of thousands of others, as Umutesi fled in a forced march across Zaire's rainforest in the middle of the rainy season. However, such external labels miss the point: this is above all a human account—the story of a person caught up, like so many others, in the whirlwind of the fierce conflicts of her time. It is seldom that we have access to these stories. In this testimony we do; it is an extraordinarily moving account, both by the almost unbelievable force of will it represents and by the simple, unpretentious eloquence by which it is made.

Born in 1959, the author is from the generation of Rwandans that grew up after colonial rule, which formally ended in 1962. With a university degree in sociology, Umutesi became part of Rwanda's educated elite. But she maintained connections with her roots — and especially with women — through her activities promoting the development of rural cooperatives. In the first part of the book she chronicles the dynamics of Tutsi/Hutu relations in the 1960s, 1970s, and 1980s; the escalation of regional tensions among Hutu under Juvénal Habyarimana's regime, when ethnic polarization diminished for a time until the late 1980s; the growing alienation of young Rwandans from the state during the late 1980s and early 1990s; and the political consequences of famine, of rural pauperization, and of the war that started in October 1990 when the Rwandan Patriotic Front (RPF) attacked northern Rwanda.[1]

While some of these themes are familiar, Umutesi provides an often-neglected perspective, that of a woman closely tied to the rural sectors of the country. She shows how these events directly affected members of her family, her professional colleagues (both Hutu and Tutsi), and other people she knew. For example, when describing effects of the war, Umutesi indicates that she became aware of torture and massacres of civilians perpetrated by the RPF in the north because this affected people close to her. In February 1993, when the RPF mounted a major offensive to seize a large swath of territory in northern Rwanda, they attacked Gatete and killed several members of the family of Umutesi's mother. In another incident, at Mwendo in the north, RPF soldiers locked local inhabitants in houses that were then set afire with grenades.[2] Hundreds of thousands of people, mostly Hutu, fled from the region.

1. The RPF was composed largely of Tutsi refugees and their children who had fled from Rwanda decades earlier during episodes of politically motivated violence against Tutsi — in the 1960s during and after the Rwandan Revolution of 1959–1961 (in which the longstanding Rwandan monarchy, dominated by a Tutsi aristocracy, was overthrown) and in 1973 when Tutsi students and salaried workers in Rwanda became the targets of pogroms. The military wing of the RPF was called the Rwandan Patriotic Army (APR); their attack on Rwanda in 1990 aimed to topple the authoritarian regime of Juvénal Habyarimana and win the right of return for Tutsi refugees. To avoid confusion, both the political movement and its military wing will be referred to here as the RPF.

2. In the 1990s most journalists portrayed the RPF in a generally favorable light — viewing their military as a disciplined, well-behaved, professional force. Umutesi, reporting what she and her friends observed, presents a different perspective: The RPF were engaged in a guerilla war in which they committed atrocities. This is now acknowledged in some analyses of the genocide written by academics and human rights organizations such as Human Rights Watch.

In the wake of the 1993 RPF offensive, Umutesi's mother and twenty-five of her relatives came to Kigali to take refuge in her house. They were among the fortunate. Umutesi describes the appalling conditions faced by most of the other displaced persons from the north, congregated in makeshift camps rife with hunger, unsanitary conditions, and lack of medical care.

Umutesi also portrays the effects at the local level of the abortive attempts to promote multiparty politics in Rwanda in the early 1990s — while the country was at war. And she describes the horror of the genocide during April to June of 1994 by referring to the experiences of ordinary people, Tutsi as well as Hutu. More than that, she captures the great confusion, helplessness, fear, and wanton violence that marked this period. In the midst of such fear and confusion, she, along with some two million other Rwandans, mostly Hutu, fled in haste and disarray to Zaire in July 1994.

The central subject to the book is the condition of the Rwandan refugees in Zaire during the 1990s. In its simple honesty and non-manipulative presentation, her account compels us to acknowledge and remember what many highly placed members of the international community tried to ignore at the time. After the destruction of Rwandan refugee camps in eastern Zaire in October and November 1996 by soldiers from Rwanda and by the AFDL army associated with Laurent Kabila, approximately five hundred thousand people returned to Rwanda through the North Kivu camps, passing through Goma and Gisenyi, while many thousands of others fled west, into the forests of Zaire's interior. Umutesi was one of hundreds of thousands of people in the camps in South Kivu, more than 150 kilometers from Goma; they were not able to enter Rwanda directly because RPF soldiers had blocked the border between the cities of Bukavu (in Zaire) and Cyangugu (in Rwanda). Consequently, those refugees were left with two options: to return to Rwanda by walking north on the dirt road along Lake Kivu, where they ran the risk of being attacked by both Interahamwe and soldiers of the AFDL and the RPF, or to flee to the west. Many chose the latter option. Seized with panic, trekking along in unimaginable conditions, those who fled suffered a veritable "martyrdom" on rough and inhospitable paths in the equatorial forest. In the process, many died of disease, hunger, and exposure. Some drowned in river crossings; others were simply massacred by their pursuers.

During two years as a refugee in South Kivu, Umutesi had emerged as a leader promoting innovative programs to ameliorate conditions for women and children in the refugee camps and to encourage discussion and reflection designed to prepare people for eventual return to Rwanda. But after the destruction of the camps, side by side with thousands of other refugees, the author fled from Bukavu to walk west. During ten months of travel, Umutesi and her companions endured inexpressible suffering. They were harassed and robbed by the Forces Armées Zairoises (Mobutu's army), hunted like game by the AFDL and the RPF, and abandoned by the international community. Along the way, the refugees stopped periodically in camps such as the notorious Tingi-Tingi, where they hoped to receive international aid in the form of food and medicine. But these turned out to be death camps, where the aid came too little and too late and where the AFDL rebels could easily attack and massacre the refugees. Umutesi and two of her companions finally reached western Zaire near Mbandaka and the great Congo-Zaire River—a journey of more than two thousand kilometers through the most demanding terrain. It was September 1997. Along the way, many Zairians nobly offered hospitality. Others mistreated and betrayed her. Only thanks to Umutesi's courage, resourcefulness, and sheer luck, was she able to survive. Scores—maybe hundreds—of thousands of her less fortunate compatriots did not.

In contrast to dry, abstract statistics, this account relates the extremely disturbing last moments of people the author knew, mostly women, who died in the Zairian forest. It is an intensely personal account, made powerful by its searing honesty: by citing their names and by telling the "little story" of each, Béatrice Umutesi asks us not to forget those who perished or were killed.

Much of the international media and some diplomats portrayed the refugees in Zaire as génocidaires. Yet, Umutesi points out, most of the people in the camps (of which about 80 percent were women and children) were not guilty of genocide. She expresses dismay and anger at the international community's treatment of the refugees. The United Nations High Commissioner for Refugees appears particularly partisan and heartless. Before the 1996 closure of the camps in Kivu the UNHCR pressured refugees in Kivu to return to Rwanda, and then later supported forced repatriation. At Tingi-Tingi and other way stations,

Umutesi and the other refugees felt the UNHCR abandoned them to be slaughtered by their pursuers — the AFDL, Banyamulenge, and Rwandan soldiers.

Then, having reached the apparent safety of villages in western Zaire, Umutesi encountered yet further betrayal. Kabila's AFDL and the UNHCR conducted a campaign to retrieve Rwandan refugees from the regions around Mbandaka. Zairian villagers faced the risk of attack from Kabila's soldiers if it became known that they were sheltering Rwandans. The UNHCR dispatched agents to locate refugees and persuade — or, if they resisted, force — them to accept repatriation to Rwanda. To encourage villagers to join in the hunt, UNHCR offered a ten dollar bounty for each refugee delivered to them. This was a substantial sum for Zairians living in extreme poverty. Umutesi barely escaped becoming a victim of this "human commerce." She lived in constant fear of being captured by the UNHCR dragnet.

It is a harrowing tale, told by a perspicacious observer. Umutesi's testimony — for that is the only term that can be applied to this heroic narrative — penetrates the complex nature of the immense tragedy that unfolded in contemporary Central Africa. It is "The Heart of Darkness" viewed from a radically different perspective, a personal story, not an allegory.

But it is more than a personal story, for it is also a stone in the edifice of the collective memory that is in the process of construction. It is yet to be seen whether such a memory will be a part of larger efforts to construct a less chaotic future, and if so how it will be integrated into that larger political architecture, that broader ongoing social process. However this may occur, it is clear that the reconstruction of a viable society in this region will require taking into account the thousands of experiences similar to those of the author — for Zairians as well as Rwandans. For in the aftermath of the events recounted here, millions of Zairians were also killed.

This individual account does not diminish the horror, the gravity, or the meaning of the genocide perpetrated against the Tutsi in Rwanda in 1994. Nor does it presume to explain the "grand politics of the homeland." Rather, the main focus is the "small politics of the individual," the often tragic fate of ordinary people in times of conflict, people jostled by armed forces over which they have no control and of which they are the targets. In living through this, and in telling the tale with such honesty and eloquence, Umutesi presents more than a story of simple survival. It is a tribute to the human spirit, a searing indictment of the agents who perpetrated these horrors, and a reproach to those who turned away.

CATHARINE NEWBURY

Author's Acknowledgments

This book would not have been possible without the encouragement and collaboration of my friends in the Democratic Republic of the Congo and in Belgium.

Hamuli Kabarhuza of the National Council of Development NGOs of the Democratic Republic of the Congo was the first to suggest that I write down the story of my experiences. When I arrived in Belgium in 1998, I was welcomed by Marie Goretti Nyirarukundo and Ivan Godfroid of Vredeseilanden-Coopibo, a Belgian NGO based in Leuven. Thanks to their help and encouragement, the idea of writing a book began to take shape.

The realization of this project was made possible by Vredeseilanden-Coopibo, which put its resources at my disposal. Their personnel unfailingly provided me with the necessary help. They also made the translation of my book into Dutch possible (2001). Later, they put me in contact with the Fundació S'Olivar in Estellencs, Mallorca. Through their efforts, the book was published both in Catalan and Spanish (2002).

Juan Carrero Saralegui, president of the Fundació S'Olivar and spokesperson for the Spanish Forum for Justice in Rwanda, understood that it was important for me, and for all those whose names appear in this book, that the book be published in English. The Fundació S'Olivar provided the funding to help me accomplish this dream and entrusted the translation to Julia Emerson. Her devotion, her attention to detail, and her perfect combination of professionalism and passion have been very moving to me.

Finally, I would like to express my appreciation to the University of Wisconsin Press. Their commitment to the publication of the English translation comes not only from academic interest. It is also an expression of human solidarity.

My deepest gratitude to all.

Translator's Acknowledgments

I would like to express my deep gratitude to Nobel Peace Prize nominee Juan Carrero Saralegui and the Fundació S'Olivar in Estellencs, Mallorca, for the grant that allowed me to begin the translation of this very important book. Juan Carrero and his organization have worked tirelessly and selflessly to ensure that all those involved in the massive human rights violations, both during and after the horrific events following the assassination of Rwandan President Juvénal Habyarimana, will be brought to justice. Their work has been crucial to bringing a more complete and balanced understanding of this tragedy to a reluctant world community.

Ivan Godfroid provided invaluable help by answering countless obscure questions about Rwanda, its history and its culture, and by ferreting out the identity of the mysterious STRIM. I would like to thank him for his patience and his dedication to the publication of this extraordinary book.

In addition, many thanks to Derrick Kardos for his work on the maps, to Catharine Newbury for her helpful comments on the translation, to Ellie Fischbacher for her careful reading of the manuscript, and to Juan Carlos Valdovinos for his encouragement.

I would also like to thank everyone at the University of Wisconsin Press for recognizing the importance of this book and working so hard to make its publication a reality.

And finally I would like to express my admiration and gratitude to Marie Béatrice Umutesi for her strength, humanity, and courage, both in surviving her ordeal and in bearing witness to it.

JULIA EMERSON

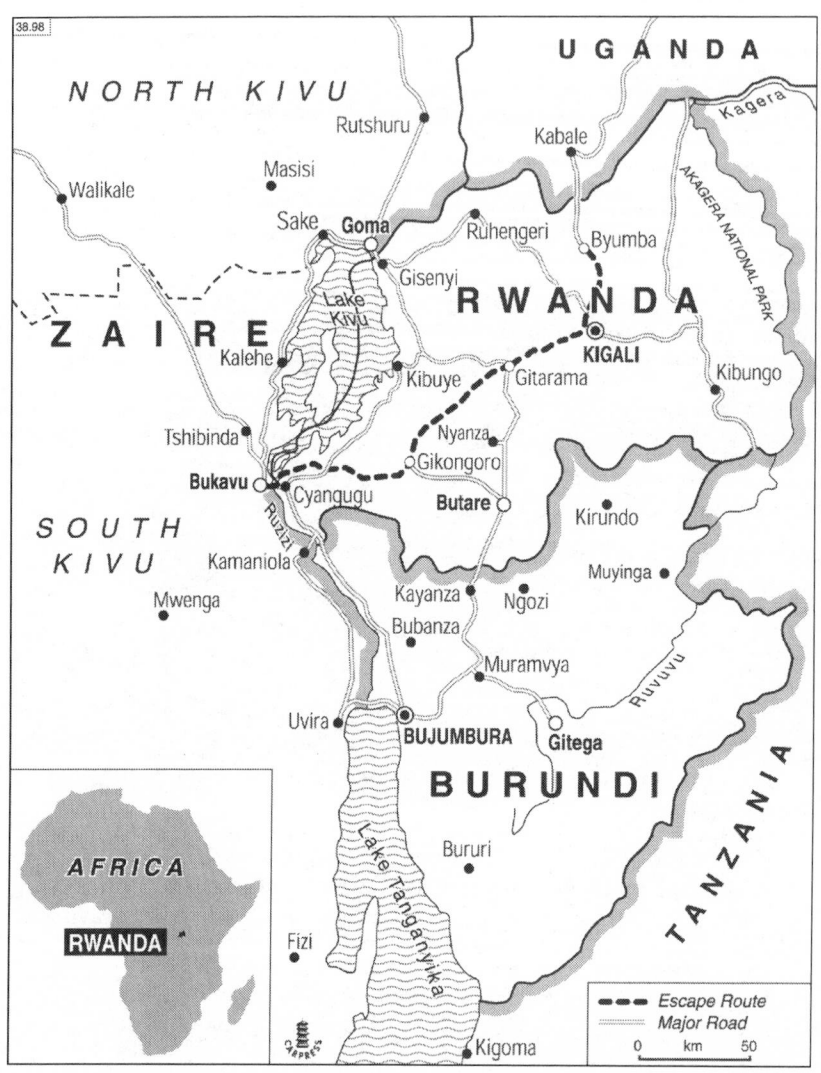

Route followed by the author in Rwanda

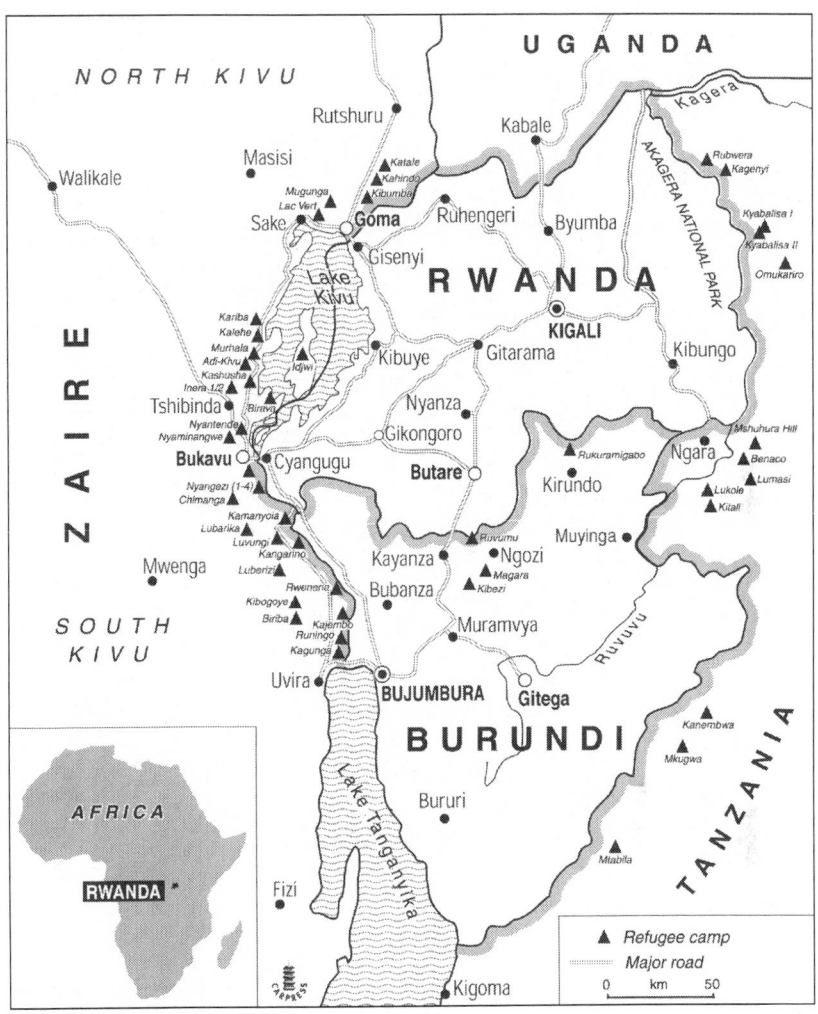

Refugee camps in Zaire, Burundi, and Tanzania

Route followed by the author in Zaire

◆
———————————————————

SURVIVING THE SLAUGHTER

Prologue

I HAVE NO IDEA how much time I spent trapped in the middle of the crowd. I am rather small, and I had to use my elbows to make a little breathing room, or I would have fainted. Just as a small group of us neared the bridge, we heard shots. At first I wasn't alarmed, because I thought that soldiers from the Forces Armées Zaïroises were shooting in the air to frighten the refugees so they could rob them. Later, the shots, which in the beginning had been sporadic, came more often. People scattered in every direction, abandoning most of their meager provisions. In this terrified mass, those who fell were trampled. There was such a crush of people attempting to cross the bridge that many of them were shoved into the river. Thousands of others threw themselves into the water, trying to swim to the far bank. Where the river was deep, children, the old, and the sick drowned.

When people began to run in all directions, sweeping before them everyone who was in their path, I tried to keep my balance and held tight to Zuzu's hand, which was covered with scabies. She in turn tugged at my hand saying, "Auntie, let's run fast. If we don't, they will kill us." We ran on, pushed from behind by those who followed, and hid in the closest huts, but there was so much shooting that these were not safe either. We entered the forest by the first path we found. After running for about a kilometer, those in front stopped abruptly, as if there were something that had frightened them, and suddenly turned on their heels. We abandoned the path and entered the depths of the forest. The branches struck our heads, and thorns and brambles scratched our arms and faces. Happily, the other girls had followed me on this mad dash. Under the dense cover of the forest we stopped to figure out what to do. We

3

couldn't stay hidden for too long, since we needed to eat and drink. Furthermore, the place where we were wasn't far from the road, and the rebels would find us during the first clean-up operation. Nor was it a good idea to continue deeper into the forest, since we were unfamiliar with the area. I decided to retrace our steps and try to find a shallow spot along the river where we could wade across. The water came up to my chest. I feel dizzy when I walk in water, and Marcelline held my hand so that I would not fall and drown. A man who was with us offered to carry Zuzu to the other side, since she was in danger of being swept away by the current, which was quite strong there.

When we finally reached Lubutu, we realized that two children were missing, a boy who left Tingi-Tingi with us and a four-year-old girl I had picked up the night before who had been separated from her mother in the confusion. I had entrusted her to Virginie. When we were running through the forest she let go of Virginie's hand and was lost in the crowd. As for the boy, Assumpta was the person responsible for him. She had succeeded in keeping him with her since Tingi-Tingi, in spite of the commotion. However, when the shooting broke out, Assumpta and the boy both fell, knocked down and trampled by the fleeing mass of people. When Assumpta finally was able to get up, she tried to find the boy, but in vain. Later we continued, unsuccessfully, to search for these two children. In light of the vast numbers of people who perished at Lubutu Bridge, I don't have much hope that they survived. During the shooting we also abandoned a large part of what we had carried from Tingi-Tingi so that we could run faster. We weren't the only ones who had to abandon part of our provisions. Mountains of peas, corn, flour, buckets, and blankets carpeted the road.

What had led us to this extremity? What are the reasons behind the tragedy of the Rwandan refugees, whose existence has been forgotten and denied by the international community? In childhood and later, at the University of Rwanda and at the Université catholique de Louvain in Belgium, I experienced the weight of all the contradictions that undermine Rwandan society. In spite of this, I never imagined that we could reach this point. Nothing had prepared me for exile and suffering. On the other hand no one can prepare to be trapped in history's torment, to be persecuted pitilessly, and harassed daily.

I have been through Hell, have known horror, and now that I have escaped, I want to testify in the name of all the men and women who did not have my luck and who died in Hell. My point of view is neither that of the historian nor of the politician. I give testimony to what I have seen and to what I have lived.

1

I Discover My Ethnic Identity

THE FIRST TIME I heard talk of Tutsi refugees was in 1963. I was four years old. It was about six in the evening, and my father was behind the house with some neighbors, listening to the news on the radio. In the early sixties, very few people owned a radio, and neighbors used to come to our house to listen to the daily news broadcast. We heard a whistle. My father ran back to the house and called to my mother: "They're here!" In his panic he dropped the radio on the floor. He had thought that Tutsi rebels were coming, but luckily it was a false alarm. Nevertheless, for a few weeks our life was dominated by fear of an attack. Even though we were far from the combat zone, people were terrified of the rebels. They took turns standing guard, and a whistle was the signal for danger. Hiding places in the marshes and the forest were prepared. All this seemed very strange to me, and it took me several years to begin to understand.

In the first place, I had to realize that I was Hutu. All Rwandans share the same language and culture, and there is no specific region that is identified with an ethnic group, no "Hutuland" or "Tutsiland." The colonial authorities, in order to simplify things, tried to differentiate between three ethnic groups, using a system based on morphology. The Tutsi are tall, slender, and have refined features. The Hutu are of medium build with negroid features. The Twa are small and have pygmoid features. In reality, these are just generalizations. There are short Tutsi and tall Hutu and Twa. After the sixties, when interethnic marriages became more common, the differences became even less pronounced.

At the time of the Tutsi genocide in 1994, Hutu with refined features were killed at the roadblocks, whereas Tutsi with Hutu features remained safe. In Cyangugu, a prefecture bordering the Congo, I found Tutsi friends who had crossed the entire country and had had no difficulty at the checkpoints, even though they had no more identification than a document certifying that they had lost their identity card.[1] On the other hand, my mother, who was Hutu but had Tutsi features, was threatened with death a number of times, even though her identity card was completely in order.

Ethnicity was never a barrier in my relationships with those who belonged to other ethnic groups, and in my family it was not considered a reason for exclusion. As far back as I can remember our house was full of Hutu and Tutsi children, neighbors and orphans that my mother took under her wing. I have no memory of preferences based on the ethnicity of one or another of the children. Only a child's character, honesty, sweetness, or obedience was important. Thus one of my parents' best friends, as well as their godparents and those of my older brothers and sisters were Tutsi. My family maintained good relations with all those who had not been carried away by the revolution of 1959.

Social revolution erupted on November 1, 1959, when I was only six months old. The Hutu rebelled against the feudal power of the Tutsi, which was based on servitude, exclusion, and contempt. It began when a band of young Tutsi attacked a Hutu subchief who had been appointed by the colonial authority. It was rumored that he had been killed, and the same day the whole country knew about this act of aggression. Revolt had been simmering since the beginning of the fifties and this was the straw that broke the camel's back.

For a long time the Hutu had chafed under the system that had been imposed on them. Every Hutu owed allegiance to a Tutsi and had to perform services that were rendered without payment. A Tutsi could even throw a Hutu out of his own home and occupy it himself if he wanted to.

One of my aunts rebelled against this system. At sixteen, while performing these obligatory services, she had to accompany a young Tutsi woman back to her family. Once there, she refused to eat for three days

---

1. A prefecture is the equivalent of a province.

because she was forced to eat alone after the members of the family had finished their meal. She was not allowed to look at the mouths of her "masters" while they were eating. She did not understand how such poor Tutsi could treat her with so much contempt when her own family was quite well off. On the way back she refused to help her "mistress" carry the gifts that she had received from her family. At this time an attitude like this was punished by a public beating called *umunani*. My aunt knew perfectly well that by rebelling she ran the risk of being beaten, but she preferred a beating to being treated with contempt. This time she was not punished for her rebelliousness.

Another time she decided to go and gather sweet potatoes in the fields before the authorities allowed it. She should have waited. It was the law. Her disobedience would once again expose her to a public beating if she were discovered, but her family was hungry. My grandfather was in jail. As expected, she was caught and they gave her eight lashes. In public. They bared her buttocks even though she was already engaged to be married. Other attitudes of the Tutsi masters infuriated her. She had to scratch herself with a stick stuck into the wall instead of using her hands to do it when she was preparing a meal for them. She had to use two sticks to carry a leaf of tobacco to her "master" because the hands of a Hutu would have defiled it. When they drank, they cleaned the straw before putting it in their mouths if she had used it. They even did this in front of her, which was a sign of profound disrespect, since a basic rule of courtesy is to never clean the straw.

My aunt was a young peasant who had never even been to catechism, but she refused to be treated like a leper. If she had been a man she would no doubt have paid dearly for her rebelliousness. I have a friend whose father had to leave and go to work in the mines of Shaba in the Congo because he could no longer submit to the abuses of the feudal powers. The father of another friend spent the prime years of his life in jail or in exile in Burundi. His behavior was considered subversive by the authorities, who faulted him for wearing a beard and not having the required *amasunzu* haircut.[2] As for my father, he left very early on to

2. *Amasunzu* refers to a variety of elaborate crested hairstyles worn by Rwandan men. The styles can have different meanings such as wisdom or virility or, as in this case, social status.

work for the colonials in order not to be forced to pay allegiance to a Tutsi. These individual rebellions did not culminate in a larger movement until the fifties, when they could be directed by Hutu who had been educated in the seminaries. In 1959 this protest movement resulted in the Hutu overthrowing the Tutsi feudal system. Bloody ethnic confrontations accompanied this change in power. Where I lived, Tutsi homes were burned and their occupants found shelter in the churches, although few people were killed. When the countryside was pacified by the colonial powers, only those who were considered by the population to have been "good Tutsi" were allowed to return to their properties. The rest were taken to Bugesera, an uninhabited area in the east of Rwanda. King Kigeli V Ndahindurwa, along with the nobles, left the country and sought refuge in neighboring countries, primarily Burundi, the Belgian Congo, and Uganda. Beginning in 1961, some of them began to engage in guerilla actions against Rwanda.

At first confined to the frontiers with Uganda and Burundi, the guerilla attacks had become more widespread by 1963, and the rebels had come within twenty kilometers of Kigali. Popular rumor held that in their advance they were killing the Hutu and that some Tutsi from the interior of Rwanda were joining their ranks. This attack by Tutsi guerillas was followed by reprisals against the Tutsi in many areas in the interior of the country. The Tutsi who had been spared in the killings and exile of 1959 were persecuted, and many were killed. Others who joined the ranks of the exiles in Uganda, the Congo, and Burundi had their lands taken and redistributed.

My cousin Laurent, who was five years old in 1963, told us what he had seen. He remembered a man running away, followed by other men armed with spears. This man wore a large overcoat that he used to gather up spears. When he had enough of them, he turned toward his pursuers, who in turn fled from him until his supply of spears was used up. Then the man again began to flee. This "game" continued for a while until the man with the overcoat was exhausted. A compassionate woman hid him under a pile of wood, but a peasant standing on the opposite hillside had seen this. When the man's pursuers had already turned to leave, the man on the hillside called to them to look again under the pile of wood. The fugitive was discovered and killed.

The killing of the Tutsi in our area was the work of outsiders from

Ruhengeri prefecture, about thirty kilometers away. When they saw our house, they thought that it must belong to a former official of the Tutsi regime, since it was the only one for miles around with a corrugated metal roof. They had already begun to set fire to it when one of my father's cousins who lived on the opposite hill intervened. One of our neighbors, whom the arsonists had questioned concerning the ethnicity of the owner, had said that he didn't know whether the owners of the house were Hutu or Tutsi. We never knew if he acted from envy or fear. Our mother had taken us to hide in the fields when she saw danger approaching. Guerilla attacks continued until 1968.

In 1973 the Hutu-Tutsi conflict, which I thought of as ancient history, suddenly flared up in our life again. It was February, and we were returning to school after a week of vacation. I had arrived at the end of the day in Byumba with a neighbor who was in my class. Downtown we met Goretti, a Tutsi friend who was with her friend Benoît, who was also Tutsi and was studying at the teachers' college. They both came from Giti, and since in those days there weren't many cars, they had made the trip on foot. It had taken them all day to reach the school. After saying hello we asked them what they were doing out so late instead of being at the school. Trembling, and with tears in her eyes, Goretti told us that the director of the school had put up a notice telling Tutsi students to return to their homes. He gave no explanation whatsoever. Goretti and Benoît had no idea where to spend the night and were waiting there hoping that someone would show them some sympathy and invite them to stay at their house. Faced with their pain we felt powerless. We didn't know what to say to console them.

At the boarding school everyone was talking about the notice but no one knew why it was there. When I was coming back from the shower I ran into a group of about ten boys from the teachers' college who had invaded our dormitory. They were armed with clubs and said they had come to throw the Tutsi out. They started poking around and looking at the ends of our noses to decide who was Hutu and who was Tutsi. They were completely misinformed. All of our Tutsi classmates had done the same as Goretti and had left the school as soon as they knew about the poster. Only Murekatete had remained at school. We told her that she should go to bed and play sick, but this trick didn't work. Murekatete and another ten students who resembled Tutsi were "selected." The following morning the students expelled them. They could not return to school unless they had identity cards issued by the Germans to their parents or grandparents.[3] This document was the only one that, according to these students, gave authentic information on the ethnicity of Rwandans.

Early in the morning on the same day that our schoolmates were expelled, about twenty students from the teachers' college arrived. They threw those of us who were still sleeping out of bed and ordered us all to put on our gymnastics uniforms. Then they made us leave the school. In the street we joined a few hundred students, some of whom were very young. A group of students from the teachers' college led the march. The rest followed, singing songs from the revolution of 1959. The group at the head of the march entered Tutsi houses and forced the occupants to leave. All the Tutsi—men, women, and children—were taken to the central prison. The politico-military authorities of the city were waiting for us in front of the jail. While they were trying to convince the students to release their hostages and return to school, an officer of the national police opened fire on the crowd, causing total panic. The officer, who, it seemed, was Tutsi, wounded about ten students, some of them seriously. Among them were three classmates. When calm returned, the wounded were gathered up and taken to the hospital, and the students returned to the boarding school. These disturbances, which lasted one day, resulted in one death, a male Tutsi nurse, and about ten wounded. Our classmates, expelled in February 1973, were allowed back in September of the same year, after General Habyarimana's coup. During the first few months, living together was difficult, even though none of us were responsible for what had happened. The Hutu feared being poisoned by the Tutsi, who in turn feared being attacked by their Hutu schoolmates during the night. Frequently they slept two to a bed.

A government-sponsored campaign of reconciliation restored order to the country, but meanwhile there had been deaths, mostly of Tutsi. Houses had been destroyed and several hundred Tutsi, for the most part members of the intelligentsia, had taken refuge in neighboring

3. Germany was the first colonial power in Rwanda and ruled until it suffered military defeat at the hands of the Belgians in 1916.

countries. The ethnic tensions that had begun to cool down since the end of the Tutsi refugee incursions in 1968, revived.

What actually happened in 1973, and why was the Tutsi population the victim of a political situation in which the refugee Tutsi apparently played no role? Although at this time I was only thirteen years old and did not understand anything about politics, I could see that the population of Byumba had, in a general way, been overtaken by events. No one seemed to understand what some were calling the "insanity of the students." People feared this mass of students that had fallen on the city, armed with clubs and sticks, singing songs from the revolution of 1959. Everyone, Hutu and Tutsi, had locked themselves in their houses. Merchants had closed their shops. Adults had not taken part in the disturbances and many Tutsi had found shelter in the houses of their Hutu neighbors. I remember meeting my sister and her boyfriend on the road going toward Byumba. She was trembling with fear. She asked me what all this meant and if we had gone crazy. I didn't know how to answer. I had no idea why I was there either. All I knew was that they had dragged us out of our beds, that they had made us put on the shorts that we normally used for gymnastics class, that they gave us clubs and told us that we should sing as we walked. Many among us followed because we, too, were afraid. Only a small group of students from the teachers' college appeared to know what was going on.

Later, I tried to understand what had happened. After the massacres of Tutsi intellectuals in Burundi in 1972, I had begun to notice the presence of small, ethnically based groups within the school. Another tragic event, the widespread killing of Hutu in Burundi by the Burundian army, which was made up mainly of Tutsi, appears to have been the catalyst for the ethnic uprisings of 1973. The Rwandan Hutu felt threatened by the killings of the Burundian Hutu. What is more, the Rwandan and Burundian governments traded insults broadcast over their national radio stations. We followed these verbal attacks between the two countries without knowing what was truly at stake. Nevertheless, the majority of the Rwandan students identified with the students in Burundi who had been expelled, killed, and buried alive. This did not contribute to a climate of understanding between Hutu and Tutsi in the schools.

Other, often contradictory, explanations were given to me of the tragic events of 1973. According to some, the northern military had organized the disturbances to destabilize the power of Grégoire Kayibanda's regime, which had begun to marginalize them.[4] Those who maintain this hypothesis explain it by the fact that the northern students were the most bitter and appeared to be the prime movers. The coup d'état of July 1973 confirms this assertion. According to others, the disturbances were fomented by those in power as a diversionary tactic to distract the population from the catastrophic socioeconomic and political situation. Be that as it may, Major General Juvénal Habyarimana and other northern officers used these events as a pretext for deposing the Kayibanda government.

Until 1990, Rwanda experienced a period of relative peace. For eighteen years there was no sign of ethnic conflict. Hutu-Tutsi relations were smooth. The number of mixed marriages grew. Even members of the military could marry Tutsi, something that was impossible in the First Republic. For a long time the Tutsi considered Habyarimana their Moses. In some Hutu circles he was accused of favoritism toward the Tutsi. Nevertheless some injustices remained. For example, Tutsi were excluded from holding important political posts, and not until the advent of political pluralism in 1991 was there an improvement in this area. The problem of the Tutsi refugees, who had fled the country in 1959, 1963, and 1973, remained unresolved.

The ethnic tensions that characterized Rwandan society gave way little by little to a new type of tension, the rise of regionalism. From then on the issue was not so much a conflict between Hutu and Tutsi but between Kiga (north) and Nduga (south). I became aware of the existence of regionalism for the first time when I was in Kigali at the Lycée Notre Dame de Cîteaux, where I had enrolled to study economics. After failing English, I had had to repeat my fourth year. The teacher who taught biology and physics was not too happy to see me again. She would rather have had me thrown out, which she made painfully clear to me. Nevertheless I always got good grades in her classes. She reminded me every day that I was a "repeater" and that I could not continue to count on the good will of the ministry. Apparently she had decided to fail me so that I could be expelled once and for all. I finally

---

4. Grégoire Kayibanda was the first president of the First Republic of Rwanda (1961–73).

understood that what she held against me were my regional origins, about which she was completely mistaken. She didn't like me because she thought I was from the south. My difficult character only made matters worse. Luckily for me, one day when she was visiting the home of some friends who came, as I did, from Byumba, she learned that I was the sister-in-law of a friend of her husband's. This was how I was saved from being expelled a second time, which would have been the end.

After the coup d'état of 1973 by the northern officers, southerners and northerners were at daggers drawn. The Second Republic concentrated all the power, both civil and military, in the hands of a small group whose origins were in the north. Southerners criticized Habyarimana's government for having removed them from power and for having arrested and imprisoned a great number of southern politicians, the majority of whom were killed in prison. For many northern politicians, a northern Tutsi was an ally whereas a southern Hutu was an enemy. Southerners held a grudge against Habyarimana's government, and starting in 1991 some of them formed an alliance with the Tutsi refugee rebellion in order to bring the government down.

I entered the Université Nationale du Rwanda in Butare in 1978. The student body in Butare reflected the same regional and ethnic problems as the rest of Rwandan society. Each group practiced rigid social control over its members, particularly over its women. When a female student behaved in a way that others from her region or ethnic group considered inappropriate, they had meetings to decide what measures to take to remedy the situation. During the three years that I spent at Butare, the council of the students from Byumba constantly called me to order. The first time they thought that I had committed the "crime" of falling in love with a Tutsi. The northern council met and a delegation of "elders" was sent to me to ask that I put an end to this unnatural idyll. I thought this was completely out of place. For one thing, the students from Byumba were wrong as to the nature of the relationship. They had mistaken a friendship for a love affair. Furthermore, even if it had been a love affair, I would not have given in to them. My life belonged to me and I had decided to live it my way.

There was also my friendship with Furaha, a young woman from Kibuye, in the south of the country. The students from Byumba considered her to be too "easy." Furaha was very generous, but too nonconformist to be appreciated by the Rwandans. She had a lot of friends, but also bitter enemies. One evening she organized a birthday party at the home of some Canadian friends in Butare. A few days later I, along with others who were at the party, was called in by the Service Central de Renseignements (SCR), a department that watched over internal security and was responsible to the president. Some classmates of Furaha's had accused us of having smoked grass. After this story of drugs, the Byumba students met again and delegated my best friends to convince me to break off my friendship with her. Once again I held firm. In 1982, together with other young women who went out with whites, Furaha was detained and interned in a reeducation center for women. They accused her of undermining morality. After her incarceration she was put under surveillance in a residence in her hometown. In 1983 she escaped the country by hiding in a truck under piles of chairs, and ended up in Kenya. From there she was able to go to France, where she now lives. She is married and is the mother of two sons.

In 1982 I received a scholarship from the Belgian government and came to Europe for the first time to earn a degree in sociology at the Université catholique de Louvain. In Louvain-la-Neuve I again ran into a bitter racism, the likes of which had disappeared years earlier in Rwanda. The Tutsi refugees refused to have any contact with the Hutu, who in turn responded with the same tactics. Only the Tutsi who came from Rwanda could hope to be accepted by both groups.

From the time of my arrival, Esther took charge of me. She came from the south of Rwanda and was Tutsi. I knew her from my secondary school where she had studied pedagogy. She had come to Belgium to study social work, thanks to a scholarship from the Episcopal Church of Rwanda. Esther was accepted equally by the Hutu and by the refugee Tutsi both because she was a Rwandan Tutsi and also because she was friendly and straightforward. Although her family had suffered in the ethnic conflicts of 1959 and 1973 she held herself above these ethnic considerations.

It was through her that I came in contact with refugee Tutsi circles. They welcomed me as one of their own. I was invited to the get-togethers that they regularly organized. Since I also moved in Rwandan and Burundian Hutu circles, some Tutsi refugees began to question my true identity. When they discovered that I was Hutu, some among them spoke of treason and infiltration and decided to exclude me. A Tutsi friend opposed this, but my relationship with the majority of the refugees changed.

This is exactly what happened with Devota, a young woman married to a Belgian. We were close friends, and I valued my friendship with Marc, her husband, who was a committed anti-apartheid militant. When Devota learned that I was Hutu, her attitude changed completely. We continued seeing one another, but our discussions, even the most innocuous ones, degenerated into arguments. One evening Esther, Devota, Marc, another Tutsi friend, and I went to a restaurant. I teased Esther about her marriage to a white. She angrily replied that she would a thousand times rather marry a white than a Hutu, because all Hutu were assassins. The discussion that had started in a joking tone rapidly degenerated. Marc accused Esther of being responsible for what had happened, since she had introduced me into Tutsi circles and had permitted me to express myself freely. He said that in Rwanda a Hutu would not have dared to speak up in front of a group of Tutsi. According to him, I should have shown my gratitude to the Tutsi refugees who had "elevated" me by accepting me into their group. These remarks made us all uncomfortable. Relations between Hutu and Tutsi had evolved greatly since the revolution of 1959 and only in certain extremist Tutsi circles was this kind of language used. No Rwandan, no matter how extremist his views, would have dared throw words like this in my face. He would have been more tactful. Marc tried to make amends later, giving me a biography of Steve Biko and a poster of Nelson Mandela.

In 1985 I finished my studies in Louvain-la-Neuve and began work in Rwanda. I very quickly found my path and dedicated myself to working with the rural population, specifically with women. I had a managerial position with the Centre de Services aux Coopératives (CSC). I helped my mother care for all the members of our large family. I had male and female friends from all races and backgrounds. In a word, I was living a full life when suddenly I was overtaken by history.

2

Increasing Violence

IN THE DECADES of silence after the first Tutsi rebellion was subdued in 1968, the entire world seemed to have forgotten the Tutsi refugees. Petitions to return to the country were examined on an individual basis by Habyarimana's regime, and this prevented any large-scale repatriation movement. For the hundreds of thousands of people who wanted to return to their country, the government proposed no other solution than that they become naturalized citizens in their host country or become permanent residents there while maintaining their Rwandan citizenship. The argument advanced to discourage the return of the Tutsi refugees was the scarcity of land. Negotiations had begun with the main host countries in which the Tutsi refugees lived, and delegates from these countries were studying the feasibility of the proposals, but in 1986 the victory of Yoweri Kaguta Museveni's National Resistance Army (NRA), which enjoyed massive support from the refugee Tutsi, changed the game in Uganda.

A new Tutsi refugee rebellion broke out on October 1, 1990. The Tutsi refugees were stronger and better organized than they had been during the last twenty years. They had leaders of the caliber of Fred Rwigema, then Minister of the Interior in Museveni's government; Paul Kagame, who is the current president of Rwanda and was at that time responsible for the Ugandan Army; and many other personalities around whom the refugees were beginning to organize.[1] With Museveni's

---

1. At the time this book was first published in French, Paul Kagame was the vice-president of Rwanda. Since March 2000 he has been president of Rwanda.

17

military victory, they could count on important armed support. Helping the Rwandan refugees recapture power in their own country was the most appealing solution for the Ugandan president. It allowed him to get rid of these allies, who were becoming a nuisance, to legitimize his power with the Ugandans and to have a friendly regime in Rwanda. It also assured that no Ugandan rebellion would come from that quarter.

Early in 1990 rumors of an imminent refugee attack began to circulate, but few gave them any credence. A lot of us thought that these rumors were hatched by the Habyarimana regime to distract the country from its real problems, which were socioeconomic and political. There was talk of economic restructuring. The Rwandan franc had been devalued and midlevel government employees risked having their buying power cut in half or worse. Political austerity, decreed by the government in an effort to reduce public expenditures, only seemed to affect the lives of those lower down on the ladder, and the powerful continued to live high off the hog. Economic scandals had been uncovered in Habyarimana's entourage. There were rumors that he had plantations of Indian hemp in the Nyungwe forest, and people who mentioned it found themselves thrown into prison. A lottery organized by his son and a Senegalese national had failed, and millions of Rwandan francs had disappeared into thin air. Scandals like this only served to discredit the regime and reinforce popular discontent.

Famine had raged in many parts of the country since 1988. People were dying of hunger and diseases associated with malnutrition. The impoverishment of the countryside was so severe that theft, both of crops and personal property, was rampant. Those in charge seemed incapable of stopping this plague. The population resorted to vigilante justice. Cases of people being beaten and even killed because they had been caught in their neighbors' banana groves or cassava fields or potato patches were frequent. The presence of thousands of unemployed young men caused ongoing lawlessness. Much later, in 1995, when I went to Belgium for a conference on gender issues, I traveled with a young former member of the Forces Armées Rwandaises (FAR) who had been blinded by an exploding shell only a few months after enlisting. He was the one who helped me understand just how untenable the situation had been for youth in rural areas. The lack of land and absence of any non-agricultural employment had left these youth without a future. Military service allowed this young man, who volunteered for the army while the war was raging, to earn a living and to feel like "someone," to respect himself. He and many others of his age and prospects had to choose between military service, with an assured salary and social standing, and leaving for Kigali to become a rickshaw driver or thief. This situation was the reason why neither FAR nor the Rwandan Patriotic Front (RPF) had any difficulty recruiting.[2] The different political parties also used these unemployed young men for the militias that they maintained for their disreputable ends.

Toward the middle of 1990, a Tutsi friend confirmed the rumor of a Tutsi attack. She said she had the information from her family in Uganda who were members of Fred Rwigema's entourage. When she had last visited her parents in Uganda, they had insisted that she not go back to Rwanda because of the impending war. They asked her to be patient for a while, since the return of the refugees was imminent. Even with this reliable information, I remained a skeptic. An attack by the refugee Tutsi would inexorably lead to massacres of Tutsi in the interior of the country, which is what had happened the last time. I hoped that the refugee Tutsi would exhaust all possible peaceful means before risking the lives of thousands of innocents. I didn't realize yet that life isn't worth much when power is at stake. As Tito Rutaremara, a leader of the refugee Tutsi, cynically remarked a few years later: "You can't make an omelet without breaking some eggs."

I heard about the attack on an international radio station. The reporters spoke of an army of ten thousand well-trained, well-equipped, disciplined men. By contrast, they referred to Habyarimana's army as a bunch of Boy Scouts. During the first few weeks, I hardly slept. Since I came from Byumba in the North, I didn't feel very safe in Gitarama, where the southern extremists could take advantage of the chaos that would follow the outbreak of war to get rid of the northerners. In addition, it often happened that I was taken for a Tutsi. If war came to Gitarama, I was in danger of being targeted by Hutu extremists who wouldn't hesitate to make the Tutsi pay for the attack by their refugee

2. The term RPF is used throughout as an umbrella term to indicate both the Rwandan Patriotic Front, which was the political movement, and the Rwandan Patriotic Army.

brothers. I knew that if the rebels took power they would use the first few days to get rid of bothersome Hutu. Being Hutu and in charge of an NGO, I had no hope of escaping the massacres. I stopped being afraid when the Zairian, Belgian, and French peacekeepers arrived. I was also comforted to learn that President Habyarimana had left a UN conference in the United States in order to return to Rwanda. I hoped that he could find a solution to the conflict before it degenerated. During these frightening days, for the first time, I had confidence in him.

The attack was followed by a wave of arrests across the country of people suspected of being enemy collaborators. In Kigali, eight thousand people were arrested and held in a stadium for several days under a blistering sun, without food or water. Many died. The Tutsi intelligentsia, wrongly considered the natural allies of the refugee Tutsi, were the principal victims. Hutu who were suspected of spying for the enemy or were the victims of account settling were imprisoned. At Gitarama, arrests happened just like everywhere else. Friends were arrested after their houses had been searched with a fine-toothed comb by the SCR, which was looking for weapons or compromising documents. The CSC did not escape their attentions. Thorough searches were carried out in the offices, at my home, and also at the home of Jean Marie Vianney, a Tutsi in charge of overseeing commercial cooperatives.

The evening before the day that the CSC was searched, I had gone to work with a women's group about four kilometers from our offices. On my way back, I stopped by the home of some friends who were priests. The driver went back alone to the office. An hour later he returned, and I saw from his face that something was amiss. His voice was shaking when he told me that soldiers had come by to see me while I was gone and that they had promised to come back the following day. At this news my throat suddenly went dry. I had to clench my teeth to keep them from chattering. I went home right away, but I was nervous. All night, I tried to think about my upcoming imprisonment with indifference, planning the clothes that I should take, and wondering how to organize from behind bars, and how to continue my work with female prisoners. Fear prevented me from taking these thoughts very far. I lay in the dark with my eyes wide open. Every five minutes I turned my bedside lamp on to check the time. Not knowing what kind of information the soldiers were interested in, I didn't know what to hide and what to leave. The only documents that seemed to me to be compromising were a photo of Sankara, the former president of Burkina Faso, assassinated in 1987, who they said resembled the head of the rebel Tutsi, General Fred Rwigema, and a biography of Fidel Castro. I thought that they could accuse me of collaboration with the enemy because I was reading a book about the Cuban revolution. At first I decided to hide them in my compost, but after thinking about it, I left them with a Swiss neighbor.

The following morning I went to the office without even drinking a cup of coffee. I was incapable of swallowing anything. The whole staff knew about the visit from the soldiers the evening before and of their promise to come back that day. You could read the fear on their faces. Around ten in the morning we saw a small truck arrive with two soldiers armed to the teeth. I stopped being afraid. The head of the court and the head of the SCR of Gitarama accompanied them. They first dug through the offices, drawer by drawer, and then went to my house and looked through all the rooms. What were they looking for? They didn't tell me. When they came across a letter from a foreign country, they asked detailed information about the person who had written it, the hidden meaning in the words, and other things. They leafed through my agendas and asked questions about what I had meant by writing such and such a thing, even if it was dated from the beginning of the year or from the year before. Afterwards they left, taking the key to our storeroom with them. Around three o'clock in the afternoon a dozen soldiers arrived in a truck. They were as well armed as the first ones and had three agents from the SCR with them. The soldiers quickly took up positions at the entrance of the office and in front of my house. The ones wearing civilian clothes entered the secretary's office. Suddenly I was very calm. The fear that had tied my stomach in knots since the departure of the first investigators left me. Three people were waiting for me in the secretary's office. One of them, who seemed to be the head of the group, wore a long raincoat that made him look like an agent from the KGB in a detective novel. The only thing lacking was a shapeless hat. The man in the raincoat informed me that they had only come to requisition our gas and to search our office supplies more thoroughly. As far as the office supplies were concerned, I didn't feel inconvenienced, but where the gas was concerned, there was no question

of their requisitioning it without authorization from the civil authorities. It was only after the prefect[3] gave his approval on the telephone
and an attorney had signed the requisition order that I allowed them to
leave with two thousand liters of gas. Following that, one of the soldiers
called my behavior "suicidal." To dare to stand up to ten armed soldiers
in wartime was either ignorance or folly.

After the departure of the soldiers and our gas, my cousin's husband,
who was the director of an agricultural project, telephoned me and told
me to calm down. The prefect of Gitarama had told him what had happened at the CSC. He had learned that those in charge of the SCR in
Gitarama wanted to lock me up because they were convinced that I
knew what the RPF was planning. Otherwise I wouldn't have office
supplies and gas. The fact that the CSC employed many Tutsi didn't
help matters. If it had not been for the intervention of the prefect himself, I would have joined my friends behind bars. Generally, people who
had had their houses searched found themselves in jail after a few days,
and I spent the following two weeks expecting to be arrested. During
this time, my movements were followed by the SCR. For the first few
days I went to visit the wives of my jailed friends, but other friends
quickly let me know that these visits weren't well thought of in high
places. I ran the risk, they said, of aggravating matters. I had to be as in-
conspicuous as possible, cut back on my field trips, watch out who I
talked to and pay attention to how I spoke. In the meantime, all of our
telephone lines were cut by the SCR. This reinforced my fear of being
arrested and not being able to warn my friends in time. As time went
on, things slowly returned to normal. The telephone worked again.
Work went on. Joseph, a Tutsi staff member of the CSC who had been
arrested, was released after a few weeks, thanks to the intervention of
our European partners. He chose exile in Burundi because he no longer
felt safe in Rwanda. At that time, I didn't understand, but when the
massacres of the Tutsi began, the wisdom of his decision became clear
to me. The victims of these arrests, who were often innocent, as well as
their families and their friends, never forgave Habyarimana's government for having singled them out unjustly. Many among them, even
those who at the beginning had supported him, joined the opposition at

---

3. The title of prefect corresponds to a provincial governor.

the time when the country opened to democracy. The majority became open sympathizers of the RPF.

After the attack in October 1990, in many areas of the country, particularly in certain districts in Kibuye, Kibilira, and Gisenyi prefectures, the Tutsi were the victims of popular vengeance. In Kibilira many hundreds were killed with machetes or drowned in the Nyabarongo River. Their houses were burned. These massacres would no doubt have spread to other prefectures if there had not been strong actions on the part of the authorities in the municipalities bordering Kibilira. For example Bulinga, in Gitarama prefecture, could have been caught up had it not been for the intervention of the mayor and a deputy, helped by the local population. For many days they organized patrols, day and night, on the banks of the Nyabarongo River. They fished out the victims and prevented the leaders from leaving Kibilira and entering Bulinga. Thanks to them, many lives were saved. Inquiries were held and about thirty people who were identified as the principal organizers of the massacre were arrested, among them the sub-prefect of Ngororero prefecture. In the same wave of repression, the Bagogwe, Tutsi herdsmen who lived in Gishwati forest in Gisenyi prefecture, were massacred by soldiers from FAR.

Beginning in 1991, the RPF changed its military strategy. It abandoned conventional warfare for guerilla warfare. For the population of Byumba, the guerilla war would be bloody. Although at the start the rebels did not attack the civilian population, after 1991 they began to systematically kill them. People began to move en masse to the areas as yet unaffected by the fighting. They told of atrocities committed by the rebels. Women were disemboweled, men impaled. Other forms of torture, each one more barbaric than the other, were perpetrated. These macabre stories created terror in the towns on the frontiers with Uganda. The rebels were no longer considered human. They were shown with horns and a tail, just like the devil in catechism books. I began to hear talk of the atrocities committed by the RPF when the first displaced people from the border towns arrived at my house in 1992. I had at first thought that these were fictions, products of the minds of people traumatized by two years of wandering. I began to believe them the day that the wife of my cousin Macali, a businessman in Kibuye, told us how soldiers from the RPF had killed him: "When the rebels arrived in Kibuye, my husband first evacuated me and the children. Afterwards he went back to get provisions, since we hadn't taken anything with us when we fled. When he arrived at the house the rebels were already there. They took him and tortured him. We awaited his return in vain. When he didn't come back, the children crept back to the house during a pause in the fighting. They found their father tied by his own entrails to a post in his store. The rebels had disemboweled him, pulled out his guts and used them for a rope." This story and others that followed affected me deeply. Life had changed: horror, anguish, and fear were present every day. Nevertheless, I had to live, work and keep the CSC going. It was a heavy responsibility. Everyday life took over. Then in February 1993, two years and three months after the beginning of the war, the rebels arrived at my house.

I had just begun a project in support of women's associations in Byumba. Every morning I left Kigali to go to different towns, and in the evening, for reasons of safety I returned to the capital where I had a temporary office. Many government and private sector employees in Byumba prefecture did the same. On my return from Buyoga, I went by to say hello to my family. My mother had just brought in the harvest, and she proudly showed me her granary, which was full of beans and sorghum. She had also begun to raise chickens along with the cows, pigs, goats, sheep, and rabbits. She reminded me that if she had left her house as her children had advised her to after the last rebel attack in June 1992, she would not have had such a bountiful harvest and would be boring herself stiff in Kigali. She didn't know that the following Monday she would be running out of her house leaving everything behind her and have to wait four years to see again this place she was so attached to. She also did not know that she would never again see the many members of her family who would be murdered by the RPF that day.

The rebels arrived in Gatete, my mother's village, around five in the morning.[4] It was Monday, market day. According to the stories told by the survivors I met on the road to Kigali three days later, they forced their way into houses, trapped the men and rounded them up. Women ran up and down all the streets calling the children, who were screaming

4. Gatete is in Rubona sector, in the commune of Kibali.

and crying, not knowing what was happening. Those who succeeded in escaping took no provisions with them. Women left their houses completely naked. Bodies of the people killed that morning were found in ditches six months later, after the agreements for the withdrawal of the RPF forces were signed and people returned to their homes. Among the dead were my cousins Bizimana Laurent, Kazimana, and many other members of my family. Bizimana Laurent was my aunt's eldest son and had been raised by my mother. He was only thirty-four years old when he was killed and left a wife and two little girls. His only crime was that he was Hutu. Like the lamb in the fable, even though he was too young to have hunted Tutsi in 1959 or 1963, his father must have.[5]

My mother had left the house carrying nothing with her after a shell fell only a few yards from her house. She abandoned everything to save her skin. Though she often complained of rheumatism, she ran the five kilometers to Rutabo without stopping to rest. Fear made her forget her pain. Then, while they started to prepare the food that they had begged from farmers who lived in the area, a shell fell in a pot on the stove. Again, everyone ran away. In the end, the fugitives walked day and night until they were about forty kilometers from Kigali. At that time my mother was about sixty-five years old. Fourteen births and rheumatism had worn her out. For many years after menopause she suffered from dizziness, and she fainted in the fields on the way. We held out very little hope of finding her alive. However, after a week she finally arrived at my house in Kigali, along with twenty-five people.

Next, the rebels arrived in the center of Kisaro, one and a half kilometers from my home. Tens of thousands of refugees who had come from towns on the Ugandan border lived there. Their camp had been destroyed in a mortar attack. Most of the farmers in my area, particularly those who didn't live close to Kisaro and who hadn't been worried by the fighting, stayed at home and continued to carry on with their normal lives. When it was clear that the area was under the control of the RPF, they didn't think they had to escape. They thought that the

5. The fable referred to here is "The Wolf and the Lamb," by Jean de la Fontaine. In this fable a wolf makes false accusations against the lamb. When the lamb tries to defend himself by explaining why what the wolf says couldn't possibly be true, the wolf says: "Then it was your brother . . . or one of your kin. You owe me one way or the other." The wolf then drags the lamb off into the forest and kills him.

fighting was over and, since they were not involved with politics, it didn't occur to them to be concerned. As to the stories that those who had left their homes told about the atrocities committed by the rebels against the civilian population, the farmers didn't believe them. On Tuesday and Wednesday most of them returned home. No longer hearing the sound of guns, these people thought that the danger had passed. They were sorely mistaken. Thursday morning the rebels began a cleanup operation in the area. Everyone—men, women, and children—was summoned, supposedly for an informational meeting. People were confident. The rebels were courteous and the peasants had nothing against them. It seems that things began to sour when they got to where this meeting was to take place. The rebels forced the peasants into houses, locked them from the outside, and then attacked them with grenades. The survivors were finished off with knives. The person who told me this story had himself miraculously survived the massacre. Finding himself alive under the bodies of his dead companions, he took advantage of the nighttime to escape and was able to join the other displaced persons in the camp at Rusine, where I met him a few days later. During these massacres at Mwendo, Nyirarukwavu, a friend of my mother's, was killed. She was a Tutsi. Her first husband had been killed in the Tutsi massacres at the beginning of the 1960s, as had her two older daughters. In February 1993, despite her daughters' insistence, she did not want to leave, as many of her neighbors had done. Nyirarukwavu was killed along with a young woman from Cyumba whom she had taken in along with her two young children. The last image I have of her is from the day my two brothers were married. She was among a group of women who had come to welcome the newlyweds as they got out of their cars. She didn't stop dancing until they arrived at the house. She was so happy that you could have believed it was her own children who were marrying. This death hurt me deeply. I found it particularly gratuitous and unjust. Nyirarukwavu did not die a natural death.

In the first days of the big rebel offensive, the roads between Byumba and Kigali were jammed. Starting fifteen kilometers from the capital, the traffic was blocked by an uninterrupted river of refugees. People didn't know where they were going. They only wanted one thing: to put as much distance as possible between themselves and the RPF. Young children walked with bare feet on the asphalt road leading to Kigali. I crossed this flood of displaced people every morning as I went to the countryside. I tried to put names to these exhausted faces. A good number of them were my family, my friends, or my neighbors. Every time that I recognized someone, I asked the driver to stop. I said hello and asked for news about one person or another and gave the news of my mother and the others. I came across a young cousin, the daughter of one of my grandfather's many sons, who had given birth on the road without any help. She was barely seventeen and this was her first child. She carried the baby, who was only three days old, on her back. Its navel still hadn't healed. She told me that she had used her teeth to cut the umbilical cord. Other women were less lucky and had died in childbirth for lack of any help. I also came across the wife of Bizimana Laurent. It was she who told me that the rebels had killed Laurent and Kazimana. She tried to hold back her tears while telling me how he had died, and I did the same to keep her from crying even more. She had her two little girls with her. The elder was the very image of her father. It was also on this road that I learned, from her daughter, that Nyirarukwavu had been killed.

With the offensive of February 1993, the RPF controlled almost all of Byumba prefecture. Out of seventeen communities, only three were untouched by the war. More than five hundred thousand people had found shelter in the refugee camps, where they lived in inhuman conditions. To protect themselves from the rain that falls from February until June, they built shelters from branches, nicknamed *blindés*.[6] These little huts, which measured scarcely five square meters, often sheltered families of a dozen people. In these makeshift camps, where tens of thousands of the dispossessed were crowded, the hygiene was abominable. The latrines were not emptied. During the first months, people did their business wherever they wanted in the fields surrounding the camps, and food scraps were thrown everywhere, creating mountains of refuse in the middle of the camps themselves. All of this let off a stench that was difficult to get used to. Every day epidemics of cholera and dysentery carried off several dozen people, especially children and the

6. *Blindé* literally means bulletproof, but throughout the book it is used ironically to refer to all the improvised shelters that the refugees built out of branches, sheeting, or whatever other materials they could find.

more vulnerable women. In the first months the only food that the refugees had was sugar cane. Most of the children were skeletal. The only thing one saw were eyes sunken in their sockets and a large head. Young girls looked like women a hundred years old. They were so thin their bones stuck out. Only their eyes showed any sign of life. Children, nursing and pregnant women, and old people died like flies of malnutrition.

In order not to suffer the same fate, some returned to their homes to look for something to appease their hunger. The majority of them were caught by the rebels and killed in cold blood. After my visits to the Gaseke camp, I met a woman who had escaped from one of the massacres. For many days the whole camp thought that she had been killed along with those who had left with her. Finally she returned to the camp with her sister-in-law. All the men who had been with them had been killed. Here is the account that she gave me of the killings in which my cousin Saratiyeri and her father were also killed: "I returned to my home with my sister-in-law to look for something to eat because I had left the house without any provisions and the sugar cane wasn't enough to calm the children's hunger. We ran into the RPF soldiers before getting to the house. They were herding about a dozen people along the road. Their hands were tied behind their backs. They stopped us and tied our hands behind our backs too and told us that they were going to take us to their commander. We went to Gatete in Rubona sector, where there were other people who had also been arrested. Everyone had their hands tied behind their backs. Then the men were separated from the women. They were thrown down on the ground on their backs. Their chests were bulging because of the ties. The rebels began to hit them on the chest with small hoes. When they were already dead, a soldier walked among the bodies stabbing each one in the ribs. Terrorized, we watched this butchery. We waited for our turn. When it was over, the soldiers told us to leave quickly unless we wanted the same thing to happen to us. We left running."

In the course of my work I made regular visits to the camps. In Gaseke camp, I went by to visit my paternal uncle, Luberete. He had tried to create an intimate family space for his wife and his many children by grouping his four blindés around a small common area. My uncle was tall, and he almost had to get down on all fours to enter his blindé. Once inside, he had to stay seated, because it was impossible to stand. The seats were made of firewood or stones gathered around the camp. The hearth was located in the interior of the huts, since it was the rainy season and one couldn't always cook outside. When the fire was lit with damp wood, the whole hut was smoky. You sneezed, you blew your nose, and your eyes got red from rubbing them. My uncle had always been a prosperous farmer. Each of his wives had several hectares of land, and food was never lacking in his house. He lived like a little potentate in his own house, where his wives took turns visiting him. To see him in these unhealthy blindés that filled up with water at the first drop of rain, forced to live bent double, and old before his time made me sick, but I could do nothing. The sight of my family living in misery was a permanent torture for me. I felt diminished in front of these thousands who had been able to save nothing but their skin. I knew that one had left a house covered with sheet metal, that another had left many cows, small animals, fields of sweet potatoes, or a banana plantation. I had often been to their homes and many times had shared a meal. They were there, in rags, filthy but too proud to ask me for a little money to buy some sorghum for a *bouillie,* which would have allowed them to hold on a few days more.[7] I watched their children die like flies without being able to do a thing. I had at least been able to study. These people, these friends, these neighbors had shown me their generosity, and I, I could do nothing for them when they were living in misery. My inability to make a gesture that would have given them a little hope made me miserable.

In spite of having almost no money, I didn't sit on my hands for long in the face of so much misery. During my visits to the Gaseke camp, the associations of peasant women from Kibali and Buyoga had approached me. There were about a hundred members who wanted to have a little money to start up economic ventures that would allow them to help their families survive. I was aware that these small loans would only be a drop of water in an ocean of misery, but, as our ancestors said: *Ubusa buruta ubuta gusa* (A little is better than nothing at all). This program was very important to me. I at least had the feeling of doing something. If, thanks to this little loan, a human life was saved, it was still a victory

---

7. *Bouillie* has no exact translation in English. It can mean any meal boiled or simmered in a liquid and can be anything from a stew to a porridge made simply of water and flour. Here it most often refers to corn meal or sorghum porridge.

of life over the death that had struck my people. At the same time as this microcredit program in the camps, I tried to do something with the women's associations of Murambi, Muhura, and Giti. These three towns had not been touched by the war, but they had welcomed many hundreds of thousands of displaced people. The economic situation there was catastrophic. There was the threat of famine. The price of foodstuffs had doubled, even tripled. Because people needed wood for the construction of the blindés and for cooking, trees had been cut down at a record rate. The hills that had formerly been covered with eucalyptus were completely bare and exposed to erosion after the heavy rains. It was complete desolation. Agricultural activity had stopped. Everyone expected to have to flee from one minute to the other. Bags were packed and those who had family living far from the combat zone had already started to evacuate part of their belongings. Under these conditions, discussing a development program that would last several months was practically impossible. The first meetings that I organized were unsuccessful. We were only a few kilometers from the front. Fleeing people and the sound of guns always interrupted our meetings.

Nevertheless, even with the approaching war, it was necessary to encourage these women. Sitting on our hands meant accepting defeat. But where to start? The women had so many problems to face. The women's associations only existed on paper and had not been active for a while. All their property had been liquidated, and the members had split the money before leaving. Little by little, I succeeded in helping the women understand that they had to prepare for flight, not by filling bags with sorghum and beans like they were doing, but instead by looking for money. With the stabilization at the front and the resumption of peace negotiations in Arusha, little by little the women gained confidence. They began with economic activities that generated short-term revenue at the individual level and in their associations. After the creation of the buffer zone and the return of some of the displaced persons to their homes, we hoped for a return to normal life.[8] We began to think about

8. After many months of negotiations between the rebels and the Rwandan government, a buffer zone (Zone Tampon) was created. It covered the whole area conquered by the rebellion following the general offensive of February 1993. The Z-T was under the military control of the Groupement des Observateurs Militaires Neutres (GOMN). This group was composed of Rwandan soldiers, rebels from the RPF, and

a medium term program and the extension of these activities to the entire prefecture. The assassination of Habyarimana, the resumption of the war, the massacres, and the genocide caught us by surprise and cut off all this energy.

My family and my neighbors stayed for months in the camps. Those who had come from the towns on the Ugandan frontier stayed even longer. All lived under conditions of misery that are impossible to describe; only the humanitarian NGOs were worried about their fate. Beyond those people who lived in Ruhengeri and Byumba prefectures, which had been touched by the war, very few Rwandans sympathized with the plight of the dispossessed. The political, ethnic, and regional divisions were such that many Rwandans did not see them as human beings worthy of compassion and in need of help. They were, after all, northerners, militants from the president's party, Hutu. Every morning several thousand starving, half naked women and children descended on Kigali. They came to beg something that would allow them to live one more day. When a woman or a child held out an emaciated hand, more often than not instead of five or ten francs, they got insults or spit in the face. Most of the inhabitants of Kigali said that the refugees were responsible for their own misery. Others told them to go home because the supposed killings committed by the rebels were only propaganda to discredit the guerillas. These peasants, many of whom had been on the run for more than two years did not understand why they were accused of being the architects of their own misfortune. How could they understand when their fellow countrymen reproached them for having escaped from the rebels when many members of their families had been killed by those same rebels? How could they understand that the political climate at the time led Rwandans to defend the executioner while blaming the victims? Personally, I will never forget the observation of a young hairdresser in Kigali about the peasants from Ruhengeri who were traveling through the town to rejoin their families in the East. From the mountains of Ruhengeri, which they left for only a few days a year to sell their potatoes in the local markets, these women proceeded on foot to Kigali-East and Kibungo. On their heads they carried smoke

---

soldiers from a few other African countries such as Senegal and Ghana. Theoretically, the belligerents pledged to abstain from all military activity in this area.

blackened pots, old straw mats, water jugs. They dragged a gaggle of small children behind them. Never having set foot in a town, they weren't used to seeing so many cars. Crossing the road took them a good ten minutes. After glancing to the left and right, the whole group would cross the street at a run, risking being run over by a distracted driver. The young hairdresser, after seeing this state of affairs, broke out in a laugh. At the time I couldn't understand how anyone, particularly a woman, could laugh at these poor people who had done nothing to deserve what had happened to them. Seeing that I was shocked by her reaction, she said to me: "Habyarimana just said in a speech on Radio Rwanda that he was going to equip the *Interahamwe* and that they were going to descend on the streets, and, voilà, he has given them old straw mats."[9] For her, these women, young and old, who carried their children on their backs were not to be pitied. They were Interahamwe because they came from the North. They deserved neither her compassion nor her help. When I remarked that these women and these children were probably unaware of the political struggles that were tearing the country apart and that they did not understand why they were in this situation, the young hairdresser replied: "Anyhow, it is the Hutus' turn to suffer. The Tutsi have already been refugees for thirty years." For her it was fitting that these women and children suffer in their turn the anguish of exile.

Instead of paying attention to the slaughter of the civilian population, both Hutu and Tutsi, that was being committed across the entire country, instead of insisting on inquiries to uncover the parties who "pulled the strings" in these massacres and excluding them from the democratic process, a large number of Rwandans denied, justified, or praised their activities. I was able to confirm and deplore this state of affairs on a number of occasions. One day a friend whom I had known since I worked at CSC was staying with me. In 1990 he had been put in prison because he was Tutsi. After leaving prison, he joined the Parti Libéral (PL). I told him about my family's misfortunes following the

---

9. *Interahamwe* was originally the name given to the youth party of the Mouvement Républicain National pour la Démocratie et le Développement (MRND). After President Habyarimana's assassination, all the different youth groups merged into one Interahamwe that was unfortunately known for their atrocities during the Tutsi genocide.

last rebel attack. He didn't want to believe me. According to him, the RPF didn't kill. The massacres of the civilian population were pure theater on the part of the presidential party to discredit the rebellion in the eyes of the population. Nevertheless, Bizimana Laurent, Kazimana, Nyirarukwavu, Saratiyeri, and the others had been killed by the rebels. Had their wives and their children invented the story of their deaths to frighten others and cause them to flee? While thinking of all those who were dead and who continued to die in the refugee camps, as their houses fell to ruin and their fields returned to the wild, while thinking of all those who couldn't return to their homes to look for a little potato to quiet their children's hunger, I decided to remain quiet. My friend did not want to accept the fact that the rebels of the RPF didn't behave like the "liberators of the people" they wanted the world to believe they were, but like assassins. Another time, I was having a drink with a friend who came from Byumba and was a member of the Mouvement Démocratique Républicain (MDR).[10] Someone told us that the rebels had killed some people in Mutura and Kanama in Gisenyi prefecture. My friend replied while sipping his glass of beer: *Nabo se babona* (They also can die). Nevertheless, he was a very nice man, a friend, a good father and an exemplary husband. It was just that the deaths were not on his side. He was Hutu and the dead were Hutu; he was from the North and the dead were also. Only he was a member of the opposition and the dead, being from the same prefecture as the president, were felt to be partisans of the latter. On the other hand, after the 1990 attack by the RPF, in many areas of the country Hutu had led reprisals against the Tutsi. In Kibilira, hundreds of men, women, and children had been killed with machetes and others drowned in the Nyabarongo River. The members of the presidential coalition said that the Hutu of Kibilira had behaved very well. They considered that the hundreds of people who had been killed, even the women and children, were collaborators of the RPF and therefore enemies, and when one is at war, killing an enemy is not a crime but an act of bravery.

During this time I suffered not only from the exile into which I had been forced and the loss of those who were dear to me but also from the

---

10. Democratic Republican Movement, formerly the only party when Rwanda was a one party state.

fact that Rwandans refused me the right to show my sorrow and weep for my dead. When I denounced the crimes of the RPF, I was treated like a Hutu extremist. For the most part, to have some peace, I had to bear my sorrow in silence. It was the same for all of the victims of the massacres no matter whether they were victims of the RPF rebels or victims of angry Hutu civilians and soldiers. No one could speak out loud about his or her pain. Only the victims were blamed. The killers had all the rights. It was only much later, in other circumstances, that I began to speak and write freely about the death of my loved ones. Since then, it seems to me that the pain and resentment that I had carried with me since February 1993 have lessened a bit.

When the buffer zone was created, many of those who were displaced in February 1993 returned home. The families of my aunt, brother, and stepmother returned to Kisaro. My mother and around ten children stayed with me in Kigali. I was able to go to this so-called demilitarized zone and visited my mother's house, which was partially destroyed and had been looted. The chairs, the tables, and the beds had been smashed. Books, school notebooks, and letters had been torn in pieces and scattered here and there. It was a scene of total desolation. My brother's refrigerator was full of bullet holes, as if someone had wanted to take vengeance and hadn't been able to put holes in the skin of the owner. This was the last time that I set foot in the family house.

On the road I met many young men in civilian clothes wearing black plastic boots. I was told that they were rebels. Apparently they came often, because they were known in the area. They often shared a beer with the young men on the corner. When I showed my astonishment, they said that they even organized political meetings. At Kigali, when someone dared to say that the rebels hadn't left the buffer zone, he was treated like an Interahamwe or a Hutu extremist. I also learned that FAR carried out raids from time to time, which created a lot of tension. An inhabitant of Kisaro, a village near Byumba, told me that one raid by FAR almost turned out badly for him: "That day I had to go to Byumba. I left very early because I had work that I had to finish that same day. Around six in the morning I got to the junction of the Buyoga and Cyungo roads, about five hundred meters from the little town of Kisaro. There I was stopped by a group of about twenty soldiers in combat uniforms carrying machine guns, Kalashnikovs, and rocket launchers. One of them asked me where I was going so early in the morning, and I replied that I was going to work in Byumba. I was shaking like a leaf. I thought that they were going to kill me. He told me to go home as quickly as possible and stay there. I ran back to my house and locked myself in. Throughout the day I waited for an attack. Happily the incident was over the same day." In fact, the buffer zone was not a safe area. It was demilitarized in name only and the supervision of the Groupement des Observateurs Militaires Neutres (GOMN) was not effective.

In 1991, in spite of the war, Rwanda had followed the political evolution of the rest of the African continent and opened to a multiparty system. Political parties were created under the auspices of the Mouvement Républicain National pour la Démocratie et le Développement (MRND), set up by President Habyarimana in 1975. In addition to the MRND, three other parties played an important role in Rwandan political life between 1991 and April 1994: the MDR, the Parti Social Démocrate (PSD), and the PL. The MDR was not a new party but was instead the party that had ruled the country since the 1960s. It had been dissolved at the time of the coup d'état in 1973. It was above all the political party associated with Gitarama prefecture, where it was called "our party," and acted as if it were the only party. "It made the sun shine and the rain come down." A peasant who did not join was relegated to the sidelines. He could be refused certain services from the other farmers, such as transportation to the hospital. He could not enter certain cafés, because no one would wait on him. Every peasant initiative needed the seal of approval of the party.

The PSD was located regionally in the prefectures of Gikongoro and Butare, in the south of the country. It was the first party to have a youth organization, called *Abakombozi*. This Swahili word means "liberators." The youth party of the MDR was called *Inkuba* or *Tonnerre*, and that of the MRND Interahamwe. Most who joined these groups did so as a result of peer pressure.

In the beginning the PL attracted members of the Hutu and Tutsi intelligentsia and businessmen. It was not identified with a particular local area like the other three. It very quickly became the principal party associated with the Tutsi and was the only party in which the Tutsi were part of the central committee. After a wave of imprisonments of Tutsi that followed the attacks by the RPF, Habyarimana and his party had lost credibility with the Tutsi. The MDR, even though it wanted to change, was seen by the Tutsi as being responsible for the massacres that had been going on since 1959. The political program of the PL was oriented principally toward the reduction of ethnic inequalities in education, administration, and politics. I believed that the most critical problems were neither ethnic nor regional. When one looked at the reality of the socio-economic conditions in which the great majority of the Rwandan population lived, there was no difference between Hutu and Tutsi. All faced the same difficulties linked to insufficient agricultural production. Rich Hutu and Tutsi both behaved equally badly toward those of their own ethnicity who were less well off. Impoverished rural youth, both Hutu and Tutsi, sought poorly paid, degrading work in the cities and made no distinction between Hutu and Tutsi employers. The PL had a superficial approach to education. They rightly questioned the system of access to secondary and higher education, which was based on ethnic quotas, but instead proposed a system based on test results. I thought this reflected the idea of Tutsi intellectual superiority that was still held by certain Tutsi extremists. It also did not address the problem of 90 percent of the children, both Hutu and Tutsi, who did not have access to secondary education. I felt that the political debate about social and economic injustice had to be played out on a larger stage, but I thought like an educated Hutu born after the revolution. I did not have, as did my Tutsi colleagues, thirty years of political exclusion behind me. For them, the debate could not be generalized, because in generalizing, they feared that the injustices that they had suffered from in the past would be forgotten amidst the numerous other injustices that the country was unable to resolve.

In other words, the interests of the ethnic and regional groups dominated. The principal problems of the day, such as the scarcity of food, rural and urban unemployment among the youth, and the war and consequent displacement of hundreds of thousands of people, were not the main concerns of the political parties. When these issues were addressed at all, it was only superficially.

I had stormy debates with my Tutsi colleagues from the CSC, all members of the PL, over their political choices. Having made the choice to work among the poorest, how could they belong to the PL? They didn't see the contradiction. They didn't even know if the PL

leaned to the left or to the right. What was important to them was that
it was the party that was concerned with the Tutsi. I had equally heated
discussions with militant members of the MDR. When I asked them
what their party proposed to do to create employment for rural youth
and increase agricultural production, they had no answer. They had not
thought about it.

In their struggle against Habyarimana's regime, the parties advo-
cated civil disobedience, disrespect for authority, and violence. Cultur-
ally, Rwandans show a respect for authority that verges on fear. When a
superior gives an order, inferiors don't argue. They do what they are told.
That was how the annual orders of the president of the Republic were
transmitted from the top to the bottom, and everyone had to mobilize
to carry them out. In rural areas, this authority protected the weak from
the strong. With this new culture of disobedience, influential families
made their own laws. The weak were attacked and their belongings
were stolen with impunity. The local authorities to whom they complained were often incapable of handing down justice. When a mayor
decided to punish someone who had broken the law, the opposition
party claimed injustice. The guilty party went free. Power slipped im-
perceptibly from the hands of the administrative authorities into those
of political leaders who used militias to impose their own law.

The MDR is the originator of the term *kubohoza*. This word literally
means "to liberate" but the meaning was perverted. When groups of
young delinquents, organized into militias and bribed by the local party
leaders, attacked the crops that belonged to the agricultural associations; when they attacked collective and private enterprises, wreaking
havoc everywhere they went; when they attacked mayors who were still
faithful to the former MRND; when the communal forests were
burned, and when water systems and roads were destroyed, the MDR
called it "liberation." In Gitarama, for example, the owner of a restaurant, a militant member of the MDR, had more power than some
mayors. He maintained a small militia that "liberated" the communal
forests and harvests from the associations and committed many other
acts of vandalism. Activities started by the peasant associations, which
would have had a positive impact on living conditions for everyone,
were discontinued in the wake of propaganda from the leaders of the
MDR, most of whom were not locals.

There is the case of the road that was to have joined Mucubira to Buhanda. The local population had wanted this road, which would have opened up Mucubira. The work had been organized under the direction of the peasant associations in the area. Oxfam had given a small grant for the construction of two bridges. The CSC had helped to find a civil engineer. The communal authorities, from the start, had shown very little interest, and the peasants had begun the project without any support from them. At the time the democratic movement began, when the road was almost finished, the MDR began to organize a group of young men against the project. The road was destroyed, or "liberated" as they were saying then.

The propaganda aimed at the public, inciting them to "liberate" the developmental infrastructures in the rural areas, went as far as convincing people to destroy their own anti-erosion measures. The example of Hasina illustrates this phenomenon well. She was president of a women's group in Nyamabuye, and she came by my house regularly to discuss her association. One day she came with a wound on her foot. One of her toes was half cut off. She had injured herself while repairing her anti-erosion ditches. She had destroyed them to "liberate herself from the dictatorial politics of President Habyarimana." When the first rains fell, all of her cassava plants were washed away. That was why she decided to replace the anti-erosion measures she had destroyed on the enlightened advice of the local party. She had had to work fast and had hurt herself. From her I also learned that the improved springs and the little roads made by communal work had been destroyed.

Only the farmers were worried about the drift of the multiparty system. When it became clear that the new politics led to discord among the farmers and the destruction of rural life, a group of about thirty peasants from seventeen districts in Gitarama prefecture, along with an aide from the CSC, met to debate the issue. By analyzing the advantages and disadvantages of political pluralism, such as it was in the Rwandan experience, as well as the goals of the different parties, they reached a bitter conclusion. The political situation in the country was deteriorating daily. Friendships between Hutu and Tutsi, cemented over dozens of years, were at the breaking point. Families disagreed with each other. Members of a single family were at daggers drawn because of party politics. The infrastructure had been destroyed. In short, the area had become the battlefield for people from the cities, and the peasants were paying the price. The groups in the population that were not represented by political parties had no voice. In order to have a place at the table, they decided to found a peasant party whose purpose was to defend their interests and those of the rural areas in general. Their approach was interesting on many levels. They assembled a large representative group that included Hutu, Tutsi, and women to reflect on the future of a rural world that belonged to all of them. For these half-literate peasants, ethnicity was not, under these circumstances, an issue. They did not allow the administrators from the CSC to participate in the debates because they did not want their analyses to be influenced by nonpeasants.

Founding a political party was not as easy as the peasants had imagined: The majority of them did not know how to read or write correctly; none had finished primary school; and since they spoke only Kinyarwanda, they could neither document their own experiences nor be inspired by the political experiences of other peasants in different places. In light of the extreme poverty in which most of the farmers lived, they also lacked the financial means necessary for the realization of a project as difficult as creating a political party and making it work. Aware of their weaknesses, the peasants of Gitarama tried to make contact with people they thought capable of advising them, such as the administrators of the NGOs and the Minister of Youth and Community Life. What a mistake. They were thrown into an inextricable imbroglio and their intentions were corrupted on every side. At the CSC, their initiative was rejected and fought by the development committee, the majority whom were members of the PL, which was allied with the MDR. They felt that a peasant party would threaten the preeminence of the MDR and its allies and wanted to have nothing to do with it. Other political groups in Gitarama saw the creation of a peasant party as an attempt by the MRND to attract adherents in districts that were hostile to them. As for the minister of youth, who was a member of the MRND, he also saw the work of the MDR behind the Gitarama peasant initiative. His reaction was categorical: if the peasants from Gitarama founded a political party, it would work against his own party. He fought it with all the means at his disposal and actively counseled the peasants to form an association instead of a political party. Thus, through lack of experience in politics, and an absence of people able to advise them in the matter, the peasants of Gitarama abandoned the idea of a political party. After several more meetings they decided to create a farmers movement for the defense of their interests: INGABO.[11] Even so, politicians from both the north and the south distrusted INGABO. In the heart of the development committee of the CSC debates were always rancorous. Supporting INGABO, as they did any other association in Gitarama that asked for help, was not automatic.

This hostility did not prevent INGABO from making progress. Today, the association has forty-six thousand members, including Hutu as well as Tutsi. After the genocide, INGABO was one of the first associations to resume its activities and to demonstrate that, in spite of what had happened in Rwanda, Hutu and Tutsi could have joint projects and organize together to see them through.

INGABO was above all the creation of one man, Manasse. I had known him since I started working at the CSC in 1988. At that time he was president of an agricultural cooperative in Ntongwe. Through his dynamism and charisma, he had been able to structure and organize the diverse associations and cooperatives there. After the advent of a multiparty system, he had been the first to be worried about the destruction of the association movement by the politicians, and he denounced the way the politicians were using the peasants for their own purposes, instead of being concerned about the interests of the rural communities. He was the first to organize a meeting of the Gitarama peasants to discuss the positive and negative effects of the multiparty system on rural life, and to try to find a way for the peasants to organize themselves to defend their interests. When Gitarama was taken on June 1, 1994, Manasse stayed in Rwanda and, as soon as it was possible, he revived INGABO. With other peasants from Gitarama, he gave meaning to the words "reconciliation" and "cohabitation" between Hutu and Tutsi by organizing them in a joint project. Manasse, unjustly accused, has been in prison in Gitarama since 1997.

With a multiparty system and the transition to democracy, there was an upsurge in criminality. Since the 1970s, criminality in the countryside

11. Ishyirahamwe Nyarwanda riGira inama Abahinzi Borozi (Advisory Association of Agriculturists and Stockbreeders of Rwanda).

had dropped sharply. The last time that I had heard of a murder in a rural community, I was still in primary school. After 1992, the situation deteriorated. People did not hesitate to kill even their own children over a few thousand Rwandan francs, a bunch of bananas, or a dispute over land. The first case I heard about was that of a woman from Masango killed by her father and his wives over land. At Nyamabuye, a few months later, a man killed his two children and his sister's fiancé because they wanted part of the insurance money that had been given to the man after the accidental death of his first wife, the mother of the two murdered children. In Giti alone, in less than a year, three other equally horrible crimes were committed. The first was a young man killed by his neighbors. After killing him, they cut him up into little pieces and fed him to their dog. Then, for the supposed theft of less than a kilo of beans, a young man was killed by people who had been bribed by his eldest brother. The third case was that of an old man killed and castrated by his eldest son. Many people seemed to be unconcerned by this rise in criminality. The murderers were arrested, but there was not much interest in their trials. Crime and death were only interesting when there were political motives. People did not want to acknowledge that if, for a few thousand francs or a couple of bottles of beer, unemployed youth would kill innocent people in cold blood, people with whom they themselves had no argument, they could kill thousands if given the means.

After 1992, in addition to these common crimes that were facilitated by the vacuum of power, we began to see a sort of organized terrorism. Every night in Kigali grenades were thrown into cafes and private houses. Bombs exploded in Kigali station and in taxis. There were dozens of victims of this blind violence. There were so many grenade attacks, and the targets were so random that you didn't know who was behind the terrorism or what it was they wanted. After the arrival in Kigali of a battalion of soldiers from the RPF following the signing of the Arusha Accords, my neighborhood became the nightly theater for grenade battles between the soldiers and the Interahamwe. At daybreak, life returned to normal and you forgot the grenades of the previous night, unless you knew one of the victims. In that case, that was all you talked about, speculating about who the murderers were and what political objectives they had in mind. Everyone's analysis depended on his or her political leanings.

Instead of denouncing this lack of safety, which was increasing every day, the various factions promoted it. You had the feeling that it worked well for them. Faced with this increasing violence, ordinary citizens didn't see any alternative to arming themselves. In every neighborhood they organized teams of night guards armed with clubs, spears, and machetes. In some areas they even had guns. The logic of violence seemed to be so imbedded in the mentality of the people that the only solution that seemed worthwhile was to arm the population so that they could defend themselves against the terrorism that the state seemed incapable of stemming. In the countryside the situation was even more alarming. Here and there mines and grenades claimed their victims. In Gitarama a grenade exploded in the courtyard of a primary school and killed a number of students. Again in Gitarama, a small truck carrying about fifty people on their way to the market exploded on a mine, killing twenty people. In Gisenyi, women and children were disemboweled in the middle of the night. People suspected the rebels. As the days went by, the number of victims of this senseless violence rose and the murderers went free.

Political assassinations began in 1993. The first to be killed was Gapyisi Emmanuel. He was one of the top leaders of the MDR and son-in-law of Grégoire Kayibanda, the first president, who was removed by Habyarimana's coup d'état in 1973. A few months before his death, Gapyisi had founded the Forum Pour la Paix et la Démocratie with Bahigiki Emmanuel, a professor at the Université Nationale du Rwanda, and with Mbonampeka, a member of the political wing of the PL.[12]

This forum wanted to unite all the people interested in peace and a true democracy in Rwanda, regardless of their political leanings. When Gapyisi was killed, some in the opposition accused Habyarimana of having ordered his assassination, because Gapyisi could have been a formidable opponent in the next presidential elections. Mbonampeka, however, accused the RPF of the crime. In his eyes Gapyisi had been killed because, during a debate that was broadcast on the radio, he had declared himself to be against taking power by force and had called for the rebels to lay down their arms and join the democratic opposition. Gapyisi believed that it was possible to topple Habyarimana's dictatorship by

12. The Forum for Peace and Democracy.

political means. He believed that if the RPF took power by force, it would maintain it with force, and would not share power with the other political parties. The rebels would have feared that these ideas would have been popular with militants in the opposition. Since Gapyisi was listened to and respected, he would have been able to rally a large number of militants to his cause. If he had succeeded, the RPF would have risked losing a large number of its allies in the interior of the country, and it was with them that they hoped to win the war. As events unfolded, Mbonampeka was proven correct, and several days later, he himself narrowly escaped a grenade attack. As for Professor Bahigiki Emmanuel, he was killed by the RPF in April 1994 along with his wife, his children, and many others who were hidden in his house. Bahigiki was an old friend and former professor. At the beginning of the 1990s he had been appointed general secretary of the Ministry of Planning. I had called him, not to offer my congratulations, but to reproach him with having sold out to "the system." He replied that not only would he never join the system, but that he would instead try to change it from the inside. He kept his promise. He was never co-opted. He remained true to himself. In a system that was daily more corrupt, he was able to maintain his moral and intellectual integrity. Bahigiki was deeply involved with the rural community and was a member of the decision-making bodies of organizations that worked for rural development. He believed so deeply in the peasantry that he organized debates between his students at the Université Nationale du Rwanda and peasants about the problems of rural life. He encouraged his students to write their dissertations on rural development. Like me, Bahigiki had lost members of his family, friends, and neighbors in the rebel offensive in 1993. So that all these victims would not be forgotten, and so that later the guilty could be brought to justice, Bahigiki had begun to assemble a dossier. Very few people agreed to tell their stories. Most of them feared being killed by the rebels if they spoke up. Many of the witnesses to the tragedy lived in the buffer zone, which for all practical purposes was under rebel control. When he told me what he was doing, I asked him if he was afraid of being killed some day. In spite of the risks that he ran, he persevered. He was killed for having succeeded with his project.

In February 1994, the top person in the PSD, Gatabazi Félicien, was killed. He was returning from a meeting between the leaders of the opposition and the RPF. The truth about this assassination remains controversial to this day. Some accuse the parties in the presidential co-alition of being responsible for this murder, while others, among them militants from the opposition, accuse the RPF and its political allies. The reasoning advanced by the latter is that Gatabazi no longer wanted to participate in the rebel plans to topple the Habyarimana government by force. It seems that he had realized that the rebels wanted to claim power for themselves once they had won. Gatabazi was highly respected by the militants in his party. A schism in the PSD was therefore possible, and this too would have weakened the RPF camp and reinforced Habyarimana. A few days later, militants from the opposition assassinated Bucyana Martin, the president of the Coalition pour la Défense de la République, at Butare when he was returning from Cyangugu, his home prefecture.[13] His assassins were said to be avenging the murder of Gatabazi Félicien.

Bucyana's assassination was followed by bloody riots in many parts of the country, but particularly in Cyangugu. In Kigali, the working-class neighborhoods were the most affected. Several militants from the RPF were killed and others hid in churches. In the Nyakabanda neighborhood, where I lived, we had no deaths, but militants of the PSD and the PL, both Hutu and Tutsi, had to leave, and their houses were ransacked. I was away, working in Germany. My family lived in fear for a week, since many of them, among them my mother, could be mistaken for Tutsi. They all stayed locked in the house and no one dared to go to the nearest store to buy something to eat. At the end of the week, a policeman who had learned from the neighbors that my mother was also from Byumba, came by to say hello to her. This unexpected visit had reassured them all.

In addition to the well-known politicians who were killed, local representatives of the presidential party were also murdered. The assassination of a militant in the Coalition pour la Défense de la République in the Biryogo neighborhood of Kigali was followed by isolated riots in which many people, particularly Tutsi, were killed. The successive murders of Hutu leaders and the bloody uprisings that followed them added to the ethnic hatred that had revived following the rebel attacks in October 1990, and positions became increasingly radicalized.

13. Coalition for the Defense of the Republic.

3

Descent into Hell

I SPENT THE TRAGIC EVENING of April 6, 1994, in the Hotel Méridien in Kigali with my roommate Goretti and a friend of hers, an officer from Ghana. He was a member of the United Nations Assistance Mission in Rwanda (UNAMIR), the force that had been created by the UN to implement the peace agreements that had been signed by the Rwandan government and the rebels. Goretti and I arrived home about eight o'clock. When we were a few yards away from the house, we heard a deafening noise. We didn't pay too much attention to it, since we thought it might be a grenade that had just exploded somewhere in the nearby area of Kabeza. During the last few months, grenades exploding in cafes and houses as soon as night fell had become part of our normal life. As long as you weren't the target yourself, you didn't worry about it too much. Around midnight, the policeman came to wake me and tell me about Habyarimana's assassination. He was returning from a meeting of the heads of state of the countries of the Great Lakes Region in Tanzania, accompanied by President Cyprien Ntaryamira of Burundi, the head of FAR, and other important members of his regime. The presidential airplane had been shot down as it was landing at the international airport at Kanombe. Lightning couldn't have struck me harder. With President Habyarimana dead, what would become of us? There was bound to be war. The reprisals would be horrific. Ethnic disturbances, which were sure to follow, would be the excuse for the RPF to resume hostilities. With the political situation in the country so degraded and the practically nonexistent government, the final confrontation, predicted by all the different political factions, was guaranteed.

The only force that would still be able to pull us out of the hornet's nest was UNAMIR. Nevertheless, their passivity during the bloody riots following Bucyana Martin's assassination did not leave much room for hope of any intervention on their part.

After the policeman left, I woke the entire family to tell them the bad news. At that time there were about fifteen of us sharing the house: my mother, many of her grandchildren, my unmarried younger sisters, and Goretti and her son. Our family also included two young servants. I was too frightened to stay alone in my room because I expected that at any moment a grenade would shatter the windows. I spread out a mattress in the hall, next to my mother's and sisters' rooms, where I felt safer. All night long I couldn't close my eyes. I was tormented by the thought that on the next day I might not be alive and that my entire family might be exterminated. I didn't spend much time wondering about the identity of those who had just condemned thousands of Rwandans to death by assassinating President Habyarimana. As far as I could see, the RPF was behind the assassination. The rebels had many reasons to wish Habyarimana dead. For the rebellion and its allies, the only way to gain power was through his assassination. The Arusha Accords had brought him back to oversee the two-year transition period, and there was a good chance that he would be reelected at the end of that time. Habyarimana still had staunch allies, such as France, which came to his rescue every time that the rebel attacks threatened Kigali. As long as he was alive, military victory by the rebels remained in question. The principal reason that the Tutsi refugees had taken up arms was to gain power. Now, the Arusha Accords only gave them part of what they wanted. With the elections, Tutsi representation in the political institutions of the country would be marginal, and it would be difficult for the rebels to return to square one after having made so many sacrifices. Like most Rwandans, the rebels expected widespread ethnic riots if President Habyarimana were killed. This was predictable, because the assassination of less important Hutu leaders during the preceding month had led to bloody riots in which Tutsi had been killed and might have served as an excuse for the RPF to renew hostilities. They were prepared. During the entire ceasefire, they had never stopped recruiting. The majority of Tutsi students had left school and joined the rebellion in response to promises of money or the chance to enroll in foreign military academies once the war was over. Still, it was hard for me to accept that the rebels did this knowing that the assassination would lead to many thousands of Tutsi deaths. I refused to believe that they had made the cold-blooded decision to sacrifice hundreds of thousands of Tutsi living in Rwanda who, during the four years of the war, had kept them going by sending their sons to the front, while carrying out a successful political campaign in the interior.[1]

Toward four in the morning the exploding grenades and bursts of gunfire confirmed what I had been expecting since the night before. The settling of accounts had begun. There would be many victims and everyone was in danger, particularly in the institutional void in which the country found itself with the death of President Habyarimana. Around six in the morning, I turned on Radio Rwanda to listen to the news. I hoped, against all logic, that they were going to announce that the president was seriously wounded, but that he was still alive. Alas, I heard a report that confirmed his death. At the same time, they asked the entire Rwandan population to stay at home until further orders. I wanted them to announce that, in spite of the death of the president, the situation was in hand, and that they would inform us of the way that the country would be governed in the interim, while waiting for transitional institutions to be set up through the Arusha Accords. Instead of the hoped for information, the national radio station played classical music. This only reinforced our feelings of fear, insecurity, and abandonment.

People were running through the streets shouting. I was afraid to go out on the road and ask what was happening and stayed locked in the house with all my family until the policeman returned at around ten o'clock. During the whole time we remained seated in the living room, not daring to speak or even get up to make a cup of tea. Even Isimbi, my

---

1. Author's note: It was only later, in the refugee camps in Bukavu, Zaire, that I began to understand. When I had myself been a refugee and daily felt the outrage of having lost my country and my identity, I understood—without admitting it—the feelings that guided those in charge of the RPF, all of whom were children of the Tutsi diaspora. I understood, because some Hutu followed the same line of reasoning, that armed struggle was the only answer. The fact that their relatives who had stayed in Rwanda would be killed if the Hutu were ever to attack did not bother them. It was a risk worth taking. They were ready to sacrifice all of them in order to return to Rwanda and reclaim their social, economic, and political rights.

niece's baby, was quieter than usual. We expected that at any moment soldiers would burst into the house. We knew that if that happened, everything would be over for us. The sound of the doorbell made us jump. We all looked at each other. No one dared to get up and open the door. When the bell rang for the second time, Nyandwi, the night watchman who was with us at the house, decided to go. It was just our policeman who had come to reassure us and say that he had mentioned us to the chief of security, who told him that we would not be bothered. From him we learned what was happening in the neighborhood, and that many houses that belonged to Tutsi and militant Hutu members of the PSD were burning. He told me of the death of Claudette, a young Hutu widow and the mother of two children, who came from Byumba. She had just been killed along with one of her daughters. The other little girl, who had a serious head wound and had been left for dead, had been taken in by neighbors. The soldiers had accused Claudette of renting one of her houses to UN officers from Ghana. The UN soldiers were disliked in the neighborhood, regardless of whether they were Belgian or Ghanaian. There was no one there to defend her. Claudette's husband had died very young, and she had first wanted to educate her children before making a life with another man. For the assassins, the extermination of this little family was profitable and risk free.

The same day I learned of Supera's death. She worked for the Inades-Formation, the NGO where I rented an office. She lived less than five hundred yards away and was killed along with a dozen other people who had come to hide at her house. She had lost her husband a few months earlier, killed by unknown people for unknown reasons. There was no known political activity on her part that could have explained her murder, although members of the militia had sought Supera's brother for several weeks because he was suspected of being a soldier in the RPF. The evening before Habyarimana's assassination, Supera was to have left for West Africa for several months of training. She had missed the plane and her departure had been put off until the following Saturday. We were petrified by the news of these deaths. Many of these people had been friends. We knew that we were at the mercy of people who killed women and children in cold blood, but we didn't know where to go.

By the end of the afternoon, the sound of heavy artillery and machine guns was added to the bursts of gunfire from small arms and grenades. This could only mean one thing: the RPF had resumed hostilities. This time the war was in Kigali and only a few kilometers away from my house. I told the members of my household to hide in a little windowless hall and to put the mattresses on top of them to protect themselves from bullets that came through the ceiling. I knew that if a shell fell on the house, a mattress, thin as it was, wasn't much help, but it was better than nothing. A basement would have been better, but, like many houses in Rwanda, mine didn't have one. Around ten o'clock our policeman returned along with two students from the Université Nationale du Rwanda who were also from Byumba and wanted to spend the night. A shell had destroyed their house on the road to the airport. Danger was moving closer. The target of the shells seemed to be the road that connected the center of Kigali with the airport and ran through the industrial zone of Gikondo, about four hundred meters away from my house.

The morning of the second day after the president's assassination, the policeman did not come to see us. Around ten o'clock, one of his colleagues came to tell us that members of the Presidential Guard had killed him. The death of the young policeman was a heavy blow for me. Not only had I just lost a friend, I had lost a protector. Who was going to prevent the militia from searching my house, and who could predict what would happen if they found out that Charlotte, one of my housekeepers, was Tutsi? While we were weeping over the death of our friend, a neighbor came to tell us that the military was asking women and children to evacuate the area because confrontations with the rebels would take place there. I left the house wearing the nightgown that I had worn since the night of Habyarimana's assassination, tights, a *pagne* tied at my waist, and a scarf on my head.[2] As for baggage, I only had the bag in which I kept my identity card. I even forgot to take the 500 Rwandan francs (three dollars at that time) that were on my bedside table, even though I didn't have any other money on me. The rest of the family also took only their identity cards. On the road, bullets began raining down on us. We got through the first hundred yards flat on our

2. A *pagne* is a traditional, multipurpose cloth used by African women. It can be worn as clothing, used to carry children on one's back, or to wrap bundles that are carried on the head.

stomachs. A neighbor who saw us running away empty-handed called out to me. He wanted to know where we were planning to go without any food or blankets to protect ourselves from the chill of the night. I replied, still running, that we were fleeing, but that the soldiers had promised to call us back as soon as the fighting was finished. It didn't occur to me that FAR could loose the battle. I had complete confidence in them, but I imagine that in such moments you need to have something to put your faith in, as slight as it might be, to be able to continue to fight and survive. On the advice of my neighbor, who seemed to be more experienced than I in these combat situations, I took advantage of a lull and returned to the house with my brother. We took a little rice and sugar and several blankets and then fled without looking back.

At our first stop, five kilometers farther along, we were among several thousand fleeing people, for the most part women and children. The men were forced to stay in the neighborhoods to warn the soldiers of a potential pincer movement by the rebels. We went toward Gitarama, a small commercial center as yet untouched by the fighting, which was fifty kilometers from the capital. Hutu and Tutsi fled together. We ran from the militias as well as the rebels. Farther down the road, the people of Gahanga were very hostile toward us. This was an unpleasant surprise, as we didn't expect anything like that. All along the road people hurled insults at us because they held the people of Kigali responsible for Habyarimana's death. For these peasants, the vast majority of whom understood nothing about politics, all inhabitants of Kigali were opponents of the regime. They had not forgotten that the opposition had said that when Habyarimana died the people of Rwanda would let out cries of joy. They wanted us to remember too. We took little used paths to avoid the main roads where we feared meeting the militias or the rebels. In spite of these precautions, several dozen roadblocks thrown up by the peasants, organized or not, slowed our progress. These people, moved by fear or a desire to rob us, checked our identity cards, or pretended to when they could not read. They rifled through our baggage looking for weapons that we might have hidden and sometimes stole things that interested them. We arrived in Gahanga at the end of the afternoon. Many thousands of other refugees had preceded us. The Tutsi of the area had crowded into the nutrition center the night before, fearing reprisals by the Hutu. All those who had come from Kigali occupied the premises of the school. You had to elbow your way through the crowd, and finding a place to stretch out for the night wasn't easy.

The next morning, my sisters went to the market to buy flour to make bouillie. They came home empty-handed. Access to the market was forbidden to outsiders. Since Gahanga was not very prosperous, people feared that the arrival of so many people would drive the prices up and would rapidly exhaust the food reserves in the area. The director of the rural NGO Inades-Formation, who had been able to bring several kilos of sorghum flour with her, helped us.

The hygiene in our improvised camp was abominable. The few toilets, built by some students, were insufficient. When you went to gather heating wood in the little woods that belonged to the parish, you had to walk through shit. Nevertheless, the problem that worried us the most was security. The presence of Hutu and Tutsi in the same place was felt to be a threat by everyone. The rupture was final. Each group suspected the presence of armed elements in the other group. The Hutu thought that there were members of the RPF among the Tutsi, who in turn believed that there were militia among the Hutu who came from Kigali. The Tutsi provoked panic in the whole camp by running away when a vehicle carrying militia or soldiers passed by on the road. The Hutu caused everyone to run when they claimed they had seen young men armed with clubs and grenades in the areas occupied by Tutsi. At each alarm, people began to run in every direction, without really knowing what was going on. They were dominated by fear and suspicion. By the end of the afternoon the tension was such that some people decided to go back to their respective neighborhoods. War was raging in Kigali, but they thought it better to risk their lives in an ethnic confrontation in which the warning signs were clearly visible.

I too decided to return to Kigali with my entire family. Another day of rest would have been good for my mother, who was exhausted by the forced march of the evening before, but our safety was more important than anything else. Many among those who decided to spend this night at Gahanga were killed. According to the stories told by those who escaped, the militia in Gahanga and armed elements of the RPF hidden in the parish fought each other with grenades. Given that there was a small number of Tutsi combatants and that they were not well armed, they could not resist for long.

Our return trip from Gahanga was more eventful. The number of roadblocks had increased and they had been reinforced with militias armed with rifles. The searches were more systematic and the robberies more numerous. Our group consisted of about a hundred men, women, and children. We stuck together. When someone encountered problems at one of the roadblocks, everyone waited until he was released. If it was necessary to pay, everyone banded together to free him. Along the way we passed French army trucks that had come to evacuate the whites and their Rwandan relations to peaceful countries. The trucks were three-quarters empty. We shouted to the French soldiers to take us with them, not to Kenya or to France but only a few kilometers farther down the road. As a response to these pleas they made a small hand gesture and the line of empty trucks passed by. When my eyes filled with tears as I saw the trucks disappear, my sisters made fun of me. They said that it was my fault that I found myself in this situation. According to them, I should have made use of my time in Europe to find myself a white husband. Then, not only would I have been evacuated like the others, but they also would have benefited.

Around six in the evening, when we were in the neighborhood of Kabeza near some cowsheds that belonged to a leader of the MDR, shooting broke out. No doubt it was Rwandan soldiers who fired on us thinking that we were rebels. We were forced to hide in the cowsheds, where we stayed for a week, sharing our beds with cows, chickens, and goats. Starting on the second day, Tutsi from Kabeza, learning that our host welcomed displaced people, began to rush in by the dozen. We stayed together, locked in the largest cowshed, the one that was usually reserved for the calves. Among these newcomers there was a young woman who couldn't have been more than twenty-five years old and had two young children. During the whole time that we stayed together we discussed the political situation in the country, and the memory of our discussions has never left me. We were two terrified young women, both of whom had abandoned all our belongings to hide in a cowshed that stank of cow dung, and yet we couldn't agree on who was responsible for this war. She fled the militias. I fled the rebels. She based her ideas on the massacres of the Tutsi in 1959, 1963, 1973, at Kibilira in 1991, and at Bugesera in 1992. My thoughts were influenced by the massacres of the Hutu in Byumba, Ruhengeri, and Gisenyi since 1990, and especially by the massacre of members of my family in February 1993. Whereas for her, the rebel advance meant that liberation was near, for me it meant, in the best case, death or exile. At the end of the afternoon of the third day, our host's wife came to warn us that the militia, having learned that there were Tutsi in the cowshed, planned to come and make a search that very day. Panic gripped everyone. Even we, who theoretically had nothing to fear, were terrified. The least doubt or suspicion could be deadly. The Tutsi left the cowshed by the back door to hide in the sorghum fields in the surrounding area. The young woman with whom I had had the long discussion left with her two children. She carried the older child tied on her back with the pagne that my sister had loaned her. Her maid, who was Hutu, carried the younger child. The two women did not return and neither did their companions in misfortune. We learned that the militia had killed many of them while they tried to reach the UN base at Kicukiro. After the Tutsi reached the cover of the sorghum, I went to sit outside with my family. It was better that the militia not find us inside, otherwise they might have suspected us of hiding something. We had our identity cards with us. A half hour later they burst into the cowsheds. There were fewer than ten of them, armed with clubs and knives. Their chief, named Gikongoro, was known in the neighborhood. Before becoming the head of the militia, he had been a delivery boy. He felt he had the right to decide who among us was a good citizen and deserved to live and who else was a bad citizen and deserved to die. As someone, a young delinquent in my neighborhood, would tell me a few weeks later, this war belonged to the *Mayibobo*—young delinquents. What wonderful revenge for this Gikongoro to see the "wealthy" trembling before him, when only a few days earlier, while staring into the distance, they had asked him to carry their packages for a pittance. Even if we had never had anything to do with him, it was people like us whom he despised, and now we had to pay. For an interminable time he would turn our identity card over and over between his fingers to extend the pleasure of seeing us trembling. My friend, who looked like a Tutsi, was saved by the fact that she had a brother in the national police force and that her father had been a well-known politician in the First Republic. We watched with relief when Gikongoro and his band departed without any of us having been beaten up or killed.

I met Sebanyambo in the cowsheds. He was married to Jeanne, a classmate at the Lycée Notre Dame de Cîteaux, who was in hiding because she was Tutsi. The militia were searching for her to kill her, and every day Sebanyambo had a visit from them. They threatened to kill him if he didn't tell them where his wife was hidden. From day to day the situation became more poisonous until finally Sebanyambo was shot in the head. Nothing could save him, even though his brother was a superior officer in FAR. After her husband's death, Jeanne had to leave her hiding place and spent the night in the sorghum field with her baby, who was only a few months old. The people who were hiding her had warned that the militia had located her.

In addition to the almost daily threats of the militia, rebel shells began to fall close to our hiding place. My sisters were almost killed when they went to draw water less than five hundred meters from the cowshed. Rumors of rebel infiltration in the area ran rampant. The least noise, even the cows pawing the ground with their hooves, made us jump. After a week, we decided to return to my house in Kigali. There at least we could count on the protection of thick walls, barred windows, and metal doors. We crawled the two or three kilometers that separated us from the house. As soon as we stood up the bullets rained down on us. On the way back I learned that two days earlier the militia had killed Musema, a friend who worked at Inades-Formation. Musema was a Hutu from Gisenyi, the same prefecture that President Habyarimana came from. He had been a party member at the time Rwanda was a one party state. While many of his friends joined the new parties, he remained faithful to the loves of his youth. In the stormy political debates during coffee breaks, Musema was often shunned by his colleagues who were active in the opposition parties. First the militia killed his Tutsi wife. Then they decided to get rid of him so that they could appropriate his house and all his belongings. His neighbors tried to intervene but did not succeed in saving him. But what could they do in the face of several dozen young thugs with weapons?

Another piece of bad news awaited us at the house. Vianney, Goretti's brother, had been killed getting out of his car at a gas station in Kanombe. The soldiers who killed him had mistaken him for one of their officers whom they wanted to do away with, because he was suspected of collaborating with the rebels. Vianney left behind a wife and a daughter only a few months old. His death was a heavy blow for our whole family. He had always been close to us, and during the bloody riots that followed Bucyana's assassination he came by the house practically every day to reassure himself that everything was all right. For several months Goretti had expected that misfortune would strike her family. A woman who was thought to be a seer had predicted to her that her brother would die during that year, as would the baby that his wife was expecting. I had not attached much importance to this prophecy of doom. Since the time when my sister had almost been the victim of charlatans, I no longer believed in stories of sorcery and divination. This time the whole prophecy became a reality. Vianney's child only survived her father by three months.

Nyandwi, the night watchman, was waiting for us at home. He had stayed there the whole time, even when bullets were falling on the house, boring holes in the walls and roof. When the neighborhood militia came to requisition my car, he objected. With the help of the neighbors he was able to protect us from being looted. All the men of the neighborhood had to spend the night at the roadblocks in order, they were told, to prevent rebel infiltration. The fighting was taking place on the other side of the airport road. The first night after our return home my brother did not go to the roadblocks. A member of the security committee had told me that it wasn't necessary. This failure of our "civic duty" nearly cost us our lives. Around midnight Nyandwi awakened me by shouting and pounding on the door. He told me, in a voice distorted by fear, to open the door right away, otherwise they would destroy the house with a grenade. Trembling, I got up. Very carefully I opened the door, which was not only double-locked but also had chains. The danger came from two young men armed with grenades. One was Majyambere, whose brother was president of the militia in my neighborhood. They must have had a lot to drink before coming to my house, because they had trouble getting their words out of their mouths. They had come to find out why my brother, whom they thought was my husband, was spending the night in the warmth with his wife while the others had to suffer the cold at the roadblocks. This made them think that we were collaborators. On top of that, no one in the neighborhood knew who we were, where we came from and what we were doing. I explained to them that I had been running from the rebels since leaving

Byumba and that many members of my family had been killed by them, but to no avail. After about ten minutes of talking with the deaf, Majyambere informed me that I would die that very night. I was condemned to death without knowing what I was accused of. Since they hadn't even asked for my identity card, I wasn't going to be killed because of my ethnicity, nor for that matter for my possessions, since besides the Suzuki I owned neither house nor television nor stereo.

Apparently they had come to my house with one idea in mind and no matter what I said they weren't going to change their plans. They had used the pretext of my brother's not having gone to the roadblocks as an excuse to come looking for women. There were seven young girls at the house, and they had attracted the unwanted attentions of the men in the neighborhood, where the lack of women was beginning to be felt.

At a certain point, Majyambere asked his colleague to go to his house and get a bottle of wine. To get into their good graces, I told them that I would be delighted to share a glass of wine with them, and they suggested that I go home with them. I immediately accepted the invitation. It was risky, but it was the only way to get them away from my family. I told myself that if they, for one reason or another, decided to kill me once I was at their house, my family would have time to go and hide in the surrounding banana groves. On the other hand, if they decided to kill me at my own house, there was the risk that they would kill everyone at the same time to get rid of the witnesses. When my sisters, who had witnessed the scene from a distance, saw me and my brother leave with the two militiamen, they believed that we would be executed, and they cried until we got back. The two young men lived a couple of doors down. In addition to a bottle of white wine looted from the stores of a Hutu merchant in the neighborhood, Majyambere had an entire collection of firearms. While I shakily drank the glass of wine that his comrade had served me, Majyambere explained to me how each gun worked. After each explanation he teased me by saying that he was going to kill me. For several seconds I would only hear the sound of him loading the gun. All movement was suspended while I waited for him to shoot. When he put the gun down on the table, my hand continued its suspended motion and a sip of wine would moisten my throat, suddenly parched by fear. After an interminable time, he finished his gun show. I quickly emptied my glass. I didn't want to stay forever with these men who, because they dealt daily with death and violence, had lost all semblance of humanity.

Alas, my troubles were not over. Majyambere had something other than the pleasure of sharing a glass of wine in mind when he invited me to his house. When he had finished showing off his guns, he asked me to follow him, alone this time, to his bedroom. His friend stayed in the living room with my brother and emptied the rest of the bottle of wine. I had heard a lot of stories about women who had been raped, but I had never thought that that could happen to me some day. I didn't know how to react. Should I run out of the house calling to the neighbors for help? Or should I follow him so as not to put my family in danger? Once again I decided to accept his invitation so that my family could survive. The truth was that Majyambere wasn't interested in me, but in my sisters and nieces. He asked me to give him one of them for the night. What saved the girls was that he first talked to me for a long time about his family, to whom he seemed to be very attached. I therefore appealed to his family feelings when I tried to explain to him why I couldn't fulfill his demand. I was astonished to see that he accepted my position so quickly and that he didn't even seem to want to use force to get what he wanted. Having agreed to leave "my" girls alone, he still felt the need for a woman for the night, so he expected certain compensations on my side. He asked me to spend the night with him. I was speechless for a few seconds. When it was a question of defending my family, I had no difficulty finding excuses, but when it came to myself, no good excuse presented itself. I could only use the risk of pregnancy to justify my refusal to sleep with him. Unhappily for me, he had a good supply of condoms. I therefore accepted his proposal, but postponed it for several days so that we could, I said, get to know one another better. For more than an hour I negotiated vigorously for this delay. After a visit of more than three long hours, our "host" let us go. His way of saying goodbye was to tell us to go home quickly because he wanted to throw a grenade right away. Of course he was joking, but it wasn't until I heard the sound of one of my sisters closing the house door behind me that I felt safe. When my mother and sisters asked me what had happened, instead of answering I burst into tears. I had been under so much tension for the last few hours that it was impossible to hold back my tears when I found myself in the warmth of my family.

The morning after our visit from the militia, in spite of the rebel shells that were falling a few hundred meters away from the house, I left the relative security of the hallway to ask advice from a friend. I was very afraid for my sisters and nieces, because many young girls in the neighborhood had been the victims of repeated rapes. The friend in question advised me to go see the president of the neighborhood militia, who was the only person capable of giving me a few guarantees. The advice seemed good to me, but I was worried about the possibility of meeting him. When I arrived at his house, I ran into his sister, who had been an old school friend. He promised that the militia would not come and threaten my family, and as my part of the bargain, I agreed to let the neighborhood health clinic use my Suzuki. I also got an agreement that members of my family who got sick would be treated for free. It was a good arrangement that took the car out of danger because there was no longer the risk that it would be stolen by the first one to happen by. Unfortunately, the protection of the president was relative and didn't shelter me from the daily annoyances of the militia. Every day there were more of them who came to the house to look at the girls. They always wanted to see all of the girls, and since as often as they could they stayed hiding in their room, I would call them one by one. It was only after the parade was over that they were allowed to go back inside. When the visitor didn't have to hurry back to the roadblocks or to the front, he would insist that the girls stay with him for half an hour or even longer. These visits, which were very traumatic for my sisters and nieces, could be repeated several times a day. Among these militiamen, I remember one very well, a young man named Braddock. He could not have been more than twenty, but he was the one we feared most. He was always grinding his teeth and fiddling with grenades. Every time he came to our house I feared that, through his carelessness, one of them would fall on the ground and explode in our faces. Every morning we had to bring him a thermos of sweet tea at the roadblocks. We had no choice but to obey him.

Around mid-April, Kanombe, the neighborhood around the airport, came under bombardment. We were completely cut off from the rest of the town. It was no longer possible to buy provisions, not only medicines but also food, a large part of which came from the market at Kanombe. To survive, we ate rotten kernels of corn that we stole from a factory that produced fodder for animals. At the end of April a way was opened to the center of town. I took advantage of this to evacuate all of my sisters to my eldest sister's house. Protecting them from the militia was becoming increasingly difficult. The most dangerous among them had already declared his love for one of my sisters and had decided to make her his wife. His name was Paulin, and he too was a brother of the president of the militia. He was feared in the entire neighborhood, even by the other members of the militia, because of his cruelty.

He told us that he himself had killed around a hundred people who had taken shelter in the L'Institute Africain et Mauricien des Statistiques et de l'Economie Appliquée (IAMSEA) in the neighboring area of Remera. The first time that he arrived at my house, it was around six in the evening. Unlike his colleagues, he did not come looking for women. He came to carry out a search. He had heard that I was hiding Tutsi and that, thanks to his brother's protection, our house had not been searched. Paulin had made up his mind to kill everyone if I were ever caught hiding someone. To enter, he did not ring the bell like everyone else. He kicked down the door. At his request I made everyone come into the living room. The adults had to have their identity cards on them. Afterwards he went through the whole house to make sure that no one was hiding. I had to go in front of him into all the rooms with a flashlight, because we had not had electric power for several weeks. To enter a room, he kicked the door open and pushed me ahead with the barrel of his gun. I had to shine the light into all the corners, under the bed, and in the closet. If I hadn't been racked with fear, I would have thought I was in an action film. With his green uniform, minus hat and shoes, his Kalashnikov pointed at the back of my neck, kicking the doors open and showing me where to shine the light by jerking his head, he could have been mistaken for Rambo. Back in the living room, he checked everyone's identity cards. Unfortunately Charlotte, like many Tutsi in those days, did not have one. She had instead a certificate of loss issued by the municipality. When Paulin began to threaten her, the whole family, even the children noisily took up her defense and he ended up by leaving her in peace. Paulin ended his pathetic life killed by other members of the militia over the question of how to divide some stolen goods.

After evacuating my sisters, I took advantage of some neighbors' departure for Gitarama to send my mother there. She had fallen ill, and she and the rest of the children were going to stay with a friend. I stayed in my house with my niece and her little daughter Isimbi, Charlotte, my brother, and Nyandwi. The latter two were forced to stay in the neighborhood until the last minute, because men who tried to leave were sent back to the roadblocks. Even though I was constantly afraid, I felt better knowing that my family was safe. I believed that, outside of Kigali, there was no danger. At any rate, the rebels continued to advance, and there were no other opportunities to leave. There was no question of my leaving in my car, because it was still being used by the neighborhood dispensary, and I couldn't risk my life by traveling on foot. Perhaps my niece and I could hope to arrive downtown safe and sound, but Charlotte was in danger of being killed at the first roadblock. I could not leave her alone. I therefore resigned myself to waiting. When I began to lose all hope of leaving in time, I learned that the president of the militia was going to evacuate his entire family. It was up to me to convince him to take us at the same time. Once again the car was the medium of exchange. He agreed to drive us personally to Gitarama, but, in exchange, he would keep the car. He promised to give it back to me later. My departure was assured, and he could use the car the way he wanted. He didn't ask any questions, even when Charlotte got into the car. Along the way, when, at the sight of her, the militias accused him of transporting rebels, he became angry. Thanks to his intervention, no one bothered us until we got to Gitarama. Ironically, at a roadblock leaving Kigali, his son, who was in the first car, nearly was killed. They took him for a rebel. With his tall stature, his refined features, and his dark skin, he had all the characteristics of a Tutsi. He was saved by his sister, who looked like a Hutu.

At Gitarama my long-time friend Spéciose welcomed me. We had studied the humanities together at the Lycée Notre Dame de Cîteaux in Kigali. My mother, who had arrived before me, was gravely ill. She had contracted a severe case of malaria, and the fact that she did not know how her children were only made matters worse. Spéciose lived in fear of the searches, which were frequent at this time. It was enough for a neighbor or an enemy to insinuate that one harbored Tutsi to have a whole brigade of militia on the doorstep. You were never sure how the search would end up. Many were killed, not because they were sheltering Tutsi, but because they had valuable possessions or money that the militia wanted to take for themselves. In order not to be apprehended after the return of law and order, they would kill the entire household. Spéciose had every reason to fear these searches. She had a Tutsi friend, whom she had been able to evacuate from Kigali with the help of a couple of government soldiers, hidden above her ceiling. In addition to the six members of my family, she had taken in Marie, a colleague from work, and her family. They had fled Butare, where they were threatened by the militia. Then there was Immaculée, a friend of Spéciose's from Kigali who was there with her family, which numbered about ten people. Finally there were the two children who belonged to the young woman above the ceiling. All these people were packed, after a fashion, into Spéciose's house and in contiguous buildings that belonged to the association for which she worked. A search would have ended in a massacre.

When I arrived in Gitarama the massacres of the Tutsi were continuing, but they were less widespread than during the month of April. A former colleague from the CSC, Nyombayire Jean-Marie Vianney, was killed after I had already been in Gitarama for two weeks. When the killings had begun, he had hidden himself in a little woods next to his home. After more than a month of living like a wild animal, he left, probably to look for something to eat, and was immediately rounded up by the militia. Then he was taken to Gitarama and shot in the head. I had known Jean-Marie since 1988. We had been hired the same day at the CSC. During the five years that we worked together, he was a friend and incomparable colleague. Far from Byumba and my own mother, his had become a second mother to me. She was an old woman, shy, but welcoming. She made very good banana beer and never failed to send me some when she made a batch. Jean-Marie had a brother who had joined the rebellion at the beginning in 1990. He had left without telling Jean-Marie, so everyone at the CSC was quite worried about him. One day he telephoned from Uganda. We were all relieved to know that he was still alive, but we were angry nonetheless. By telephoning from Uganda, the country from which the rebel attacks were launched, he risked putting his brother in danger. Jean-Marie wasn't the only Tutsi colleague to be put to death by the militia. Rugeruza Etienne was killed along with his entire family, despite the fact that his wife was a Hutu from Ruhengeri. When Etienne spoke to me about his family, I was astonished that a southern Tutsi had married a northern Hutu. He laughingly told me that he and his father had been the only Tutsi to come to his wedding. His friends had declined the invitation because they thought that his marriage was a misalliance. The husband of Pelagie, the cashier at CSC, was also killed during my stay in Gitarama. Only a few days after my arrival, other friends were killed too. Among them Esther's parents, her brother-in-law who was a teacher, and his eldest son. Her sister, Ibyishaka, had been able to escape and hid in the parish of Kabgayi.

I stayed at Gitarama for the whole of the month of May. Almost all of the heads of the NGOs involved in development had come there. We were overcome by the extent of the tragedy. In addition to the Tutsi genocide, which was happening before our eyes, the rebels undertook widespread killing of the civilian Hutu population in the zones that they occupied. Thousands of people, the majority of them women and children, roamed the streets without any humanitarian aid. All of the humanitarian organizations had deserted the country just at the moment when the Rwandan people needed them the most. The Red Cross was the only one that had stayed, but their resources were limited. It was going to be impossible for them to help hundreds of thousands of people in distress. Thinking about these events today, more than four years afterwards, I am unable to explain to myself what the attitude of either the humanitarian NGOs, the United Nations, or the international community in general was. I remain convinced that if UNAMIR and the humanitarian NGOs had stayed in Rwanda, it would have been possible to avoid the genocide. The armed conflict could have been stopped and transitional political institutions put in place. The international community seemed more interested in gross acts of war than in the plight of the people who were being killed every day, of those who were hiding in the ceilings, woods, ditches, and swamps, and of those thousands who were wandering along the roads. The weak, children, pregnant and nursing mothers, and old people were condemned to die of starvation, sickness, and exhaustion. As for those of us working for the Rwandan NGOs, we were aware of our inability to face this tragedy alone. Nevertheless, we were convinced that staying in hiding in our little corners and continuing not to speak up made us accomplices of the militias and the rebels. We began to meet in order to denounce the massacres of the Hutu and Tutsi populations and the resumption of the war and also to see how we could come to the aid of those who had been displaced. We were in the process of preparing emergency plans to submit to our backers when Gitarama was attacked. That day Spéciose had gone with Frans, a representative from our donors, to Kamonyi camp, where several thousand refugees who had come from Nyacyonga were living in absolute misery, without any humanitarian aid. When they came back, the town was already beginning to empty. I left with Frans and a group of people who were at Spéciose's. The rest of the group crammed into a small truck from the Gitarama CSC driven by Marie.

There were roadblocks every ten meters guarded by young men armed with clubs and rifles. Charlotte, whom we could not take with us, remained hidden at a house that belonged to an old woman in the Muslim neighborhood. Spéciose's Tutsi friend stayed hidden in the ceiling and left her hiding place when the rebels arrived. Today she is working again in Kigali. Spéciose took her friend's two little girls with her and passed them off as her own children. The departure from Gitarama was a nightmare. The thousands of fleeing people, cars, and trucks full of soldiers created monstrous bottlenecks. Shells fired by the rebels fell in many parts of town. The rat-a-tat-tat of the heavy machine guns mingled with the cries of babies. The militias threatened the fleeing people with blood-stained clubs. People had their throats slit at the roadblocks at the slightest hesitation or suspicion. At one roadblock more or less five kilometers from the city, a woman was stabbed and killed with spears while we watched. Our car moved at a snail's pace. My stomach knotted with fear, I wished I could have flown far away from this Hell, but we had to be patient, creep along with the others, praying that we would not be the next victims of the militias' clubs or the rebels' shells and bullets.

We spent the first night of our wandering on the premises of a high school at Muyunzwe, a place about twenty kilometers from Gitarama. The local population was very hostile. In the psychotic situation in which we lived, people suspected everyone who came from somewhere else of being rebels or their accomplices, come to infiltrate their area. In the face of the approaching danger, instead of the pity that they would have felt in different circumstances, fear and suspicion dominated them. They went so far as to destroy bridges to prevent vehicles from crossing. Since leaving Kigali I had noticed that fear, instead of bringing people together, separates them. People who had lived together peacefully for years began to suspect each other to the point of making denunciations. I also observed that the will to totally exterminate the Tutsi grew with the approach of the rebels. Tutsi who had been spared in one neighborhood or another because their neighbors didn't have anything against them were killed when rebel shells began to fall. It is human nature to see enemies everywhere and think that the only way to stay alive is to kill them. The locals reproached us with what they called our cowardice. For them, these thousands of people who flooded in were deserters, cowards who abandoned their houses and their possessions without presenting any resistance. I understood them, because our flight put them in the line of fire, making them the next victims. After Byumba, I had noticed the same attitude everywhere that the refugees passed through, but this didn't prevent their detractors from following them the next day, when war fell on them. When you haven't yet heard the sound of a shell landing a few meters away, when you haven't heard the sound of heavy artillery and Kalashnikovs, when you haven't yet seen your friends, neighbors, or even your own family members torn apart by a grenade, when you don't know what it feels like to walk over dead bodies or even hide under them to save your own skin, you think it would be possible to stay bravely in your house or even pick up a stick or some stones to fight soldiers who are armed to the teeth.

We arrived at Gikongoro the second day after our precipitous departure from Gitarama. We were so famished that we plunged into the first restaurant we saw. I was one of the first ones in along with Frans, the Dutch friend who had been such a great help when we left Gitarama. On seeing us, a soldier and several civilians who were eating started to make rude remarks about women who went out with whites, holding them responsible for the defeat of the government forces. Since 1993 in Byumba, I had been disappointed in the behavior of FAR. Many soldiers deserted their posts to plunder houses and stores. With the resurgence of regionalism in the army, certain soldiers from the south did not want to fight for a northern power. They openly declared that the war was an affair between the Tutsi and the people from the north, and that it was in no way of any concern to them. They didn't see, they said, why they had to continue to die to keep northerners and Habyarimana in power. They should just take care of themselves. When the war arrived in the south, the northern soldiers reacted the same way. Since 1993 the only thing that everyone seemed to be able to agree on was plundering. Instead of fighting, they preferred to pillage small towns and commercial centers, which they then left in the hands of the rebels. In short, when I heard the accusations of the soldier and his companions, I was so disgusted that I thought neither of the pistol he carried in his bandolier, nor of the necklace of bullets he wore around his neck, nor even of the grenades he had in his pocket. All I saw was the injustice and irresponsibility of what he was saying. I had no desire to bear the blame for the defeat of FAR. They had failed in their mission and it was up to them to assume the responsibility and not look for a scapegoat. I reacted, forgetting that it was wartime and that a soldier in the middle of losing the war could prove very dangerous. As was to be expected, he didn't much appreciate my attitude and he pushed me out of my chair with the butt of his gun and made me leave the restaurant. If not for the intervention of another soldier, who arrived a few minutes later and calmed him down, I don't doubt that he would have put a bullet in my head without a second thought, convinced that he had rid the country of an enemy. Nevertheless he was too angry with me to let me clean off. The punch that he gave me as a lesson for my recklessness made me zigzag between the tables, and I found myself sitting in my chair without really knowing how I had gotten there. I suddenly wasn't hungry any more, despite the fact that I hadn't eaten for two days. I left without eating and went to the Gikongoro Agricultural Project, where we had temporarily found shelter. Lying on a mattress, staring at the ceiling, I realized that I had narrowly escaped death. It was only at that moment that the horror of what I had just experienced became clear to me. I began to tremble like a leaf. I looked back on what would have happened to my mother and little sister if I had been killed. I swore to myself that I would keep quiet, no matter what kind of provocations I would be confronted with later. But it is always easier to make promises than to keep them.

At Gikongoro our group split in two. Frans, Marie, and her family went toward Bujumbura, where they expected that there would be representatives of a Rwandan NGO to help facilitate contacts with the outside world. The means of communication no longer functioned in Rwanda since the resumption of the war. As for me, Spéciose, Immaculée, and our respective families, we continued on to Cyangugu, a town on

the border with Zaire. After Gitarama was taken, without much resistance, by the rebels, we were convinced that the defeat of the government forces was inevitable. Rebel control of all of Rwandan territory
was only a matter of time. Cyangugu had a double advantage. Being far
from the front, we would be able to have a rest from the noise of the artillery and machine guns. In addition, since the town was located on the
frontier, we would easily be able to leave the country the day that there
was no other alternative. In a normal situation the trip from Gikongoro
takes a maximum of two hours. It took us two days to cover the same
distance. At each roadblock we were stopped and thoroughly searched.
At Pindura in the Nyungwe Forest, we were held up for several hours.
The forest guards who were at the roadblock discovered a badge in
Spéciose's bag with a picture on it of Gatabazi Félicien, the leader of
the PSD who had been assassinated in February. They wanted to know
who this man was and what his connection to Spéciose was. It was a
trick question; we didn't know if he actually recognized Gatabazi or
whether Gatabazi was considered to be an ally of the rebels or not. As a
result, we kept quiet. While one group of guards continued to interrogate Spéciose, the others carried out a systematic search of all the baggage in the car. To explain the reason for the search, one of the forest
guards, joining his words with deeds, wanted to show us that it would be
easy to hide a grenade in a bag of clothes. At the sight of this weapon,
his colleague, who had not been present for the "demonstration," began
to shout that he had just found a rebel and started to beat the owner of
the bag. Luckily, the one who had planted the grenade intervened and
the young girl was released. As for Spéciose, her interrogation continued until she finally said that it was Gatabazi whose picture was on the
badge. Very fortunately, he was not considered to be a rebel collaborator.

At Cyangugu a staff member of the Centre IWACU welcomed us.[3]
He was married to a Tutsi woman and was terrified by the idea that some
day the militia could turn up at his house. This dreaded visit happened
the day of our arrival. It seems that the militia came from Bugarama.
They were known in the entire prefecture of Cyangugu for their cruelty.

---

3. Centre IWACU is a Rwandan research and development center. In Kinyarwanda, Iwacu means the equivalent of "at our house."

Fortunately for us and for our host, everyone had an identity card. They left, even excusing themselves for having disturbed our host's wife, who had just given birth. During their entire visit she had her face turned to the wall and the blankets pulled up over her head, pretending to be asleep. We greeted their departure with a big sigh of relief. With the staff of the Centre IWACU, we continued the plans begun in Gitarama and laid out an emergency aid project for the camps at Cyangugu and Gikongoro. Without any way to communicate with the outside world, it was impossible to send the dossier directly to our European partners so that they could help us find financing. We had to go to Uvira, a Zairian town located about one hundred kilometers to the south. Bukavu, the capital city of the Zairian province of South Kivu, was only a few kilometers from Cyangugu, but there as well, the means of communication had not functioned for several years. I went to Uvira with Spéciose and the administrator from the Centre IWACU to try to telephone Marie, our colleague whom we thought was in Bujumbura, to see what the best way would be to send the dossier. It was a useless trip. Since the situation at Bujumbura was very tense, Marie had not been able to stay, nor had she been able to open an office as we had hoped. She had been evacuated to Belgium. Hutu were not welcome in Bujumbura.

To coordinate the projects of the groups from Cyangugu and Gisenyi, a meeting was organized in the Zairian town of Goma. I left for Goma with Spéciose, traveling via Gisenyi. That June, a trip in the interior of Rwanda was dangerous because of the roadblocks. To minimize the risk, I could not wear a chignon, which made me look like a Tutsi. Spéciose had to take out her braids, because popular opinion held that Hutu women did not braid their hair. Despite these precautions, suspicions fell on us. At one roadblock in Kibuye, for example, a member of the militia exclaimed when he saw me, "Look, a Tutsi woman!" To defend myself, I became angry. I didn't want to show him that I was afraid. Going and coming, we passed trucks full of militia. People said that they were coming from Bugarama to bring reinforcements to their colleagues in Kibuye, to fight the Tutsi who had hidden in the mountains of Bisesero. French soldiers from Operation Turquoise, a humanitarian zone set up by the French and later taken over by the UN, saved only a few hundred of them. Many thousands of others were killed. We met the first contingent of soldiers from Operation Turquoise on our way to Gisenyi. They came from Goma to assure the security in the humanitarian zone created by France in conjunction with the United Nations in the prefectures of Cyangugu, Kibuye, and Gisenyi. Their main mission was ensuring the safety of the escaping Tutsi and the humanitarian NGOs, so that they could resume humanitarian assistance to the thousands of displaced people. I watched them pass by with a mixture of great pleasure and a little bitterness. They were going to prevent the massacre of around ten thousand Tutsi packed into the camp at Nyarushishi; they were going to permit the humanitarian NGOs to help thousands of people who found themselves in the newly created humanitarian zone; but they had arrived too late to prevent the total disintegration of Rwandan society. They had arrived too late for the hundreds of thousands of dead crammed into common graves that littered all of Rwanda. They were also too late to prevent the exile of the thousands of people who were jammed into Gisenyi and Cyangugu once the rebels took over power in Kigali. The town of Gisenyi was crowded and we had enormous difficulty finding a place to spend the night. It was already dark when we found a bunk bed in the men's dormitory in the Protestant Welcome Center where we spent the night with about twenty men who were terrified by our presence. Maybe they thought we were spies from the RPF and that we were going to kill them in their sleep!

Our donors were also represented at the meeting in Goma. The most important decision taken during this meeting was to create the Collective of Rwandan NGOs with two hubs: one at Gisenyi and the other at Cyangugu.[4] Once back in Cyangugu, we tried to set up concrete programs with the help of French humanitarian aid, but the situation deteriorated so badly that we had to escape to Bukavu before carrying out the activities we had planned.

---

4. The Collective of Rwandan NGOs (hereafter the Collective) was finally formed when individual staff members of several Rwandan NGOs, all members of the umbrella organization Conseil de Concertation des Organisations d'Appui aux Initiatives de Base (CCOAIB), found each other again in the refugee camps in eastern Zaire. They used the term "collective" because they all wanted to retain their primary identification with their employer-NGOs in Rwanda, although eventually their former employers in Rwanda disallowed the use of their names and required their staff either to return to Rwanda or consider their nonreturn as a formal resignation.

Cyangugu, a little town of ten thousand, had seen its population expand ten times in just a few weeks. Tension had reached a peak. Rumors ran rampant that the rebels were going to block all the accessible borders and prevent the Hutu from escaping to Zaire. We were reminded that at Byumba they were already telling people that they would push all the Hutu into Lake Kivu. In spite of the presence of French troops, who held meetings and distributed communiqués to calm the population, the fear that reigned in Cyangugu continued to grow.

At the beginning of July, the RPF, which controlled almost the entire interior, set up a transitional government. After they took over Kigali, everyone gave in to panic. Very early in the morning, lines of vehicles and thousands of people pushed and shoved on the little frontier bridge across the Ruzizi River, trying to be the first ones over. The value of the Rwandan franc fell dramatically. People saw their money, which they counted on to survive until the arrival of humanitarian aid, evaporate. Whereas a week before you needed ten new Zairian francs for one Rwandan franc, now it was the reverse: you needed 10,000 Rwandan francs to get 100 Zairian francs. On the other side of the Ruzizi, a reception center had been set up by the Forces Armées Zaïroises (FAZ). This center seemed to have as its one objective robbing the refugees of all their possessions of any value, particularly vehicles and money.

Rwanda emptied itself of its population at the border posts at Cyangugu and Gisenyi. Old and young, men and women, ministers, bankers, teachers, students, pupils, delinquents, and criminals fled. Rwanda was like a sinking ship that even the rats were leaving. Only those under the protection of the French in the Turquoise Zone could enjoy, one last time, the pleasure of feeling at home, of having a country, a homeland, putting off for later the moment of crossing the border, of becoming a refugee. A large number of them would join us in exile a few months later, at the time when the French troops retreated and the Turquoise Zone fell under the jurisdiction of the UN, which was returning to Rwanda to count the dead. Those who thought that the UN soldiers would assure their protection, as the French soldiers had, paid dearly for their confidence in an institution that had already shown its incapacity to protect the innocent during the Tutsi genocide in April 1994. In April 1995, at least eight thousand people were killed in the displaced persons camps at Kibeho by the new Rwandan army, in the presence of the UN troops charged with assuring their protection. Neither the UN, which watched this massacre of the innocents without lifting a finger, nor the RPF, responsible for the death of many thousands of people, mostly women and children, were disturbed by this. The dead of Kibeho were buried in common graves and forgotten.

4

Survival in the Camps
at Kivu

WHILE THESE EVENTS were unfolding on the other side of the
Ruzizi River, I was trying to survive with my family at Bukavu. We
spent the first week at a primary school. There was no room in the
classrooms, so we slept in the dust of the courtyard. During the night,
those who slept inside urinated on us. In spite of these miserable conditions, I slept deeply, something that hadn't happened to me since April
6, 1994. Fear of the rebels and the militias no longer kept me awake until
dawn.

The second day after our arrival I got to work. I knew Bukavu well
and had addresses of contacts, principally among the NGOs, in my head.
I very quickly found members of the Collective of Rwandan NGOs.
There were about twenty of us, and later we heard that other members of
the Collective had been seen on the other end of Lake Kivu at Goma. We
spent a lot of time in meetings, looking for things to do, looking for
ways to make ourselves useful. We contacted the local NGOs to try to
assess the situation together and establish a minimal aid program for the
refugees who were crammed by the hundreds of thousands — the census
had not yet been made — into the streets of Bukavu, without food, without health care, without adequate sanitation.

First of all we had to find housing because, like everyone else, we
had to take care of our families. The NGO ADI-Kivu (Action de Développement Intégré du Kivu) let us use its training center in the village of

Kavumu, about thirty kilometers from Bukavu. In the beginning each family had one room, but as the number of families grew, we needed to squeeze more in, and several families had to share the same room. In the meantime, my brothers and sisters, from whom I had been separated since Kigali, had rejoined me. Even though there were around fifteen of us in one room, we were happy to be together again safe and sound. Few Rwandan families had the same good luck as we did. In spite of the overcrowding in which we had to live at ADI-Kivu, our situation was far better than that of other refugees, who lived in the courtyards of public buildings and the streets of Bukavu with no shelter from the sun and rain. They defecated in broad daylight in holes in the ground over which someone had thrown a couple of boards to stand on. I can still see these young girls and old mothers who had to answer the call of nature in public, trying to hide their faces.

Once housed and assembled at ADI-Kivu, the Collective was able to begin work. Supervision of the thousands of unaccompanied children living in Bukavu was one of our first accomplishments. Most of the time they ate garbage and slept in the gutters or on the roofs of cars. Caritas and UNICEF, which were ready to put money and expertise to work for these children, tried to count and assemble them. Caritas negotiated with the local authorities to find land, and the Collective equipped it and organized the reception. It was comforting to see these children, brought from Bukavu in a state of unspeakable misery, covered in rags and filth and ulcers, their hair full of lice and traumatized by all that they had lived through in Rwanda, become the children that they had been before knowing the horrors of war, genocide, and exile. To see them play something besides war games; to hear them laugh like children should laugh, without the blank stare of those who have watched their families slaughtered; to see them run, gamboling like young goats, warmed our hearts, although at the beginning many of them hid in corners and didn't even want to open their mouths.

At the same time we laid the foundations of a program for the reunification of families. Most families were separated at the time they crossed the border between Rwanda and Zaire. Every day mothers in tears searched all through the town, going from one group of refugees to another, calling the names of their children and asking passersby if they had seen a child of a certain age, a certain height, dressed in a particular way and answering to such and such a name. These inquiries, for the most part, came to nothing. Looking for a five-year-old child in such a vast number of refugees was like looking for a needle in a haystack.

To help these mothers locate their children, we set up the program for the reunification of families with Maendeleo, the NGO radio station at Bukavu. We went among the camps and distributed forms, and Goretti read information over the radio, where we negotiated thirty-minute time slots.

Since the postal service in Zaire had been inoperative for quite a while, the Collective set up a messenger service with letter boxes in every camp so that the refugees who had located their families could re-establish regular contact with them in the camps in North and South Kivu and, later, in the camps in Tanzania and the rest of the world.

After Habyarimana's assassination in 1994 and the ensuing genocide, a large part of the world saw all Hutu as genocidal, from the old woman who could hardly walk to the baby still nursing at his mother's breast. As we saw it, this negative perception explained, in part, the lack of urgency manifested by the humanitarian NGOs and the international community in coming to our aid.

As the Rwandan NGOs had not taken part in the genocide and the massacres that had enveloped Rwanda since 1990, we were well placed to provide better information than that disseminated either by the sources close to the new government in Kigali or by those close to the old regime of Jean Kambanda.[1] With this in mind we organized, beginning in August, several seminars on the Rwandan problem in which Zairian and local NGOs as well as our European partners participated. The Rwandan tragedy is complex. There are not simply victims on one side (Tutsi) and guilty (Hutu) on the other as we have been led to believe. In our meetings we always proposed that all the guilty, regardless of their ethnicity, be identified, judged, and condemned for their crimes, and the innocent rehabilitated. Ignoring this reality would only impede

---

1. Jean Kambanda was prime minister of Rwanda from April 9, 1994, until July 19, 1994. In 1999 he was found guilty of war crimes by the International Criminal Tribunal of Rwanda (ICTR).

progress toward reconciliation and a durable peace for the Rwandan people. As was to be expected, though we wanted to be as objective as possible, we were misunderstood. On the one hand, we were accused of complicity with those who had committed genocide, and on the other we were treated like collaborators with the powers in Kigali.

We began to distribute, via our partners, a regular publication, *La Lettre d'Information* (The Information Letter), under the logo of the Collective. We provided information on the camps, which had been characterized in the international media as hiding places for the perpetrators of genocide, where the former officials held the other refugees hostage and prevented them from returning to Rwanda. We showed another view of the camps, the one that we saw every day. We did not want to deny the presence of those who were guilty of genocide among the refugees, we simply wanted to remind people that the vast majority of the refugees in the camps had played no role whatsoever in the tragedy. We thought the best way to marginalize the guilty was to recognize the existence of the innocent majority, thereby lessening the appeal of the genocidaires.

By the end of August, the majority of the refugees had been installed in the camps. There were between 350,000 and 500,000 Rwandans and Burundians crammed into about twenty camps in the areas of Bukavu and Uvira.

After a failed attempt to relocate a small group of refugees to Bunyakiri, in which members of the Collective were attacked by a crowd of people who suspected them of having been sent by the RPF to repatriate them to Rwanda, we realized that in order to organize in the camps, we had to live there. Since we couldn't start everywhere at the same time, we chose the two camps that were closest to ADI-Kivu: INERA and Kashusha.[2] I therefore left the relative comfort of the room in ADI-Kivu that I shared with my family and went to live at INERA.

INERA was located about thirty kilometers from Bukavu toward Goma, and, along with the neighboring camps of Kashusha and ADI-Kivu, housed a third of the refugee population of South Kivu. Groupe Jérémie, a Zairian human rights NGO, had offered their services to

2. INERA camp was built near the offices of l'Institut National d'Études et de Recherches Agronomiques (INERA).

Caritas for managing the camp. They let me use a small plastic blindé located in an area that the refugees had nicknamed "the neighborhood of the prefects" because it was inhabited by former officials from Habyarimana's regime. Because of the fear and suspicion that ruled the camps at that time, some inhabitants of the area did not want a neighbor whom they did not know and who, in addition, was called Umutesi, a name normally associated with Tutsi. They bribed some young men from the neighborhood who took advantage of the dark to destroy my blindé, and I had to construct a new one in another part of the camp.

INERA was the first place where I slept in a sheeting.[3] On this first night I had taken every precaution to protect myself from the cold, since at night the temperature could drop to 10 degrees Celsius. It was worse than I thought it would be. I was wearing pants, a flannel nightgown, a sweater, and socks, and in addition I was covered with a blanket and a thick bedspread. In spite of all these precautions the cold kept me awake most of the night. My nose and ears were frozen. Around six in the morning I was awakened by drops of water falling in my ear. I thought at first that it was raining and that the water was coming through a hole in the sheeting, but it was only the condensation of my breath during the night. My neighbors, when I told them of my early morning misadventures, advised me to put covers on the ceiling and walls of the blindé so I could protect myself from heat during the day, cold at night, and drops of water in the morning. These coverings had another great advantage in that they protected me from the curiosity of my neighbors. When night fell and lamps were lit, passersby could see everything that went on in a blindé. The covers allowed a semblance of privacy.

My blindé was both home and office and was spacious in comparison to those of my neighbors. I was able to have a small bedroom for myself, and another for Bakunda and my three nieces, the four children who had followed me. The rest of it served as an office and a meeting room. For the refugees who had some money it was always possible to make a more spacious home, but the poor, that is to say the majority, had to make do with one sheeting. In such a small space, parents and

3. The standard issue sheeting distributed by the humanitarian NGOs is a white, green, or blue plastic tarpaulin four-by-five-yards square. With this one piece one has to construct a shelter for a family of at least five people.

children slept on the same mat. Children had to witness fights between their parents and other scenes not normally associated with childhood. The children were not the only ones to be present for the fights and lovemaking of their parents. The neighbors were there too. As a rule, a blindé was only separated from the neighboring ones by about a yard. Since the sheeting was thin, everything that was said in one blindé was heard by all the neighbors. It was common during the night to hear all the people in one area debating the same subject as if they were all in the same room. There was an element of security in this proximity. In case there was a problem, the neighbors could intervene right away. But from time to time, it was frustrating to live so publicly.

Little by little I settled in, gradually discovering the other problems of life in the camps. More than one hundred of us shared one toilet. In the absence of a rigorous cleaning schedule, it quickly became useless. People relieved themselves all around the hole. Since there were swarms of flies everywhere, I was concerned about fly-borne disease.

There were no showers in the entire neighborhood. I had to wait until night to wash myself. Every time that someone passed by with a flashlight, I stopped washing and covered myself with a towel, but since I washed in the dark, I was never sure that I was completely clean. I had to find a solution. My blindé occupied an entire three-by-four-meter area. Every household had the same amount of land, but my neighbor had a smaller blindé and had some space left over where I was able to build a small shelter. I asked some children to collect stones to put on the ground, and since there was a source of water nearby, I dug a small ditch in front of my blindé for the water. Finally I could wash myself in peace. Everyone in the area was happy about this, because they could use it too.

In the area of cleanliness there was another feminine matter about which I could do nothing. Those in charge of humanitarian aid had not thought of feminine hygiene, and during their periods women used old rags or skirts. Soap was only distributed sporadically and it was almost impossible to find enough to wash oneself and one's soiled underwear. After several days of washing with water alone, it became hard and abrasive. If you had the misfortune of having to move around during your period, you became chapped. In addition, since men ran the camp, they had not thought of private places where women could go to wash this laundry away from the eyes of passersby. We had to wash it late at night or early in the morning in front of our blindés. The bloody water snaked in little rivulets between the blindés and here and there made bloody little puddles. To add to the discomfort of the situation, many women were obliged to wash these bloody rags in the same pots in which they prepared food for their families. I couldn't help asking myself what evil we had done to be condemned to these extremities.

Once every two weeks we received enough corn, either as grain or flour, as well as beans or lentils, salt, and oil to survive for a week at most. Malnutrition was rampant among children under five and among pregnant and nursing mothers, particularly those who lived alone and did not have the opportunity to hire themselves out to the locals. Among the many children with bloated stomachs, huge heads, and frail limbs whom I met every day at the nutrition center at INERA, I remember Muhawe, my little four-year-old neighbor. His mother had died on the way to Zaire while giving birth to his little sister. The baby had only survived her mother by a few days, and Muhawe now lived with his widowed grandmother. When Muhawe left Rwanda, he was a chubby three-year-old. Bad food and dysentery had made him into a little old man whose huge head was all you noticed. He was too weak to get up and walk even a few steps and just sat in front of his grandmother's blindé. To go back inside he crawled on his hands and knees like a baby. His grandmother brought him regularly to the nutritional center, but the diet he was given didn't have much of an effect. He either vomited it all up or else refused to swallow. When I arrived in the neighborhood, Muhawe had reached an advanced state of malnutrition. To save him, we had to find meals with meat, the only thing he still was willing to swallow and that didn't cause him to vomit. Unfortunately, the nutrition center didn't give him any, and the grandmother was too poor to buy any, even once a week. I therefore began to feed this little boy myself and prepared meals with vegetables and potatoes and made him eat them first before getting a piece of meat, in spite of his tears and nausea. The first days were the most difficult, but later he ate everything I gave him without my having to force him.

I was happy to see him get stronger and be able to cross the distance between his grandmother's blindé and mine alone, but rebellion gnawed at me. What had Muhawe and the thousands of other Rwandan children who were dying in the camps done? Was Muhawe guilty of genocide to deserve this fate? Why was he condemned to die? One day when I was on the verge of cracking, I took a pen and began to write down everything that was in my heart. I described the suffering of Muhawe and the other children, who, like him, were starving and whose graves lined the long road into exile. I described the tragedy of the old women who lived alone in plastic blindés riddled with holes, and the suffering of the street children of Bukavu who lived by begging. I imagined the horror experienced by the young RPF soldier who, back from the war, found that the militias had exterminated his entire family. I spoke of the murder of my cousin Laurent and my mother's friend Nyirarukwavu. I made a habit of writing so that people could know and break their silence, but also to stop my own pain. I often wept while I wrote, but when I had finished I felt comforted.

To deal with the lack of food aid, many of my neighbors went to work for the locals. In return they received cassava, bananas, and a little money. For a day's work they earned on average the equivalent of twenty-five cents in American money. I happened to run into old school friends who had to work for a couple of beer bananas to provide some variety in their families' diet. Women, who in Rwanda had been civil servants or had worked in the private sector and who had left beautiful houses and cars in Kigali, allowed themselves to be insulted by potential employers because the survival of their families was at stake. Some locals took advantage of the abundance of female workers to force the women to sleep with them prior to hiring them. Some, particularly those who had sole responsibility for their families, accepted this and a few months later found themselves pregnant, with no possibility of terminating these undesired pregnancies. In addition to working for the locals, women planted kitchen gardens in the spaces between the blindés. The sight of this greenery brightened up the misery. Other economic activities such as small businesses, production of banana beer and corn fritters, basketwork and carpentry took place in the camps. Those with a little money even opened small restaurants, boutiques, butcher shops, cafes, sewing ateliers, hair dressing salons, and so forth.

The provisions of heating wood from the humanitarian organizations were also insufficient, and a week's ration lasted at most three or four days. As a result, the refugees went to the Zairian eucalyptus plantations to make up this deficit, which contributed to tensions among the two communities. Men risked being beaten to death if they were caught, but women were in greater danger. They ran more slowly than the men and weren't strong enough to defend themselves when they were caught. The number of women raped while gathering firewood in the plantations of Zaire is incalculable.

In addition to the practical problems, we were confronted with constant threats to our safety. The great majority of Hutu of all classes had left Rwanda when the rebels took power. This meant that in the camps bandits, ministers, bankers, assassins, businessmen, simple peasants, and soldiers lived side by side, and victims lived with those who had persecuted them in times past. I often met Braddock, the young soldier who, at Kigali, had forced us to bring him tea every morning at the roadblock. He had become a refugee in rags, like so many others. Without a gun to make himself important, he had returned to being the young delinquent he had been before the war, no longer the feared killer who had made us tremble. One day he begged money for food from me. Even unarmed he was a potential danger and his presence in the area didn't make me feel secure. I knew what he was capable of doing for a little money.

The presence of weapons was another factor in this insecurity. The disarmament had worked well enough, but not every little street had been searched. There were people with weapons and grenades everywhere. The situation was most dangerous in the camps of Panzi and Bulonge, where there was a large concentration of soldiers. Grenades exploded there every night and in the morning you mourned the dead, victims of jealousy or account settling. In other places this happened too, but less regularly. My uncle barely escaped death at Panzi. A grenade had been tossed into his blindé. His wife escaped unharmed, but his arm was mangled. At any rate, with the continuing impoverishment of the refugees, those who had weapons began to sell them to the Zairian military and the Burundian rebels. These sales, dictated by the need to survive, solved the problem of weapons. The last year there were almost no deaths caused by firearms or grenades.

Repeated attacks by soldiers from the RPF were an additional cause of uncertainty and created a state of generalized psychosis. The camp at Birava, located on the shores of Lake Kivu, across from Rwanda, was attacked at the beginning of 1995 by a commando group made up of about one hundred Rwandan soldiers supported by mortars located on a small Zairian island in Lake Kivu. More than sixty people were killed with grenades, mortars, and knives and more than a hundred others were wounded. Following this attack the camp at Birava was deserted. The camp at Panzi was also the target of regular attacks from Rwanda. Twice, when shooting broke out, I was at Panzi. The first time, I was presiding over a meeting of women delegates from the camps in South Kivu making preparations for International Women's Day on March 8, 1995. At first we attempted to keep calm and I continued to moderate the debates as if nothing were happening. Then someone called out that it would be better to take shelter and we rushed to the hall, since the meeting room had large bay windows. Bullets whistled above us. After a few hours the shooting stopped, but we had lost interest in our meeting. After this experience, I didn't want to take the risk of going to Panzi again. Nevertheless, a year later, pressured by the women's organization there, I had to return. What a mistake! Around three o'clock, I began to hear the sound of machine gun fire. As we were close to a Zairian police station, I thought the noise came from there and wasn't worried. Another woman commented that the "Rwandan music" was starting but she didn't seem to attach too much importance to it either. In the marketplace it was business as usual. A few minutes later, however, the shooting became louder. The market emptied in no time. The blindés emptied too. Everyone ran to the ground floors of buildings or to houses with concrete roofs. Around five o'clock the gunfire stopped and I was able to go home. Every attack on a camp by the RPF was followed by a period of generalized fear, even in the camps that had not been targets.

Suspicion and fear themselves created insecurity. When an unknown person entered a camp, he was in danger of being lynched. Often it was enough for someone to simply shout that someone was RPF for him to be killed. Even the employees of the humanitarian NGOs were threatened. Camps like Kashusha, where there was a large concentration of bandits from Kigali, were among the most dangerous. A friend of mine and her sister were very nearly lynched when they returned from visiting me. They left at about six o'clock, and when they got to the Bukavu-Goma road, which separated INERA from Kashusha, two strangers began to follow them, and they began to run. At the taxi stand they slowed down. The two crooks started to yell, "Catch the rebels" and pointed at them. They found themselves surrounded by menacing onlookers. The robbers took advantage of the situation to steal their watches and glasses. A passerby who recognized them saved them from being lynched. If you wanted to appropriate someone else's possessions, you only had to accuse them of being RPF. By this simple word you could activate a blind killing machine, guided only by fear, resentment, and vengeance, though as time passed these feelings diminished.

At INERA, I was considered to be "pro-RPF" because, among other things, I looked like a Tutsi and had a Tutsi name, and I preferred the company of the old women in my neighborhood to that of the directors of the camp. They also held it against me that I organized meetings in my blindé without permission. INERA was organized by Father Carlos of Caritas-Spain, who ran the camp with a firm hand, and lynching, possible at Kashusha, was impossible at INERA. Nevertheless I was afraid, particularly when people came by my blindé asking if this were the place where the RPF woman lived. It was so easy to place a grenade in a blindé. All you needed to do was cut the sheeting near the bed with a razor and put the grenade next to the sleeper, and it was all over. Some days I had trouble sleeping. I wouldn't have been the first woman to be killed by a grenade. About five hundred meters from me, a grenade had killed a young woman and a little girl, and a visiting priest had lost an arm. The assassins were never found. Another family that had escaped death lived in the "prefects" neighborhood. Around two in the morning the woman heard a noise, and she awakened her husband. They got up to see if someone had entered the sheeting to steal. They lit a light and saw that the sheeting had been cut in several places, but everything seemed to be in order. The neighbors, who had heard them speaking, came over to hear the news. The woman got up with her baby in her arms, but as it was cold outside she went back inside to get a cover from the bed to wrap around the baby. It was dark in the blindé. While groping around for the cover she felt something round and cold. She called her husband to bring a flashlight. They discovered a grenade with the pin half out. If it had fallen on the floor it would have exploded.

The deterioration of conditions in the camps brought with it another type of criminality. Killings, for vengeance or out of fear, began to give way to killings committed for the purpose of robbery. A priest who was visiting his parents was killed in Kashusha camp and robbed of two thousand American dollars. While walking around the camp one evening, to see for himself what the reality of life there was, he was approached by a well-known bandit, Pariti, and his gang. The next morning they found his body in the camp cemetery. In Mudaka camp a young man tried to strangle his friend with a rope for a hundred American dollars. Neighbors who heard him yelling intervened and saved him. Security was precarious, and the numbers of rapes, killings, and robberies stayed relatively high despite the introduction of new efforts to maintain order.

The arrival of the Contingent Zaïrois Chargé de la Sécurité dans les Camps (CZSC), at the request of the United Nations High Commissioner for Refugees (UNHCR), created hope that was dashed a few months later when the CZSC became a principal source of insecurity. Like all soldiers, those of the CZSC loved women and money too much. When women didn't come of their own accord, or when they didn't have enough money for prostitutes, they entered the blindés and took women by force. In Kashusha camp, for example, women didn't go out any more after six o'clock. When they went to the bathroom, they had to arm themselves with a razor blade. That way, when a soldier from the CZSC tried to force the door they could cut the sheeting and leave by the back. Pauline, a colleague from the Collective was the victim of an attack of this kind but was able to escape. Not every woman was so lucky. After multiple rapes by soldiers from the CZSC, a young woman from Mushweshwe camp was hospitalized. Another young girl's brother was arrested for something or other. Taking advantage of his guard's inattention, he ran off. Believing that he had returned to his sheeting, the soldiers followed him there, but finding only his sister, they took her in for questioning. The next morning the young woman was hospitalized. She had been beaten and raped. At the same time they recovered the body of a young girl near the CZSC at INERA camp. She had been raped before being stabbed.

A refugee suffers, not only from having been torn from her land, her house, her work and her country, but also from having to beg to survive. For someone who has had work that allowed them to live decently, it is difficult to accept someone else deciding for her what she should eat and how much. It is even more difficult to spend the entire day sitting around with nothing to do but wait for the distribution of aid. Feeling useless is the worst thing imaginable. To forget their uselessness, the refugees threw themselves headlong into drink and debauchery. Alcohol and sex became their major pastimes. Marriages took place younger and younger and were less and less stable. The majority of girls over fifteen were pregnant or had already given birth. Almost every family with daughters had this problem. When she was barely sixteen years old, my niece became pregnant. She was in her second year of secondary school and lived with me at INERA. International opinion tried to explain the phenomenon of the increasing number of single mothers in the camps by saying that it was a deliberate plan on the part of the Hutu to recapture power in Rwanda in the future. I think that this situation, which all the women found deplorable, had roots elsewhere. The lack of anything to do and the absence of privacy allowed children to learn about sex too young. Poverty led young women to give themselves to anyone in order to get food and money to buy cosmetics, shoes, and clothes. There was a crisis of parental authority. Parents were no longer obeyed because children no longer depended on them economically. Whenever a child did not get along with his parents he could always go to the humanitarian organization that was running the camp to get his own blindé and identity card, which gave him the right to receive his own food aid. In a context where sex education was more or less nonexistent, one saw the proliferation of venereal diseases, which often go side by side with AIDS.

With the goal of helping the refugees to put the brakes on this moral self-destruction, the Collective set up a self-organization program in the camps to begin to establish more credible leadership and to organize for return. The first thing we did was to establish a small credit fund to permit the refugees to take care of those needs not covered by humanitarian aid, such as buying clothes, soap, vegetables, and so forth. When we launched these small credit activities, some people thought we were wasting our time, but we succeeded and they provided an entrée for the other programs of the Collective. When Kambanda came to the camps he discouraged the planting of vegetable gardens, saying that return was imminent. We thought this was hot air, words spoken to maintain his credibility, but many believed him.

With groups of rural women who had benefited from the small credit program, we had our first workshop to study the causes and consequences of the Rwandan tragedy at Bukavu at the beginning of

1995. It may have been too soon to begin a debate on such a controversial issue, and the women, because they feared the consequences of speaking openly among strangers, found it difficult to express themselves with confidence. To get around this problem, they were encouraged to express themselves anonymously in writing. This allowed them to identify all those who had played a positive or a negative role in the Rwandan tragedy, but as a result it was impossible to engage in substantive discussions.

A similar problem arose when a group of educated women wanted to disseminate information by and for women. They felt that women did not participate actively in discussions on return because they weren't sufficiently well informed. Their attempt to start a newspaper was blocked by the camp authorities, who themselves had just started their own paper and would not tolerate any competition. It was the kiss of death for the enthusiasm of the women, who didn't want to run the risk of being expelled from the camp for having disobeyed orders. Above all else, the mothers worried about the daily survival of their children, and they were ready to make any concession in order to ensure their safety.

International Women's Day in 1995 was an opportunity for us to encourage the women to organize and participate more actively in bettering the conditions in the camps and to engage in discussions on return and reconciliation. Cultural, self-help, and other women's groups were created. Female representatives were elected for the camps. From then on, in most of the camps, the female representatives were consulted by the humanitarian NGOs and even by the UNHCR when they planned something for women. They were also consulted on distribution of humanitarian aid. The representative structure of the women also played an important role in the social life of the refugees.

While preparing for Women's Day in 1996, we tried to set up representation for women on the regional level, but the women showed very little interest in taking part in this process at that time, though the idea was brought up again later. This experience, which followed the problems encountered with the groups of women who joined small credit unions and the association of educated women in INERA camp, led me to understand that the women, generally, were not yet ready to come to the forefront and denounce the injustices of which they had been the victims. They were even less ready to fight for a lasting peace in Rwanda, which was the only guarantee of security for themselves and their families. Many women were still convinced that politics had to be handled by men and they continued to wait for them to act.

Nevertheless, with time, I became more and more convinced that a determined, aggressive group of women had to take the lead. The rest would follow the movement once concrete action had been taken. In 1995 with the help of several other women, including Frieda, Louise, Judith, Fébronie, and Véronique, La Ligue des Femmes Rwandaises Pour la Defense de la Droit de Vie was founded.[4] The goal of the League was twofold: it was committed to denouncing all acts that ran contrary to the right to live, in Rwanda and in the camps, and to creating a forum in which women, in the interior and in the camps, could speak out about the problems of the day and about the tragedy they were experiencing. The League produced and distributed two magazines, one in French, *Le Reveil* (The Awakening), and another in Kinyarwanda, *Ijwi ry'umunyarwandakazi* (The Voice of the Rwandan Woman). Periodically we also produced tracts on specific subjects: repatriation of refugees, the massacres at Kibeho, the situation of women in Rwandan prisons, lack of security in the refugee camps, the causes and consequences of the Rwandan tragedy as seen through the eyes of rural women, conditions of life for women in the camps, the human rights situation in the camps, and so on. Our sources were personal testimony and information that we gleaned from the international press. We also denounced the crimes committed on the civilian population in Rwanda by the RPF and the "infiltrators."[5] We made statements that we sent to the press and to the associations dedicated to the defense of civil rights.

The issue of camp security was so worrisome that it was dealt with in every issue of the League's publications. Certain articles on the subject in *Le Reveil* were even reprinted in well-known newspapers in Bukavu, such as *JUA*.[6] Taking these positions almost had us arrested as intimidators.[7] In the face of the alarming increase of rape in the camps,

---

4. The League of Rwandan Women for the Defense of the Right to Live (hereafter the League).

5. Infiltrators were people who returned to Rwanda from the camps and carried out attacks.

6. JUA (Sun in Kiswahili), was the name of a local newspaper that has not been published since 1996.

7. Those suspected of trying to prevent the refugees from returning to Rwanda were called intimidators.

we wrote a letter to the UN High Commissioner for Refugees in Geneva denouncing this phenomenon and proposing actions to limit this plague: notably, distancing soldiers of the CZSC from the camp, providing sufficient supplies of firewood for the camps, and bringing to justice those guilty of rape, whether they were members of the CZSC, refugees, or locals. We gathered about a dozen signatures from different camps. The delegation of the UNHCR at Bukavu, to whom we gave a copy of the letter for informational purposes, did not appreciate this initiative. Since the High Commissioner was personally concerned about the problem, the delegation at Bukavu feared they would be criticized if, in high places, it was thought that nothing had been done in the camps to stop this plague. Along with Frieda and Louise, I was summoned by the UNHCR at Bukavu to give an explanation. They tried to frighten us. According to them, by writing this kind of letter, we risked being classified as intimidators. Anyone accused of being an intimidator was arrested and sent to prison in Kinshasa. Threats did not have the desired effect. Louise and I were single, and Frieda only had one child, and life in the prison at Kinshasa could not have been much worse than life in the camps. At least in Kinshasa we would not be under the permanent threat of forced repatriation or an armed attack from Rwanda. In addition we would be sheltered from the annoyance of the Zairian soldiers. When the people from UNHCR realized that their threats weren't working, they agreed to discuss the problem seriously. We decided to set up a monitoring station in each camp, where the female victims of rape would be listened to and taken care of and where it would be possible, as well, to gather enough information to indict the rapists. The delegation from UNHCR asked us to put together a dossier showing all the crimes that elements from the CZSC had committed on the refugees. The delegation, on its side, agreed to distance the CZSC from the camp if the dossier showed that their presence did the refugees more harm than good. That letter really worked.

Even though many women in the camps appreciated the work we were doing, at the beginning few among them dared to send us information. But, little by little, many had the courage to express their views, either by writing articles themselves or by giving us interviews. Each time that I saw women leafing through *The Voice of the Rwandan Woman* while cooking, or when the Zairians complimented us on some article that had appeared in *Le Reveil,* or when the director of *JUA* came to ask my permission to reprint articles from *Le Reveil* in his own newspaper, it encouraged me. Even if recognition of these actions remained limited to the refugee camps and the population of Bukavu, there was hope. After all, the pen and pencil were the only weapons available to the women, and it was a way to show that there were other ways to make oneself heard than through violence.

Later we had the idea of expanding our activities among the youth in the camps. In 1995 we launched a successful Youth Festival in the Bukavu and Uvira camps as well as in the town of Bukavu. Youth representatives, elected in each camp, were responsible for the organization. There were panel discussions on Active Non-Violence (ANV) and sexuality among youth as well as cultural and sporting events.[8] Sports teams were organized and playing fields were cleaned up in the camps. Representative structures for youth were initiated on the regional level in Bukavu and Uvira, as were the program Active Non-Violence and a youth newspaper.

We finally were able to begin a system of loans for agricultural equipment and seeds for the farmers. We wanted to be more connected to this group, but, in the context of the camps, it was particularly difficult. These loans allowed us to begin setting up representative groups of farmers in the camps and on the subregional level.

At the same time that women, youth, and farmers gained representation, other members of the refugee population also continued to organize, but their efforts were very dispersed and lacked collaboration. To be effective these efforts needed to be coordinated so that the voices of all those who are used but never consulted could be heard. A coordinating committee was set up and an old school friend from the Université Nationale du Rwanda, Jean Damascène, was made president. He was president of L'Action pour la Réconciliation Nationale au Rwanda (ARNR), which had many publications on Rwandan problems to its credit. I remember him as an intelligent, hard-working man of great integrity who was always there for his work and for his friends. The goal of the forum was to facilitate meetings between Rwandan refugees and Rwandans in the interior concerning concrete problems of survival. The

8. Active Non-Violence is a specific technique for conflict prevention and resolution that can be adjusted to local conditions.

organization also sought to arrange cultural and sporting activities so that people could meet each other, learn to talk to each other again and recreate trust, and renew ties broken by the war, genocide, and exile. A first meeting was organized in Nairobi by the European and regional NGOs in December 1995. It brought representatives from the interior and exterior Rwandan NGOs together. I participated in this meeting as a representative of the program supporting the socioeconomic promotion of the women of Byumba.

Recent events had affected every participant. Passion often dominated the debates. Reaching conclusions was difficult. In spite of all these problems, a follow-up committee was established. It was supposed to meet regularly and propose concrete actions to take, for the European NGOs as well as for the Rwandan NGOs. The goal was to facilitate return, reintegration of the refugees with their communities, reconciliation, and the reconstruction of the NGO movement.

The committee was unable to reach its goals. The obstacles were insurmountable. It was impossible for someone living in Rwanda to maintain good relations with refugees who were living among the perpetrators of genocide. Many of the members of the interior Rwandan NGOs shared the opinion that all the refugees who did not come back to Rwanda had something to be ashamed about. They did not want to believe that we simply feared for our safety. It was truly difficult to have a common program or even to decide where to meet. The refugees ruled out the idea of meeting in Rwanda. The Rwandan NGOs, for their part, thought that all these trips abroad were useless. Attempts were made to revive the process, but they were unsuccessful.

In 1995, when I left for Europe to attend a seminar on gender issues, many of my colleagues thought that I was going to use the trip to seek asylum in Belgium, because the situation in the East of Zaire continued to degenerate. Nevertheless, for many reasons, I decided to return to Bukavu. The work of the Collective and the League were important. My departure would have been cowardly, with hundreds of thousands of refugees still in the camps and my colleagues still working in Bukavu. In addition, my mother and all of my family were still in Bukavu. I could not abandon them.

5

A Difficult Choice

IN AUGUST 1995, the Forces Armées Zaïroises led an operation aimed at forcing the refugees in the areas of North and South Kivu to return to Rwanda. It lasted three days. The morning that the operation began, we noticed, without being unduly alarmed, an unusually large presence of well-armed soldiers in Bukavu. We had such good relations with the Zairian NGOs that we were informed of all political decisions concerning the refugees as soon as they were made. As we had not heard about a large-scale military operation, we believed that the soldiers simply wanted to take the last vehicles that were still in refugee hands. We continued to work as usual, and at two o'clock I went, as planned, to a meeting. It had hardly begun when someone from the Collective came to inform us that Zairian soldiers were arresting Rwandan refugees in the streets, and forcing them to get into trucks taking them to the Rwandan border. We all were upset, but we didn't know what to do. We couldn't go get more information because we were in danger of being arrested and taken like the others. Our colleagues from the Société Civile Zairoise[1] met and drew up a statement condemning the operation, during which the camps at Hongo were destroyed and their occupants, more than six thousand people, were forcibly repatriated to Rwanda. At the border between Rwanda and Zaire, many of the refugees committed suicide by throwing themselves into the Ruzizi River rather than return to Rwanda.

1. Zairian Civil Society.

During the first two days I remained hidden at the home of Zairian friends along with other colleagues from the Collective in Bukavu. The third day, disguised as a local farmer, I got back to the camp at ADI-Kivu in a car that belonged to a Zairian friend. Crossing the town, I was struck by how calm it was. No refugee-owned taxis were driving around, and the children who usually wandered the streets of Bukavu begging from passersby had disappeared, the majority of them repatriated and the others still in hiding.

Place du Vingt-Quatre,[2] at the edge of town where the road goes toward Kavumu airport, was completely deserted. This was where the repatriation operation had begun. The young thieves who usually loitered there waiting to relieve travelers of their wallets; day workers taking their midday rest; refugees from the camps trying to do a little business; all had been shipped off. Thomas, a member of the Collective, had been repatriated when he came to Bukavu to wait for his wife, who was returning by boat from the camps at Goma. A boatman had hidden her and their baby, who was only a few months old, in the hold during the entire operation.

In the two camps at Hongo there was total desolation. Apart from a few bodies, there was no one but locals rummaging in the debris, trying to recover the abandoned sheeting, pots, and provisions. The camps at Hongo were built on three little hills overlooking Lake Kivu. The morning of the second day of the operation, soldiers encircled the camp leaving open only the way to the many dozens of trucks stationed on the road at the shores of Lake Kivu. Even for those who knew how to swim, the lake offered no safety, because on the other side was Rwanda. To dissuade the refugees from fleeing, the soldiers had placed machine guns at all four corners of the camp. They entered the sheetings and forced everyone to leave, kicking them and beating them with their rifle butts. Children cried and screamed, hiding in the skirts of their mothers, and women called to their children to make sure that no one was left behind. The men stayed silent glancing from left to right to see if there were a small breach where they could escape. Many of those who tried were killed, but a few succeeded in getting back to the camps in the area that had not yet been destroyed. A few days later

2. Named for November 24, 1965, the day Mobutu came to power.

dozens of children whose parents had been repatriated roamed the streets of Bukavu.

At Mudaka, the camp was empty when the soldiers arrived. The refugees had left before they came, in order not to fall into the same trap as their compatriots at Hongo, and had fled into the neighboring mountains. They had gone without enough to live on and without any medicine. In INERA and Kashusha camps it was a total rout. The refugees, carrying some provisions on their heads, left without knowing where to go. Some came back to camp, chased off by locals who feared reprisals from the soldiers and didn't dare hide them. Pygmies attacked the refugees who had fled to Kahuzi-Biega National Park, and they also had had to return. It was chaos. Those who had left had taken their sheeting with them and, having returned, did not dare to reconstruct their blindés. Others had also taken their shelters down but had delayed their departure due to the pervasive misinformation. All these people stayed on the road, seated on their belongings waiting to see what would happen. A crowd of disoriented people wandered around. Our car had great difficulty making its way through. There was no violence in the air, only a palpable malaise. My friend was well known in the camps, but people did not greet him as they usually did. They were silent. The only ones who seemed happy with the way things were going were the soldiers from the CZSC. They waited impatiently for the operation to begin so they could pillage Kashusha camp, where everyone said the rich businessmen had lived.

At ADI-Kivu there was the same desolation as in INERA and Kashusha camps. The people didn't dare escape through the main entrance to the camp for fear of the CZSC, who prevented the refugees from leaving with their belongings because they were afraid that they would find nothing valuable to steal once the forced repatriation operation reached ADI-Kivu. When I arrived at my mother's house, I found my family very disoriented. For three days she had had no news of me. My arrival comforted them, but the situation was worrisome. The Zairian friend who had brought me offered to take my family to his mother-in-law who lived in a neighboring village. Since there were too many of us, my mother and the youngest children went to hide with another family of friends who lived near the airport, while I went with the rest of the family to the mother-in-law.

Bands of young thugs robbed refugees who tried to hide in the countryside near the camps. I met two of them when I was taking baggage to the old mother-in-law's house. While they were threatening us with knives, I was so unnerved that I began swearing at them in Swahili. Normally I could speak only a couple of words in that language. When they saw that we were prepared to defend ourselves, they ran off. My friend's mother-in-law must have been around seventy years old. She was happy to have us come, but she was worried that unscrupulous neighbors would attack her during the night and steal our belongings. Around noon the old woman, who had gone to the spring to get water, came running back to tell us that the Zairian government had decided to temporarily suspend the forced repatriation operation. When the news became known, everyone returned to the camps.

These three days of terror showed us just how precarious the situation we found ourselves in was. The majority of the members of the Collective had been on a black list in Kigali ever since we had a meeting in Bukavu where we brought up the responsibility of the RPF in everything that happened in Rwanda. Part of the conclusion and recommendations of the meeting were published in the newspapers of Kigali along with the complete list of participants. Since there were files on us in Rwanda, none of us could let ourselves be forcefully repatriated if the operation were ever taken up again. To escape this threat, many of the members of the Collective, from North Kivu as well as South Kivu, decided to leave Zaire. At Bukavu more than fifteen, among them the top people, left for Kenya, West Africa, and Europe. There were many candidates for departure, but you needed money. A one-way ticket from Bukavu to Nairobi cost five hundred American dollars per person. For someone who had a family of five, it wasn't easy to find the two thousand five hundred American dollars for the tickets, not to mention that once in Nairobi or somewhere else, you had to rent a house and get food. After the departure of so many of the leaders of the Collective, I was chosen as the administrator in Bukavu. I left INERA in February 1996 and moved into a house in Bukavu. My stay in a blindé had lasted eighteen months.

Most of the refugees who had money left Zaire. Those who did not want to leave, because of their businesses or their political pasts, evacuated their families. The young, particularly the university students who did not have money but were not afraid of adventure, went on foot or by truck to Zambia or the Central African Republic. Even officials from the former regime, such as the former minister of justice, the former minister of women's affairs, the former prime minister, and former administrators began to leave. They risked being arrested and brought before the tribunal at Arusha, but they didn't have a choice.[3] Whereas forced repatriation, which often happened out of sight of the international media, gave them little chance of survival, imprisonment in Arusha was at least public. Little by little the camps were emptied of the intelligentsia and businessmen. This process continued until the time when the Banyamulenge rebels destroyed the camps in 1996.

For the great majority of the refugees, who had neither financial means nor diplomas they could make use of once they had arrived in another country, the only solution was to return to Rwanda. Even then they had to get around the obstacle of the lawlessness that still reigned in the country. Tens of thousands of prisoners were awaiting trial. In April 1995, four months before the effort at forced repatriation began, RPF soldiers had killed around eight thousand people in the camp for displaced persons in Kibeho, many of them women and children. Political assassinations, disappearances, and arbitrary arrests continued. The refugees knew about this situation thanks to the stories brought by the new refugees who still arrived daily in the camps as well as through the Rwandan and international media. Radio Rwanda was the most listened-to station in the camps.

There were two opposing opinions concerning the immediate return of the refugees to Rwanda. For some, particularly the young, the only solution was to fight. They saw the massive return of the Tutsi refugees after the victory of the RPF as a good example to follow. For those who believed this, it was better to die trying to regain power in Rwanda than

3. The ICTR was established by the United Nations Security Council Resolution 955 of November 8, 1994, for the prosecution of persons responsible for genocide and other serious violations of international humanitarian law committed in the territory of Rwanda between January 1, 1994, and December 31, 1994. It may also deal with the prosecution of Rwandan citizens responsible for genocide and other such violations of international law committed in the territory of neighboring states during the same period. So far, it has only prosecuted those Hutu who committed crimes against humanity during the genocide inside Rwanda. The crimes committed after these dates, both within Rwanda and in the neighboring countries, have not been prosecuted and the perpetrators have enjoyed impunity.

to be delivered, bound hand and foot, to the RPF or to be killed by pygmies while trying to hide in Kahuzi-Biega National Park. It is probable that some who returned took action very quickly. After the forced repatriation, Radio Rwanda began to speak of major operations involving sabotage and the assassination of politicians in certain districts in Cyangugu and Kibuye. These actions were attributed to infiltrators from the refugee camps in South Kivu. Many prisons were also attacked and prisoners set free. It wasn't a question of an organized military force. These acts seemed to be led by small groups probably organized by former members of FAR.

The RPF often used these acts of sabotage as a smokescreen to rid themselves of certain "undesirable people." This was most notably the case in Bugarama Prison, where soldiers from the RPF simulated an attack in order to be able to do away with about forty prisoners. A Rwandan newspaper that published the testimony of a survivor of these massacres confirmed that many of the prisoners had been killed by soldiers with knives.

During the days that followed the forced repatriations, I had several opportunities to have serious discussions with those who held out for armed attacks. Their argument was that they had the means to regain power immediately, because they had fled with an army, generals, and weapons, but a former superior officer from FAR told me: "Personally, I could see leading an attack on Rwanda if I were assured of having an army of at least five thousand well-armed men, weapons, ammunition for the first three months, and a rear guard. Zaire is too disorganized and the Zairian officials are too fond of money for them to be counted on."

Those who were for fighting thought that the refugees would agree to sell part of their humanitarian food aid to finance this rebellion. Some in the international media also speculated about this possibility, but it was unrealistic. There was not enough food aid to feed the refugees, and they had to sell their labor to make up the difference. It was therefore unthinkable for most of them to deprive themselves of food by selling it.

In these discussions, those advocating armed resistance continually brought up the model of the RPF victory, but the situations were not comparable. The RPF had won the war thanks to massive support in men, materiel, and ammunitions from Uganda. It was daydreaming to expect any support from the Zairian government.

The second option was that of a peaceful return, one organized and carried out in a way that guaranteed security to those returning. The majority of the refugees favored this option. The political will of the Rwandan government was the unknown factor. Was this government going to install a democracy and promote representation of all the political, ethnic, and regional factions in the running of the country? What guarantees would one have of safety? The news was bad. The new government had just excluded Hutu ministers from government. Faustin Twagiramungu, the prime minister designated by the Arusha Accords, had been driven out. Jean-Baptiste Nkuliyingoma, the minister of information; Seth Sendashonga, the minister of the interior; and Marie-Alphonse Nkubito, the minister of justice, had also been dismissed. Like Faustin Twagiramungu, they had been longtime allies.

Rwanda's donor countries seemed to have opted for an immobility that looked like complicity. There was no pressure exercised on the government in Kigali to induce them to create the conditions necessary for a large-scale return of the refugees.

As far as Rwandan civil society was concerned, it was still too unstable to play a role that would lead the government to a more flexible position. There were organized groups such as the NGOs, the associations for widows of genocide, human rights organizations, and farmers groups that rendered appreciable help to the population, but the civil society still clung to the ethnic and regional divisions, and to fear. In short, one did not know which way to turn, and the issue of return seemed insoluble.

To address this new situation, the Collective decided to review its strategies and focus all its energies on return and to that end organized meetings in all the camps. The principal axes of the program were discussions about return, preparing the refugees for reconciliation, training in ANV, informing the refugees on the situation in Rwanda, and sensitizing international opinion on the issues of return for the refugees.

So that the refugees would not be completely cut off from the realities in their country of origin, and in the hope of preparing them for return, we made available to them Rwandan newspapers, both pro- and anti-regime, as well as clippings on Rwanda from European magazines, no matter what their opinion. Reading rooms had been set up in the camps for this purpose. In each camp a program for listening to the radio was begun. A group of refugees, mostly young men, would listen to a radio every morning and would hang up notices about what they heard, to make the news accessible to the greatest number of people. The refugees who could not read depended on those who could. The important thing for us was to provide enough information for them to decide for themselves on the most opportune time to go. In the beginning some people in the camps did not appreciate what we were doing. They went as far as to think of us as collaborators with the regime in Kigali, but we persevered despite the risks.

With education in nonviolence and reconciliation, we were aiming to lead the refugees, particularly the youth, to understand the origins of the tragedy that had been shaking Rwanda since 1994. We also wanted to show them that it was possible to fight effectively against dictatorial and criminal powers, without resorting to the same weapons they used. Violence breeds violence. Since we wanted to contribute to a lasting peace in Rwanda, which would be the only guarantee of an equally lasting reconciliation, it seemed to us to be important to destroy the "logic" that had been preached to them since they were young through such slogans as: "All power kills," or "Power that doesn't kill is like an empty gourd." We were aware that it was a long-term project and that it would take months, maybe even years, to see tangible results, even more so because the recent histories of Rwanda, Burundi, Uganda, and Eritrea showed that the use of arms had allowed excluded groups to take power in their respective countries. We hoped to help these young people understand that democracy was the only path capable of bringing a lasting peace to Rwanda, and that you couldn't achieve this with weapons. In the beginning some people accused us of teaching the young people to accept the law of the jungle, but little by little they began to understand what ANV really was, and more youth began to be interested in these ideas.

As a complement to the ideal of ANV, we mounted a program to prepare the refugees for reconciliation through cultural activities. The children made comic books based on the theme of peace and reconciliation. This project was done in collaboration with a Zairian NGO. There was a competition, and the five winners were to be published. Among the five comic books that won, three were from the refugee camps. During the same time, we established the Monseigneur Thaddée Nsengiyumva

Trophy for Peace and Reconciliation. Monseigneur Thaddée Nsengi-yumva had been killed, along with three other bishops, in May 1994 at Gitarama by the RPF. The choice of Nsengiyumva was motivated by the fact that he was not controversial and that he was known to all Rwandans for his courageous efforts to find peace and reconciliation. When he was murdered, he was on the point of organizing a meeting between the youth of the RPF, when they were still an underground movement, and young men from political parties in the interior of the country. With this trophy we wanted not only to render homage to a man who had preached peaceful coexistence among all Rwandans, but also to give the youth an image of a peaceful hero. Heroism in Rwandan culture had always been tied to violence.

For many months we organized dancing and singing competitions in the camps of South Kivu: ballets, choirs for adults and children, and soloists who produced works about reconciliation and the return of the refugees. Since people had made use of song and dance to preach violence and ethnic confrontation, we could use the same channels to transmit the messages of tolerance, peace, and reconciliation. We had planned to produce a CD, cassettes, and videos with the best works and distribute them in the camps in the interior of Rwanda. In the town of Bukavu and in the camps, the main bars and restaurants had agreed to help us with the distribution. Some songs were already being played on Radio Agatashya, the station set up by Reporters Without Borders.

In short, at the Collective we struggled and we believed in the possibility of return and reconciliation. We counted a great deal on the support of our European partners, and from the beginning of our collaboration, we often discussed with them what their role should be during the process of resolving the conflict in Rwanda. I based a lot of hope on their involvement in helping us to escape from the impasse in which we found ourselves. They could continue to support the economic efforts of the poorest in Rwanda and in the camps, support activities to reinforce Rwandan civil society and pressure European governments so that they, in turn, could put pressure on Kigali.

Unfortunately, these discussions came to nothing. After the failure of the initiative in Nairobi, some of our European partners began to be less interested in the Rwandan refugees. Many of them, discouraged, took up their traditional role of research and financing and barricaded themselves in this position. Behind this withdrawal, there was a feeling of uselessness, and there was also the wish not to be seen in a negative light by the authorities in Kigali. Many of the Belgian NGOs that supported the efforts of the refugees were forbidden by the government in Kigali to continue their activities in the interior of Rwanda.

Forced repatriation was a warning shot on the part of the Zairian government. It was supposed to frighten everyone and then be followed by massive voluntary returns. All the camps were to have been empty by December 31, 1995. Faced with failure, the Zairian government and the UNHCR got together and invented a panoply of constraints on the refugees to force them into a return that would still qualify as "voluntary." In reality these measures made life in the camps difficult to bear. One of the first measures taken was the suspension of all organized youth activities in the camps. Since 1994, some humanitarian NGOs such as Caritas and Jesuit Refugee Services (JRS) had established school programs for children and youth, and in addition, the refugees themselves had organized to assure minimal schooling for their children. To facilitate the refugees' adaptation in the host country, language clubs, especially French, English, Swahili, and Lingala, sprang up in almost all of the camps. Already in 1995 and 1996, the JRS and Caritas had received permission from the Inspector of Secondary Schools at Bukavu for the refugee children who were in the last year of humanities to sign up as auditors and take the official final examination. With the decision to suspend all group and educational activities in the camps, all these efforts came to a halt and thousands of children found themselves, once again, in the streets.

Banditry, sexual promiscuity, and early marriages were more widespread than ever. The NGOs tried to organize clandestine schools, and teachers began to give classes in their own sheetings. It wasn't easy to hold forty students captive in a sheeting that was barely four-by-five-yards square, in the terrible heat, while waiting to be interrupted by members of the CZSC. When they discovered one of these clandestine schools, the teacher who had been caught in the act had to pay a fine if he didn't want to be arrested and sent to Kinshasa as an intimidator.

After group activities and schools were forbidden, economic activity in the camps was prohibited. The markets, which were held every day, were suppressed and food rations were cut drastically to one thousand calories per day per person, even though the recommended number of daily calories per person is two thousand. Malnutrition, which had nearly disappeared, resurfaced.

Despite their inhumanity, these measures did not convince large numbers of refugees to return voluntarily to Rwanda. The Zairian authorities, with the blessing of the UNHCR, decided to proceed with the gradual closing of the camps. In the Bukavu area, the first camp to be closed was Nyangezi Deux, in February 1996. Soldiers encircled the camp for two weeks. People couldn't leave to look for something to eat from the local population. Inside the camp the refugees were forbidden to have meetings. The Collective's reading room was closed. The radio monitoring activities were suspended, as were the program for education in Active Non-Violence and the preparation for International Women's Day 1996. In the other camps, study groups were suspended. Meetings led by people from outside the camps were prohibited. Even Mass had to be celebrated by priests living in the camps. Nevertheless, most of these activities continued underground.

When an administrator from the Collective came to a camp to check on our activities, he knew that he could be arrested at any time and sent to Kinshasa as an intimidator. That is what happened to Ndagijimana Cyprien, a member of the Collective arrested by soldiers from the CZSC when he held a training session on ANV in the ADI-Kivu camp for youth representatives from all the camps in the Bukavu area. Before being sent to Kinshasa, he spent a night in the dungeon of the Security Services at Bukavu with another trainer who was Belgian and who was working in the camps at Goma on a project dedicated to peace and reconciliation in Rwanda. At first they were both released. The charge of being intimidators didn't stick, since education in ANV was part of a larger program preparing the refugees for return. A few days later Ndagijimana Cyprien was rearrested and taken directly to Kinshasa. When we were informed of this second arrest, we immediately contacted a friend in the Security Services to see if he could do something. Unfortunately it was too late. He had already been transferred to Goma. Our friend told us that Cyprien had been rearrested at the request of UNHCR. Along with many other refugees imprisoned in Kinshasa, Ndagijimana Cyprien was set free at the beginning of 1997. He was later killed while trying to locate his wife and children.

Two days before the implementation of the decision to close the camps, Administrators from the known refugee organizations were invited to Goma for a meeting with the Zairian minister of the interior, who had come especially from Kinshasa to inaugurate the operation. I had been invited to participate in the meeting as the person in charge of the Collective. Damascène had also been invited as the representative of the Société Civile Rwandaise en Exil au Sud Kivu. For the first time, not only was I able to go to Goma without paying the ticket myself, but I also left Kavumu and Goma airports without having to leave a fortune there, and without spilling all the tears in my body trying to soften up the soldiers and employees of the Immigration Bureau, the Department of Roads and Airports, Health, and other services that only existed in the Zairian airports and had been created solely to legally rob the poor people who had had the unfortunate idea of transiting there. At Goma, we were driven around the whole time in cars that belonged to UNHCR, and before we returned to Bukavu, they paid us for our time.

The meeting with the minister of the interior was designed to let us know that we were all known to the Zairian administration. We were called upon to collaborate with it to encourage the refugees to return. If not, we would be considered intimidators and sent to Kinshasa to be imprisoned there. In short, it was more a meeting to intimidate us than a debate about encouraging the refugees to return. When we asked questions about guarantees of safety and what had been done inside the country to facilitate the return of the refugees, the minister informed us that the UNHCR had confirmed that these guarantees existed. If we wanted more precise information, all we had to do was go ourselves to the UNHCR station in Goma. At the UNHCR office at Goma we were treated to another session of intimidation. They told us that if we tried in any way to countermand the decisions of the Zairian government, we would be considered intimidators.

Accepting the decisions of the Zairian government would mean that we could no longer object to the prohibition of group activities, training, and economic activity, or any of the other coercive measures accompanying the closing of the camps. The UNHCR considered that our interest lay in helping them to repatriate the great majority of the peasants, who didn't have much to fear from the RPF, while we who were educated, who would risk a lot if the Zairian government took over the forced repatriation, would benefit from their protection. Even if Zaire did not want refugees on their territory, they said it would be possible to negotiate a welcome for us in other countries, because there would be fewer of us.

I returned to Bukavu with a bitter taste in my mouth. How did they dare to ask us to accept this logic, we who were supposed to represent the interests of the refugees? My role, as head of the NGO, was limited to informing the refugees as objectively as possible about the situation in Rwanda and in the Great Lakes Region in general, so that they could decide to return when and if they saw fit. It was not my job, nor was it that of UNHCR or the Zairian government, to decide for the refugees. They knew better than anyone else what the situation was in their areas of origin because they had contact with people who had stayed in the country, and they followed everything that was said about Rwanda on Radio Rwanda, Radio Agatashya, and on the international radio stations very closely.

The most annoying thing about the proposal from the UNHCR at Goma is that they asked me specifically to convince Gaudence, Marie, and the other rural women to go back. They asked me to disregard all the reasons why they hesitated to return to Rwanda, to turn a deaf ear to everything they had said in the workshop at Bukavu. They wanted me to disregard the testimony both of the new refugees and the human rights organizations about the massacres of the civilian population, arbitrary arrests, and disappearances that continued in the prefectures of Kibuye, Cyangugu, Gisenyi, and elsewhere. And if, ignoring all this information, I were able, against all odds, to convince a few of these women to return, if some among them or members of their families were killed or put in prison, wouldn't I have these deaths and these imprisonments on my conscience? Even to save my life I felt incapable of betraying these women.

Once back in Bukavu, I wrote an article on the complicity of UNHCR in the adoption of the coercive measures that were impacting the refugees, and I continued with the usual activities of the Collective. We had to revisit our strategies. From then on, since organizing large-scale demonstrations and seminars in Bukavu or in the reading centers was forbidden, we needed to go back to semiclandestine activities. Even meetings of the representatives from the different camps, around forty people, took place in the blindés or in the fields. After the arrest of Ndagijimana Cyprien, we began to take threats from the UNHCR seriously. We were constantly afraid that we would one day see the soldiers from the CZSC entering our offices to arrest us all. At one time we thought of moving the services of the Collective to the offices of the various Zairian NGOs. Negotiations were in progress, but the idea was abandoned. We had to keep our offices because the refugees felt at home there, which would not have been the case in the facilities of the local NGOs.

The CZSC and the UNHCR were not the only factors in the state of perpetual insecurity in which we worked. Every morning several members of the Collective came from the camps to work at Bukavu. When our finances still allowed us to provide a car for them, the trip could be made without much trouble. When that became impossible, they had to use the refugee-owned minibuses, which made the trip between Bukavu and the camps. These minibuses were a favorite target for the police and the civilian guards. Whereas the police were always stationed in the same places and demanded predictable amounts of money from the drivers, the civilian guards changed places all the time. You always came upon them when you expected it least. They then proceeded to systematically frisk the passengers in the taxi down to the women's underpants. The women often arrived in the office complaining about this morning groping.

The soldiers regularly arrested the leaders of the Collective when they went to the camps. Each time we had to spend enormous amounts of money to get them released. After having been beaten, Déo, our financial administrator, had even been taken to the Rwandan border for repatriation. We negotiated for an hour and had to hand over four hundred American dollars to free him. Nevertheless, neither intimidation by the UNHCR nor terrorism on the part of the police, civilian guards, and CZSC could have made us give up our work.

6

Pursued Westward

I FLED BUKAVU on Tuesday, October 29, 1996, around eleven o'clock in the morning. Two nights earlier I had left my house to hide with a family of friends who lived on the outskirts of town. Five young people, the three girls and two boys who lived at my house, came with me.

After the beginning of October, Bukavu was in a state of siege. There were military roadblocks at every corner. The authorities feared that soldiers, who were running away from the fighting by the hundreds, would sack the town. In addition Banyamulenge rebels had opened hostilities a few weeks earlier in the mountains above the town of Uvira.[1] In the beginning the Banyamulenge rebellion was not taken seriously. The locals in the Ruzizi plain spoke of large movements of armed people coming nightly from Rwanda to the mountains of Mulenge, but no one listened to them. It was only when the rebels attacked the hospital at Remera, a few kilometers from Uvira, killing doctors, nurses, and patients, that public opinion began to change. To prevent the budding

---

1. Author's note: The Banyamulenge are Tutsi of Rwandan origin who left Rwanda toward the end of the nineteenth century, bringing with them their families and their herds of cattle. They went to the mountains of Mulenge, to the south of Bukavu, because the climate was good for raising cattle and reminded them of the country they had just left. Over the years other Tutsi fleeing Rwanda came and increased their number. The last immigrations dated from 1959. With time the Banyamulenge were integrated into their host country and adopted Congolese nationality. During the Sovereign National Conference at the beginning of the 1990s, some Congolese began to question the citizenship of their countrymen who spoke Kinyarwanda as well as that of the Banyamulenge, the Hutu and the Tutsi from North Kivu. This questioning of their citizenship was the reason put forward by the Banyamulenge for taking up arms.

rebellion, the military authorities in the area mobilized about one hundred poorly armed soldiers who had no means of communication. On top of that, these soldiers were not provided with rations and had to live off the backs of the villagers.

A detachment consisting of about thirty civilian guards and old policemen was sent to Kaziba, a little village at the foot of the Mulenge mountains where my mother had lived since 1995. She had left the refugee camp at ADI-Kivu so that my sisters and nieces could continue their studies, since it was impossible for them to follow a normal course of study in the camps. The climate in the Kaziba area is similar to that in Byumba and my mother fit in very well there. Zairian neighbors had lent her fields, which she had begun to cultivate.

When the soldiers came to Kaziba, they hunted out the Rwandans, who, according to them, were conniving with the Banyamulenge rebels. My family was their first victim. One morning the girls were getting ready to go to school when five armed soldiers erupted into their rooms. They kicked them and hit them with their rifle butts and forced everyone to go with them. In addition to my mother, there were four of my younger sisters, four nieces, my adopted son Bakunda, a young woman my mother had taken in and a friend of my sisters'.

All twelve were led to the administrative office of Kaziba, where the soldiers made them lie down in the dust. Then they took sticks and began to beat them. The more the girls tried to explain, the more they beat them. One of the soldiers went to get a machete, ignoring their screams and explanations. My mother put herself between the man and the children and demanded to be killed first. She did not want to watch, powerless, as her children and grandchildren were massacred. Fortunately, a neighbor, who had seen their arrest, went to alert the chief, who quickly sent someone to demand that the soldiers let my family go. This is how they were saved.

After this unhappy incident, it was impossible for my family to stay in Kaziba. My sisters and nieces, who were in secondary school, were in danger of being raped. I had first thought of taking them with me to Bukavu, because it seemed safer. However, while I was preparing for their arrival, Bukavu went through two consecutive nights of fighting between the Zairian army and the Rwandan army based in Cyangugu. I spent the first night underneath bunches of bananas, sacks of potatoes, and coal. The next morning I left the house to hide with friends who lived on the other side of town.

After this it was obvious that South Kivu offered no security for Rwandans, and I decided to evacuate my family to a more peaceful country. Since I didn't have enough money to get everyone out at once, my mother left first with the girls who were in secondary school and the youngest children. The others were to have followed as soon as the means were available. Unfortunately I had to flee Bukavu before that project could be completed.

In the meantime the Banyamulenge rebellion continued to advance and the Zairian army seemed incapable of containing it. In Bukavu some people began to prepare to leave. The refugee camps in the Ruzizi plain were among the first rebel targets and were destroyed by mortars and heavy artillery. Tens of thousands of refugees were again thrown out on the roads, leaving behind them hundreds of dead. They fled over mountain roads, trying to get to the camps near Bukavu, where they hoped to find safety. The UNHCR sent them toward the camps at Nyamirangwe and Cimanga, one hundred kilometers north of Bukavu. On the road they didn't receive any food aid, although they had fled empty-handed. Returning for provisions was impossible. The rebels were already in the camps and had begun to kill the remaining refugees with knives. When the refugees asked the UNHCR to find them a little corn flour, at least for their children, the delegates replied that they would be helped once they arrived at their destination. Thousands of men, women, and children walked one hundred kilometers under a burning sun without food. The humanitarian organizations watched their suffering and did nothing.

At the Collective we were able to gather up our personnel who were based in the camps, but those who were in Uvira were stuck there. Faced with this new influx of refugees in the camps around Bukavu, we held a crisis meeting. History was repeating itself. As in July 1994, when hundreds of thousands of Rwandan refugees had descended on Bukavu, families were separated, people were hungry, food was unavailable, the infrastructure to receive them was overburdened, and, in addition, everyone was terrified.

Although we didn't have much, we decided to open orientation centers in the camps, make forms for searching for missing persons available, and begin organizing the new arrivals. After the destruction of the camps at Uvira, the rebels advanced and destroyed the camps at Nyangezi, located only about thirty kilometers from Bukavu. The refugees in this camp added to the number of those who had taken to the roads in their exodus. Some left for Cimanga while others went to the camps at Kashusha and INERA, which little by little had become large cities, like the camps at Goma.

People began to flee Bukavu toward Kinshasa. Only Zairians could take a plane. For the refugees, the camps that were still in operation were the only places to go. As the rebels advanced, the humanitarian NGOs packed their bags, leaving us in total disarray. Even the CZSC abandoned their posts and headed for Kisangani. At the end of the last week in October, the rebels took control of the power station at Ruzizi, which was less than ten kilometers from the camps and provided electricity to Bukavu, Rwanda, and Burundi. The locals also warned of the presence of small rebel groups in the mountains above Bukavu.

On Friday, October 25, 1996, I asked a friend what he thought of the situation. He replied that, because of the way that things were going, it was likely that Bukavu would fall during the weekend and that it would be good for me to leave that very day. Despite this wise advice, I didn't leave Bukavu right away. I had received a fax informing me that our European partners had transferred money for the Collective. This money could give the personnel of the Collective, who hadn't been paid since March, a little money for the road. I decided to visit Kotecha, the shopkeeper into whose account the money had been deposited. Unfortunately, that day his store was closed because the shopkeepers feared looting. Until Tuesday, October 29, I went every day to the shop, but with no luck.

We spent the weekend of October 26–27 listening to the sound of shooting, mostly heavy artillery. The fighting was unfolding a few kilometers from the refugee camp at Panzi, which was on the outskirts of Bukavu on the road to Uvira. Monday, October 28, the firing became more intense as the fighting came closer and closer to the town. The neighborhoods nearest the Rwandan border began to empty. Sitting in front of my friends' house, I could see groups of fleeing women and children on the road. They were empty-handed. Rumor had it that several hundred well-armed soldiers had been sent from Kinshasa and that they would make short work of the rebels. Young men from the town and the surrounding area had begun to form Mai Mai militias and controlled some neighborhoods.[2] Rwandans, particularly Tutsi, were pursued. Many of them were taken by force to Rwanda. Some were killed.

Tuesday, October 29, after checking that Kotecha had not opened his store, I went back to my friends' house. The sound of heavy artillery had grown louder. I learned that Panzi had fallen and that the rebels were already in the town. It was only then that I began to think seriously about leaving. At about ten-thirty, the machine gun and small arms firing intensified. We weren't immediately alarmed. We thought that Zairian soldiers were looting the center of the town. People were running by on the road carrying boxes of biscuits that they had taken from the Red Cross stockpiles. A few minutes later Zairian soldiers passed by on the road. They seemed to be running away from something. And then someone called out to us that the rebels were already at the Institut Supérieur Pédagogique,[3] only a few hundred meters away from us. By the time I went in to get my bag, the whole neighborhood was in turmoil. Everyone was running and screaming. Those who had just looted the Red Cross abandoned their booty in the roadway. Even the soldiers were running. It was every man for himself. The shooting got closer and closer. I called Bakunda and we began to run behind the soldiers. I didn't even have time to warn the three young girls who lived with me, Assumpta, Alvera, and Vestine, who were staying with one of my friends a few houses away. Only Assumpta was able to catch up with us farther along. Alvera and Vestine were stuck in Bukavu.

Alvera was Généreuse's little sister. Généreuse died in 1985 in the United States. Like me, she came from Byumba. We studied humanities together and went to the university at the same time. She was the youngest in our class and was only seventeen when we finished. After three years at Butare we both were hired at the Office National de la

2. Mai Mai are local defense groups, very often initiated by traditional leaders, and were originally created to protect isolated communities against foreign invaders and the rebel groups they support. They are found in North and South Kivu, including the Maniema, Northern Katanga, and Ituri. Unfortunately, in an environment characterized by impunity, they often act for personal gain and behave as badly as the rebels.

3. A branch of the National University of Zaire.

Population.[4] We shared the same office and the same room and were inseparable. In 1982 I got a scholarship to go to Belgium, and the next year Généreuse left for the United States. I saw her again in March of 1985, in a coffin. Until my father's death in August 1986, I dreamed of her every night. In memory of our friendship, I, together with two other friends, paid for schooling for Alvera, who resembled her mother closely. In 1994 Alvera had become a very pretty young woman and worked at the Société des Transports Internationaux du Rwanda.[5] Vestine is my aunt's granddaughter. Her mother had her very young, at sixteen, and after her birth she separated from Vestine's father. A few months later she remarried and left Vestine with her grandmother.

I left Bukavu at a run in a hail of bullets and shells. By good luck I had seventy American dollars with me. At Place du Vingt-Quatre a group of young men took the small amount of Zairian money that we had. When we had left our house the previous Saturday, we had been careful to take enough with us to survive for a few days: clothes, plates, glasses, blankets, and a little jerry can for water. I left Bukavu with nothing but the clothes on my back and my identity card. I even forgot to take some sugar to snack on on the road. I covered the eight kilometers that separate Bukavu from Bagira at a dead run. It was the first time I had run so far in my life, but unfortunately it wasn't to be the last time. Every time that I was on the edge of complete collapse, I begged the others to go on without me, but every time they told me to hang on. The danger was still very close. Shells whistled overhead and at every step we expected to have one land on us. For several kilometers the paved road, which linked Bukavu and Kavumu Airport, ran along Lake Kivu, and the flood of refugees made a nice target for the Rwandan artillery. At the main hospital in Bukavu we passed by many who had been wounded, some of them severely. They said Rwandan soldiers from Cyangugu who had entered the country at Ruzizi had shot them. The Banyamulenge and Rwandan troops who were fighting in Bukavu were supported by heavy artillery in Cyangugu. Bukavu was not the first place in South Kivu to be taken with the support of Rwandan troops. Kamanyola, on the road between Bukavu and Uvira was taken in the

4. National Office of Population.
5. Society for International Transport in Rwanda.

same way. Eyewitnesses claimed that they had seen tanks crossing the Kamanyola Bridge coming from the direction of Bugarama in Rwanda.

I arrived at Bagira tired, but happy to have escaped the bullets. Since we were not yet out of danger, we had to continue to walk, trying to get to Mudaka camp, about halfway between Bukavu and Kavumu. We left the paved road, where we were an all too visible target for the artillery positions in Cyangugu, and hid in the banana groves of Kabare. With me were Bakunda, Assumpta, Augustin, who had worked in my house since the beginning of the year, and Serge, the oldest son of the family we had stayed with outside Bukavu. We had lost track of Serge's parents and sisters. The last time we saw them they were running out of the house, but they disappeared in the crowd. Serge's whole family was reunited when we left INERA the following Saturday. It was the last time I saw them. All the members of this family were reported missing.

Walking through the mountainous banana groves was not easy. We had to go up and down the hills following paths that had been soaked by the torrential rains that had beaten down on us all the afternoon and drenched us to our bones. This forced march lasted until late into the night, when we found refuge in the buildings of an elementary school. Trembling from cold and hunger, we arrived at the school around ten. The night was black and we couldn't even see where to put our feet. Several times we lost the path and found ourselves among thorn bushes. I don't remember how many times I tripped and fell. Every time, Augustin came to pick me up and get me back on the road. At the school we were met by youth from the former Mouvement Populaire de la Révolution,[6] which had been revived and made nightly patrols in the village. We showed them our identity cards and they let us into one of the classrooms where there were already some Zairians who were running away from Bukavu. I acted as if Assumpta, Bakunda, and Serge were my own children saying that they had left Rwanda before they were old enough to have identity cards. The two boys spent the night on benches in the classroom while a farmer agreed to put Assumpta and me up for the night.

I had just gone to bed, our host having spread a tarp on the ground in a room that we shared with a few chickens, when I heard a discussion

6. Popular Revolutionary Movement.

between him and some other people. These people wanted to know if I were really Bakunda and Serge's mother. The youth who were in charge of security suspected Serge of being a Munyamulenge who had taken advantage of the flood of refugees to infiltrate the area of Kabare.[7] It is true that Serge resembled a Tutsi. I got up and, accompanied by my host, I returned to the school where the boys were spending the night. I once again presented my identity card and reaffirmed that Assumpta and the two boys were my children. Afterwards I returned to sleep in the house that belonged to this Shi peasant, whose name I didn't even know.[8] He was one of a chain of Zairians who, during the whole length of my long journey, shared their roofs and what little food they had with me.

Wednesday in the very early morning I got back on the road, but with great difficulty. After the night's rest, the muscles I hadn't used in so long made me suffer terribly, but I thought that I was almost at the end of my troubles since Mudaka camp was near by. We arrived there at the end of the morning, but the camp no longer existed. The refugees had all left the night before and had joined up with other fugitives in the camps at Kashusha and INERA, another ten kilometers farther down the road.

With the influx of new refugees, the two camps, which normally housed one hundred thousand people, now held two hundred thousand. All the trees at the edges of the camp had been cut by the new arrivals to construct shelters, provide heat or cook the food that they begged from the other refugees. INERA camp swarmed with people. When I arrived at around three in the afternoon, I was welcomed by the sound of automatic weapons. At first I thought that the rebels were attacking the camp from the inside and I told my little family to go back to the road. After a few minutes, the shooting stopped and we were able to reenter the camp and go to Frieda's blindé. I later learned that the shots came from some elements of the CZSC who had stayed at the camp and who wanted to create panic so they could loot in peace.

I knew INERA camp well since I had lived there for over a year before going to Bukavu at the beginning of 1996. I, along with Assumpta and Bakunda, stayed with Frieda. Serge went to relatives at Kashusha

7. The Munyamulenge are Tutsi of Rwandan origin.
8. The Shi are an ethnic group living in South Kiva.

and Augustin went with his sister. In addition to being my closest collaborator at the Collective, Frieda was a friend. We were both active working for women. She was always willing to take part in discussions and projects concerning women. She was one of the founders of the League in 1995, and we had planned the organization's first project together. To the same extent that I was carried away by ideas and theories and speculation on the role of women in the Rwandan issue, Frieda was concerned with concrete actions that the Collective could take to justify its existence. It was probably due to her hard work that, from the beginning, the Collective was operational. Even if the whole team made important contributions and dedicated their weekends to producing publications and declarations, Frieda did more. It was natural that, having been thrown out of Bukavu, I would stay with her. I needed a roof over my head and food, but even more I needed a friend to boost my morale and a colleague to talk to about what the Collective should do in this situation.

Conditions at INERA were worse than I had imagined. In place of the serenity and tranquility I had hoped for, there was total panic. It was worse than what we experienced during the last days in Bukavu. People were completely disoriented. They didn't know what to do or where to go. When the CZSC were shooting and trying to create panic, people thought that they were being attacked by Banyamulenge rebels and began to run. These stampedes led to accidents. Frieda, who was near the spot where the shooting happened, was trampled. She came out of it with a broken arm. The camp hospitals were not operating, so a traditional healer who worked in the neighborhood treated her. I thought that this panic was exaggerated, because the rebels were still in Bukavu, but when I talked about this with people, I understood that there were a number of reasons that I was unaware of that contributed to and exacerbated the panic. Among them were the massive arrivals from other camps; the torture that the rebels inflicted on the refugees that they caught; the departure of the CZSC and the humanitarian organizations and particularly of Father Carlos, who had been in charge of INERA camp; the flight of the Zairian soldiers, some of whom, newly arrived from Kinshasa, didn't even report to Bukavu, preferring to return by the road that went by Kisangani; the fall of Bukavu in one day; and the feeling of having been abandoned by the international community. The list was endless. The materiel left behind by the soldiers was later taken by former members of FAR and by the Banyamulenge rebels. Even the new military governor of the South Kivu area had left.

On top of that, the refugees who with the approach of the fighting would have liked to return to Rwanda could not. The rebels were between them and the frontier at Bukavu and Goma. The only remaining way out was through Kisangani to the frontier with the Central African Republic a thousand kilometers to the north. To escape by this route, we had to go by Bunyakiri, a little village about thirty kilometers from the camp, which was occupied by Zairian soldiers who were running away from the fighting. Completely without pity, they sent any Rwandan who tried to pass by back to the camps.

After Friday, November 1, the rebels were only a dozen or so kilometers from the camps and everyone was ready to leave. But where to go? The question was on everyone's lips, in everyone's thoughts.

Around eleven at night, I was awakened by the sound of the neighbors taking down the sheeting from their blindé. The whole household got up at once and we went to find news. We learned that the rebels were already at Miti, a little village less than two kilometers from INERA. From eleven until six in the morning no one closed an eye. At four in the morning we started folding the sheeting and waiting for the first shots so that we would know which way to run. Those who weren't too afraid began to make bouillie. In the beginning, the gunfire was sporadic. Then bullets began to rain down on us. Light weapons alternated with heavy weapons and grenades. Having left Frieda's blindé at the first shots, I was able to take a sheeting and a small mattress with me. Bakunda took a few kilos of sugar and some rice and Assumpta a small amount of flour, peas, and cooking utensils. In addition, we each carried a blanket. When the shooting got closer and more sustained, and when we began to see the wounded, we abandoned most of our provisions in the banana groves of the Shi.

In our headlong flight, as everyone wanted to put as much distance as possible between themselves and the rebel shooting, we were separated very quickly. Assumpta left in one direction and Frieda and her family in another. I found myself alone with Bakunda, running with people we didn't know. Trying to make sure that we weren't found, we avoided the roads. We ran under cover of banana groves and fields full of beans and sugar cane and sweet potatoes. You couldn't even stop to go to the bathroom. We did it on the run. At one moment I felt like my bladder would burst but I couldn't stop because the shells were falling all around us. It was only after a few more kilometers, feeling my wet panties, that I remembered what had happened. But in the end, what difference did it make?

We were slowed down a bit by torrential rains that beat down on us when we arrived in the village of Katana, fifteen kilometers from INERA camp. From Katana we continued on toward Kahuzi-Biega National Park, where safety lay. We spent the first night of our flight in a hut that a Zairian family let us use at the entrance to the park. We were joined there by Chantal, Frieda's neighbor. Since the borrowed hut was in poor condition, Bakunda covered it with the sheeting while Chantal went to get water to make bouillie. She had been able to save a little flour and we had some sugar. At nightfall we were joined by four young people who would be our companions as far as Walikale. Denise and her cousin Charles were from Ruhengeri; Lily and her sister Fauvette were Burundian refugees born in Kigali.

We entered Kahuzi-Biega National Park on Sunday, November 3, in the late morning. Around ten thousand of us took this route, a rarely traveled path used mainly by hunters. Often we had to carve out secondary paths when it was too crowded. In the places where the forest was so dense that it was difficult to make our way, even with the help of a machete, we waited for hours, standing, unable to sit down, stuck together. The rough terrain and the rain that fell each day made the march even more difficult. When we left the forest on Monday in the late afternoon, we looked like pigs after a mud bath. And we stank.

We spent the week after leaving the park with a Tembo friend of Charles's, named Ngengeri.[9] They had met at Goma and for a while had been friends. I took advantage of these four unexpected days of peace and quiet to have my sore legs massaged. Charles was in charge of this delicate job. He massaged everybody with a cloth soaked in boiling water, and we left this massage crying because it hurt so much. I had also gotten diarrhea in the forest. It was annoying because I had to stop every half hour and go to the bathroom. I always tried to find a bush to go behind, but when I could not, I hid my face. Many times I stood up

9. The Tembo are an ethnic group living in Zaire's eastern highlands.

before I had finished because I was afraid of being bitten by a snake. When I was sure that it was just the grass that was tickling me, I sat down again. At Ngengeri's there was a hole, but the toilet hadn't been built. Everyone coming back from the fields or the spring passed by the hole. When I saw them coming I looked in the opposite direction.

Ngengeri, who was a traditional healer, cared for me with medicinal plants. To house us, the family had let us use the hut that belonged to their oldest son. It was small, with two little rooms. I shared the bed with Chantal, and the others slept on the sheeting in the other room. In order not to get wet when it rained, we covered the roof with another sheeting. After the second day, other refugees began to come looking for something to eat in exchange for work. Ngengeri took one and the others went to look elsewhere. The family was not wealthy, and we ate white cassava without vegetables, salt, or oil. The evening before we left, Chantal found her brother. They had been separated since INERA, and they continued on together.

We left the Ngengeri family on Saturday and traveled on toward Bunyakiri. We hoped to arrive there before the rebels. Our final destination was Kisangani, where we wanted to get a boat to take us to the Central African Republic. When we were a few kilometers from Bunyakiri we were stopped by the Tiri militia,[10] who did not want Rwandan refugees in their territory. During this obligatory stop I found Assumpta. After two days in a transit camp, they let us continue on our way to Hombo via Bunyakiri. The area was under the control of Tiri

10. Author's note: After the collapse of the Mobutu government, Zaire fell prey to innumerable militias that made the eastern part of the country completely ungovernable. The Tiri were among them. All of these militias came from North Kivu, a region that had been inhabited by the Hunde, the Nyanga, the Tembo, and the Nande. After the partition of Africa in Berlin by the great Western powers, and the creation of modern nation states, part of Rwanda was tacked on to North Kivu. This, in addition to the aforementioned ethnic groups, added two more groups to the area, Hutu and Tutsi, the Banyarwanda. The exploitation of the mines and the value of these regions to the colonizers brought large migrations of Rwandans to many areas of Zaire. In 1959, with the social revolution that brought the Hutu to power in Rwanda, the Tutsi, along with their cattle, sought refuge en masse in the area of North Kivu. The areas of Ruhengeri and Gisenyi were overpopulated, so the Hutu in these areas emigrated to Kivu. With these successive waves of Rwandan immigrants, certain parts of North Kivu such as Rutshuru and Masisi found themselves with a population the majority of which spoke Kinyarwanda. These new arrivals bought land from the locals, often for a crust of bread,

fighters, who had erected roadblocks everywhere. At each one of them, the refugees were searched and sometimes robbed. On the whole, though, very few Tiri were thieves, since according to their beliefs those who stole died in battle.

We spent the first night in a village about ten kilometers from Bunyakiri where the pastor of a protestant church gave all seven of us shelter. During much of the night we talked with him. He was very worried about the fate of his children, who were studying in Goma.

We spent the second night under the roof of a peasant who came from the region of Burega. The third day Bakunda fell sick. He could hardly walk. Ever since Rwanda he had had problems with his liver. The last crisis had been when we were fleeing Kigali, where an old woman had treated him with herbs. He later underwent a draconian diet without salt or oil. At Kaziba he partially regained his health and stopped the diet. The headlong flight from Bukavu, followed a few days later by INERA, in addition to the fear, hunger, and fatigue, had had their way with him. Assumpta had also been suffering from malaria since the night before. We had to adapt our plans to them and could only manage about twenty kilometers a day.

The second Thursday after leaving INERA we arrived at Irangi, eight kilometers from Hombo. All those who had preceded us had once again been forced to stop. This time the Tiri did not want to let us continue on. There was talk on the international radio of creating a humanitarian zone to help the refugees. By keeping us with them, the Tiri made the cynical calculation that, on the one hand, they would receive financial compensation from the humanitarian organizations once the zone was set up, or on the other hand, if they reached an agreement with the rebels, they would deliver us up to the Rwandan soldiers. This last bit of information was passed on by one of the Tiri to a refugee.

---

and after a few decades most of the land in these areas had passed into the hands of the Banyarwanda. The locals were not only dispossessed of their lands but were also gradually marginalized in other areas. In schools, for example, almost of all the instructors were Banyarwanda. It was the same with the priests, nuns, nurses, and doctors, and so on. Only the government was left in the hands of the locals until the day that the Banyarwanda wanted to take that over too. This was, no doubt, the straw that broke the camel's back. Feeling threatened, the locals began to organize militias to combat the Banyarwanda.

Irangi, where we stayed for about two weeks, is on the stretch of paved road between Bukavu and Kisangani, about ninety-two kilometers from Bukavu. The place where we had parked ourselves was bordered on one side by the road and the other by a river. The refugees had put up their blindés all around a former hotel. It soon became a camp that was really a prison. In the event of a rebel attack we had little chance of escaping. There was only one exit and a few well-armed Tiri guarded it. Those who tried to leave were robbed of all their belongings, molested, and even killed.

This underpopulated area was situated at the edge of the equatorial forest, and accommodating and feeding more than twenty thousand people was not easy for the local population. Often we had to content ourselves with a few roots, and we were almost out of salt. Since Bukavu was inaccessible, the local merchants could not buy provisions.

A few days after arriving in the camp, I came down with a horrible toothache and a bout of rheumatism. After the long march that I had just made, the feeling in my legs was diminished. This phenomenon, which had begun in my feet, progressed every day. After a week it reached my knees. At the rate that it was progressing I feared that I would lose the use of my legs and not be able to continue on if the Tiri ever let us go. There were doctors and pharmacists and a dentist in the camp, but I did not have enough money for them. Of the seventy American dollars that I had had when I left, only ten remained. It was hardly enough to appease the hunger of my large family, which, in the meantime had grown. Virginie and three orphans who came from the camp for unaccompanied children at Kashusha joined us.

Luckily for me, Marguerite, the secretary of the Collective, arrived in camp. When she learned through friends that I was there, she came to see me and found me moaning. I was suffering horribly from the toothache. Having assessed the state of my health, Marguerite left right away to look for a dentist and a doctor for my rheumatism. A few hours later she came back. She had found a dentist who had the basic equipment to pull my tooth, which he said was the best thing to do in the present situation. He even had painkiller. What a luxury! The cost of the operation and the antibiotics to prevent a possible infection was twenty American dollars. Along with the visit to the doctor and medicine for my rheumatism, the cost would come to thirty American dollars.

I thanked Margot[11] for the trouble she had taken to find care for me, but I had to tell her that I didn't have the money. Even though she herself didn't have anything to feed her two children, she assured me that she would find a solution. I did not share her optimism. I didn't believe in miracles, especially at such a time. The majority of the refugees in Irangi were in the same fix as I was. Many had already begun to sell their clothes, bedding, sheeting, kitchen utensils, and so forth to buy something to eat. Even those who had a little money had to spend it very carefully, because we did not know how long we would be without humanitarian aid. There couldn't be that many people who would give thirty American dollars to someone they didn't know with no hope of ever being repaid, but you have to believe that saints exist, even in Hell. This person, whose existence I didn't believe in, existed and even had a name, Egide. In Rwanda he was a journalist for Radio Rwanda. At Bukavu he had continued his trade on Radio Agatashya, set up by Reporters Without Borders. Egide knew the Collective well, but he did not know me personally. Because of the information that Margot gave him about me, he decided that my death would be a loss to the entire community. He sent me an American fifty-dollar bill so that I could get medical attention and buy food. Thanks to the generosity of this man whom I didn't even know, and thanks to Margot, my bad tooth was pulled and my rheumatism treated.

Margot came to the Collective during the first months of 1996. She was, for me, not only the secretary of the Collective, but also a friend and companion in arms. We began to work together in 1995, even before she was hired by the Collective and spent many sleepless nights together hastily stapling a report together every time there was someone leaving for Europe. When she was hired to be the secretary for the Collective, she continued to help me in her free time, after work hours or on the weekends. And when, with Frieda, Pauline, Marie-Louise, and others, we created the League, Margot volunteered to do the computer data entry and layout for our publications.

In the prison of Irangi I rediscovered prayer. As far back as I could remember, the members of my family were practicing Catholics, even though, like the majority of Rwandans, we still believe in magic, spirits,

11. Familiar form of Marguerite.

and other evil forces. My father was very devout. Every day, before going to sleep, the whole family gathered together on our knees and said the evening prayers. Even if we were already asleep, they woke us up to pray. After my father remarried, we abandoned this practice, which was for us children an act of obedience and not of faith.

I had no idea what lay in store for us, or whether the Tiri were going to let us go on our way before the Banyamulenge rebels and the RPF caught up with us. Even if the RPF did not attack us in the coming days, hunger was waiting to kill us if we didn't succeed in leaving the camp. The arrival of an international force and the creation of a safe humanitarian zone where the NGOs could resume their work became more and more a matter of conjecture. We were caught like rats in a trap. No doubt it was finding myself at such an impasse that led me to prayer. Like many others, I thought that only divine intervention could get us out of there.

It was thanks to Immaculée that I again found the words that had been lost for so long. I couldn't have found anyone better to help me in this path. Immaculée was a very devout woman, a member of the Legion of Mary and many other charismatic groups. With her I again learned the right way to say the Lord's Prayer, the Creed, the Gloria, and other prayers that I had forgotten. But the most important thing that Immaculée taught me, which continued to help me even when we were no longer together, is to accept God in everyday life. To accept him like a loving father, who comes to our aid every time that we call on him, even for the smallest things in life. This faith would be my greatest support during the year spent in the equatorial forests of Zaire. Immaculée only asked us to pray and to hope, because, she said, God will see that we did nothing to deserve the misery we are enduring. She had such a great confidence in God that she didn't doubt for a moment that he would find a solution to our problems. At her suggestion, the prayer group that we began with the young women and the old mothers in our area began a novena.[12] She was convinced that before three days were up we would have a satisfactory answer to our prayers.

Three or four days after the beginning of the novena, around twenty young men arrived at the camp. They were barefoot and dirty. Some carried automatic weapons. Some wore military uniforms. I was expecting

---

12. A nine-day devotional practice.

the arrival of the rebels so strongly that I told myself that it was no longer necessary to wonder where I could run to, since the rebels were already inside the camp and more of them had no doubt encircled us already. I left for prayer as I usually did. Everyone was at the meeting, but our hearts were not at peace. No one had any information on these newest arrivals and rumors ran rampant. The prayer meeting was very short. Each one of us wanted to return home to pack our bags and make plans with our families for a last minute escape.

When I got to our room in the former hotel, I was too agitated to talk about anything. I was counting on divine intervention to get me out of this hornet's nest, as it had ever since 1994. Stretched out on the sheeting, I was thinking about these things when a child came to tell me that one of the soldiers who had just arrived was looking for me. I went out trying to keep my hands from trembling and my teeth from chattering. The first thing I saw once I was outside was a group of people around a ragged soldier. Several days' growth of beard covered his face. I didn't recognize him right away, but his face reminded me of someone. It was only when we began to talk that I recognized him. I knew his father, whom he strongly resembled. They were our closest neighbors in Byumba, and when I was a child I passed their house when I went to get water from the spring. After reassuring myself that he was indeed the son of our neighbors in Byumba, I let out a sigh of relief and thanked the good Lord. Our "liberators" had arrived.

These badly dressed, dirty young men had gotten out of the camps at Goma safe and sound two weeks earlier, which was a miracle. They had weapons and ammunition taken from fleeing Zairian soldiers. After entering the forest they had had to fight the Banyamulenge rebels and soldiers from the RPF to make their way to Masisi. From there they went through the forest towards Walikale, where they were attacked several times by the Tiri fighters. A few kilometers from Hombo, they began to come across refugees coming from Bukavu via Shanji, and they decided to go along with them and protect them from the Tiri attacks. When they were around twelve kilometers from Irangi on the Bukavu-Walikale road, the Zairians informed them of the presence of refugees who were stuck in Irangi. They decided to make a little detour before going on to Kisangani. The Tiri took flight when they arrived, though they continued to attack refugees when they found them in small groups.

The rebels destroyed the camps at Katale and Kibumba first. The refugees from these two camps went to swell the numbers at Mugunga, which within a few days became what was no doubt the largest camp in the world. To get there the refugees from Katale had to follow little used tracks through the forest and spent many days without water. To quench their thirst they chewed the roots of certain shrubs. They had sores in their mouths from chewing. When they were only a few kilometers from Mugunga they came upon rebels who split them up, letting some, mostly women and children, go and keeping others, mainly men and women who were well-dressed or wearing jewelry. These they killed after robbing them of their money and anything else of value.

My neighbor's son told me that my sister Marie-Rose and her children were among those who had been lucky enough to get to Mugunga. Unfortunately, her husband was not with her. They thought that the rebels had killed him.

During the few days that the camp at Mugunga had survived the other camps in the area, the living conditions became unbearable. The population had tripled, there was no food and the noose of the rebels and the RPF soldiers tightened every day. The latter had taken up positions on all the hills above the camp and led attacks from Lake Kivu. Small groups of rebels who infiltrated the camps took advantage of the night to assassinate refugees in their sheetings.

A few days before the destruction of the camp at Mugunga, a mission of American soldiers came by. With the help of megaphones, they asked the refugees to take advantage of their presence in order to go back to Rwanda, because afterwards it would be too late. It was after this that there was a massive return. The only exit that wasn't blocked by the rebels was the one that led back to Rwanda. Even though they controlled the movements of the people and could take whomever they wanted aside and kill them, they let the great majority of the refugees pass. At all the other camp exits, they shot anyone who moved on sight. Put in the position of having to choose between returning to Rwanda and death from rebel bullets, many chose the first alternative. Everyone knew that they ran a very real danger by returning, but they thought that it was their last chance at survival. And in Kinyarwanda they say, "It is always better to die tomorrow than to die today." Families met to decide who would leave for Rwanda and who would try to get past the nets of the rebels. In many cases it was decided that women and children should return because they ran a smaller risk of being killed or thrown in prison. Those who chose to attempt the impossible and find a way to Sake, Walikale, and Kisangani were mostly the educated: people who had had important political jobs in Habyarimana's regime, former politicians, students, former soldiers, and former militia members. Some women decided to follow their husbands, even though the husbands would have preferred that they return to Rwanda so that they could move more freely. According to eyewitnesses, on the road back to Rwanda many men were taken by the rebels to Lac-Vert camp where they were killed and their bodies dumped in the lake. Several weeks after the destruction of Mugunga, the NGOs said that they buried 6,700 bodies.

Those who had decided to continue their flight left the camp silently under the cover of night so as not to be seen or heard by the rebels surrounding the camp. Even the children held back their tears. They no doubt felt their parents' fear. Despite all the precautions, many groups were attacked before reaching the forest. It was a group of these refugees from Mugunga who had arrived to "liberate" us from our prison at Irangi, and it was in their company that we took the road to Walikale, one hundred seventeen kilometers from Irangi, the next day. Their presence protected us from the Tiri, who were unhappy to see their prisoners escape.

7

Hunted by the Rebels and the RPF

IT WAS DIFFICULT to make much progress. Zairian soldiers had gone ahead of us, and provisions were practically impossible to find. The soldiers arrived in the villages shooting in the air, took women by force, and robbed the population of everything they had—clothes, bicycles, food, and money. People fled to the forest. We passed through dead villages, abandoned by their inhabitants weeks before. We contented ourselves with green papayas cooked like vegetables or a few leaves and tubers from the colocases, which grew around the abandoned houses.[1] We spread out our sheetings in the courtyards of houses to sleep. The area swarmed with snakes of all kinds, and sleeping under the stars was dangerous. One night a woman was bitten in the eye by a snake and died the next morning, her face so swollen that even her family did not recognize her.

Between Hombo and Walikale, I was hungry all the time. One day I was resting in the square of a small abandoned village. There must have been a few hundred of us who had stopped there. Some tried to protect themselves from the noonday sun by looking for shade under the trees or in the ruined houses, others prepared a few tubers. I was stretched

---

1. *Colocasia Esculenta,* a kind of taro, is very high in protein and rich in vitamins A and C as well as calcium and phosphorus. The corms (roots) must be cooked for at least an hour to remove an irritating substance. The leaves are also edible but must be boiled for at least forty-five minutes over low heat.

out on a sheeting in the shadow of the trees, but hunger and ants kept me from closing my eyes and tasting the rest that I had been longing for. To pass the time and keep my spirits up I began to look at the people around me. That was how I noticed a young man who was preparing beans. I could not take my eyes off of him. I hadn't eaten beans for weeks. Beans had never been my favorite dish, and even less beans cooked in palm oil, like those the young man was cooking. And there, in a little abandoned village in the middle of the equatorial forest, my mouth was watering watching him stirring his spoon in the pot and bringing it to his mouth to taste if there were enough salt. I wanted to ask him to give me a little, but I was afraid he would refuse, even though it would have been only one more refusal among the many I received every day when I asked for some water to drink or some sugar. I was so hungry and the beans looked so good that I didn't stay where I was for long. With a smile and a little voice that didn't resemble mine at all I asked the young man if he would give me a few beans. I spoke so softly that I had to repeat the question. To my great astonishment he went to get another pot, into which he put half of the beans. He handed me the pot and a spoon. I couldn't find the words to thank him, so I muttered my thanks and fell on the beans. I devoured the first mouthfuls without raising my eyes. I was so astonished that someone would give an unknown person half of his beans, something so rare and expensive, in the total destitution that we found ourselves in, that I wanted to know who he was and where he came from. I found out that he was from Ruhengeri and, like me, was a refugee.

To reach help as quickly as possible, we raced the 117 kilometers between Irangi and Walikale. We wanted to get there before the rebels who were coming from Goma to attack Kisangani. Goma was only about one hundred kilometers from Kisangani, and the maps that some of us were using showed a road between Goma and Walikale. In reality, this road, which had existed during colonial times, had returned to its natural state because it wasn't kept up, but we didn't know that. We ran with hunger and fear in our stomachs. A few kilometers from Hombo, we met some Zairians who had picked up a tiny baby just a few weeks old from the road. They asked all the refugees who passed by if they knew the child's parents or if someone would take it. I didn't know the parents and I didn't feel capable of taking charge of such a young baby since I didn't have anything to feed the six children I had with me already. In addition, I told myself that the baby had a better chance of surviving with a Zairian family than with a Rwandan family that wasn't its own.

During the morning everybody talked about the baby. We asked ourselves what could have led the parents to abandon such a young child on the road. Later, I learned from some refugees that the father had abandoned the baby after its mother died the day before. These people knew the parents from having spent the last few nights in the same places and from having been on the road together. The couple had two children, the baby who was only a few weeks old and an older child who couldn't have been more than two. When the mother was still alive, she carried the baby on her back and the father carried the other child as well as the baggage, since the mother was ill and couldn't carry anything more. The husband took good care of his sick wife, helped her walk, and tried to do the best for her. When she died, he had buried her with the help of a peasant. He had probably realized that he couldn't carry two children by himself, and since he had no milk for the baby, it did not have much chance of surviving. Instead of watching it die before his eyes, he had decided to abandon it on the road, covering it with a blanket so that it wouldn't suffer from the cold. Perhaps he hoped that someone would save it. Afterwards I learned that a refugee woman had taken the baby.

In this race against the clock, when someone fell, rarely was a hand stretched out to help him get up. If, by chance, he wasn't trampled, he was left thrashing around on the ground. One day, when we were taking advantage of the cool of the morning to cover as much distance as possible before the sun slowed us down, an old woman fell. She must have been seventy years old. She carried a mat on her head in which she had wrapped a blanket and some ragged clothes. She had cut her forehead and the blood made a red spot on the road. People gasped when they saw her lying motionless on the road as if she were dead, and then continued on their way, making a little detour so as not to step in the blood. Her little grandson, who was probably seven years old, wasn't strong enough to help her up himself and was waiting for her. At first I did the same thing that the others had done, but a few meters on I retraced my steps. I was ashamed of what I had just done. How could I have dared to pass someone by who needed my help without even trying to figure out what had happened or seeing if there were something I could do? I helped her get up and sit down on a stone by the side of the road and mopped the blood that had dried on her forehead and wrinkled cheeks with one of the socks I was wearing. The cut wasn't as deep as I had thought. Little by little the old woman recovered, and she told me that her son had died at INERA and she was traveling with her daughter-in-law and her children. She hoped that at Walikale she could rest her old body, which was beginning to fail her. A half an hour later her daughter-in-law and granddaughter arrived.

All along the route from Hombo to Walikale the forest stank. In some places, particularly Itebero, bodies rotted in the houses along the road. We learned from Zairians we met that there had been bloody encounters between the Tiri and the Zairian soldiers after the Tiri had accused the soldiers of running away from battle. The victims were either thrown in the forest next to the road or abandoned in the village squares.

Once in Walikale, a young Rwandan girl who had escaped these encounters told us that there were also Rwandan refugees among the victims. They had come from Bukavu and had convinced the Zairian soldiers to let them continue on toward Kisangani by giving them large sums of money. Among the refugees assassinated by the Tiri were three young men who had had an air transport business between Kavumu and Nairobi. I knew them from the time I used their services when one of my sisters left for Kenya. This young woman, whose name was Shani, was a friend of Denise and Lily. She had escaped death by a miracle. The trip from Bunyakiri to Walikale was a nightmare. She had left Bukavu on Tuesday, October 29, when the town was taken. On the road she had met the three young men, and they had gone on together along with other Zairian friends. At Bunyakiri their group was stopped by Zairian soldiers who let their countrymen go on, but who refused passage to the Rwandans, telling them to join the other refugees at Kashusha camp. After long negotiations and the exchange of a large amount of money, they finally allowed them to pass. They were afraid to go on alone and stayed several days at Bunyakiri waiting for the Zairian soldiers to get back on the road so they could travel with them. The situation began to go down hill after Hombo.

Here is how Shani told the story herself:

The Tiri ambushed us and the soldiers had to battle their way through. I was in a truck with their wives and children. When there were ambushes, we would get out of the truck and hide under it until the end of the fighting. There was no place else to hide. On both sides of the road there were forests. At one point the Tiri got the upper hand. After a lot of negotiating, the soldiers and their families were allowed to leave and they kept the Rwandans. They took the three young men who were with me to the forest. Afterwards I heard three shots, and I knew that my friends had been executed. I waited for my turn. I didn't think they would wait long to come back. A Tiri who wanted to rape me saved me. The same day another group of Zairian soldiers came by. I took advantage of this by hiding among their women. A few kilometers before Walikale, we fell into another ambush. I had a bad case of malaria and had taken advantage of a short stop to lie down in the shadow of a vehicle. When the Tiri attacked, everyone took cover behind the vehicles and in the ditches. I stayed alone on the road, not knowing what was happening. I heard shooting, but I was too weak to move. I expected to be shot at any time. I wasn't afraid. After everything I had been through in the last days, death would have been welcome. Since I was wearing green the Tiri thought I was a soldier and shot at me. A Zairian soldier dragged me away during a moment of calm. After that day, this group of Zairian soldiers took me as their mascot. They were convinced that I had supernatural powers. They couldn't understand how I could have survived the Tiri, who were using me for a target. They had heard that soldiers from the RPF and the Banyamulenge rebels owed their victory to one-breasted women who preceded them when they went into battle. The Zairian soldiers, who believed in sorcery, included me with the one-breasted sorceresses. Every time that the Tiri attacked, I touched the guns before the soldiers went into battle. Fortunately they won every time.

Four days after leaving Irangi, we finally got to Walikale and found out, to our great disappointment, that no NGOs were waiting for us. Nevertheless we were happy to have arrived before the rebels. Refugees from Goma began to arrive. There were several thousand of us in the town. Since Walikale had not been completely abandoned by its inhabitants, we were able to trade for food. It was there that I began to sell the few things that the children and I had been able to bring from INERA, like blankets, some clothes, and kitchen utensils. We rested for two days and everyone paddled in the two rivers that ran through Walikale. The characteristic modesty of the Rwandan women was forgotten. Bare breasted women bathed themselves alongside men and children and no one was shocked. The first time I took a bath in public was before we got to Bunyakiri, in one of the many places where we stayed for a few days waiting for the Tiri to let us pass. Denise and Lily told me that they had discovered a place where it was possible to bathe in peace, out of sight of passersby. I went with Denise. When we arrived, the place was already occupied by a man who was washing his clothes after having washed himself. He only had his underwear on. I began to wash my feet while waiting for him to go, but he didn't seem to be in a hurry. Finally I asked him if he intended to stay for long. He burst out laughing when he understood that we didn't want to disrobe in front of him and suggested that he could take all his clothes off too if that would make us more comfortable. Since we had to wash, we got undressed after he promised not to turn around. A promise he didn't keep, because every time I raised my head I saw that he quickly turned his and pretended to be busy with his washing. Before the end of our bath, several children and two other men came to watch this spectacle for free.

After I had been in Walikale for a day, other members of my family joined us from the camp at Shanji, which was destroyed three days before I left Irangi. Many of the refugees in Shanji camp were killed, others taken by force to Rwanda and many others still dispersed in the forest. Among them was Marcelline, a young girl we had met at INERA and who had lived with me after 1995. She was with Gisimba, my nephew Mukunzi, his cousin, and two other young people from Byumba.

When the camp at INERA had been destroyed, and I was hiding in the banana groves of the Bashi near Kahuzi-Biega National Park, Marcelline was at ADI-Kivu. She and my nephew, along with about one hundred thousand other refugees, went toward Goma. Pursued by the Banyamulenge rebels and the RPF, they hid in the mountains above Lake Kivu, where they had hoped to be rescued by the international force that had been mentioned on the international radio stations.

As I said before, the Bukavu-Goma road separated the camps at INERA and Kashusha. ADI-Kivu camp, named for the Zarian NGO ADI-Kivu, near whose headquarters it had been set up, was about five hundred meters away and was built around the buildings that belonged to the NGO. When the rebels attacked the camp at INERA, the three camps were immediately evacuated. While many of the inhabitants of INERA sought cover in the banana groves to escape the bullets, shells, and grenades, at least three quarters of the refugees from Kashusha and ADI-Kivu, among them Frieda and her family, fled down the road to Goma, since you could travel more quickly, particularly when you had children. An outdated map showed the road I mentioned before that joined Goma to Walikale and Kisangani and passed through Sake, and many wanted to take it. People who owned cars were far ahead of the others even though the roads were bad, but those at the head of the convoy fell into a Mai Mai ambush. Some were killed and others turned back. Since taking the Sake-Walikale road was impossible, they had to find an alternative.

Shanji lies in the hills that run from Lake Kivu to the Kahuzi-Biega National Park. The place where the camp was set up is an eight-hour walk from the village of Nyabibwe, on the shores of Lake Kivu. It took women and children two or three days to get there. The Shanji region is mostly inhabited by Hutu originally from Ruhengeri and Gisenyi. They are called the Bakiga and had been there since the colonial period. The refugees were welcomed, even though there were about one hundred thousand of them. The first to get there got free milk. When more arrived, the Bakiga continued to give them various things including potatoes, colocases, beans, bananas, meat, and milk at affordable prices. While the refugees set up camp at Shanji, where they hoped to stay until the arrival of the rumored international force, the Banyamulenge rebels, supported by the RPF, continued to advance. One Thursday, three weeks after we left INERA, the camp at Shanji was also destroyed. Groups of rebels waited for the refugees on the roads that they had to take while fleeing the camp, particularly in Ntumbi and Shambusha. Frieda and her family had left the night before the attack, trusting the locals who had said that the rebels weren't far away, but they walked slowly because of the children. The broken terrain and the soaking rain that poured down on them slowed them down even more. The rebels and the RPF had gotten to Shambusha before them, and they were welcomed with machine gun fire. In the pandemonium that followed the fusillade, Frieda went one way and her husband and son the other. Her niece went alone, and her sister and her husband took another direction. Frieda found her family many days later. Only her niece was missing.

The destruction of the camp at Shanji and the attacks at Shambusha and Ntumbi caused heavier losses than at the earlier camps. Thousands of refugees were forcefully repatriated to Rwanda, others were killed, and tens of thousands of others were lost in the forest, where they died of hunger, cold, and exhaustion. Among those who disappeared were many members of the Collective, including Edouard and Félicien along with their families. Later I met a man who had miraculously escaped the massacres at Shanji. He told me the following story:

I was in Shanji camp when it was destroyed by mortars. I fled with my entire family. Along the road we fell into a rebel ambush. I was taken when I tried to escape through the bushes. Along with many others, mostly men, we were sent along the road to Kavumu airport. Our hands were tied behind our backs. At the airport there were other soldiers who were not Rwandan. They must have been Ugandan, because they didn't understand Kinyarwanda. A discussion about us was going on between the Rwandan soldiers who were escorting us and the foreign soldiers. Afterwards they untied our hands. They even gave us something to eat. Then they forced us to get into a vehicle, telling us that we were going to go meet their leader. They took us to l'Institut National d'Études et de Recherches Agronomiques (INERA) where they locked us up. Other Rwandan soldiers came by from time to time to see us. Among them was a soldier who, as I did, came from Kibungo prefecture. When I saw him, I was happy because I thought he would set me free. He knew that I had not been involved in the genocide. But when I asked him to help me, he said that he wasn't the one who made the decisions and that he could do nothing for me. A few days later the Rwandan soldiers made us leave the INERA buildings. They took us to a small forest below Miti. They beat us with sticks until they thought we were all dead. I was left for dead among the bodies. The cool of the evening woke me up. I began to touch myself to see if I were still alive. I pushed my way through the dead bodies of my friends and crept into the nearest banana grove. I spent the rest of that night and all of the following day there. When night fell, I went on toward Kahuzi-Biega. I met another fugitive and we continued down the road together as far as Walikale and Tingi-Tingi. The Zairians gave us food and pointed out the road taken by the other refugees.

The other eyewitness story is from a young woman who lived at ADI-Kivu. I knew her well, because her husband often drove me to Bukavu in his car. When Shanji was destroyed, her husband went one way and she another. She found herself alone with their only daughter and a young boy who lived with them. Everyone thought that she had been killed, along with her daughter, at Shambusha. Many claimed to have seen their bodies lying alongside the road. Her husband was like a madman. He blamed himself for having abandoned them and thought that, had he been there, he could have protected them. But how could he have prevented the bullets from finding them? He held himself guilty, but he was not responsible for this tragedy. When shells fall, even mothers are separated from their children. When we had given up hope of ever seeing her again, she arrived.

I had just entered the village of Shambusha along with my daughter and the young boy who lived with us, when the shooting started. I didn't know what was happening until the moment when the boy dropped to the ground, killed by a bullet. I shoved my daughter and both of us fell next to the body of the boy. Everyone who passed by us as they fled thought we were dead. After an interminable time the shooting stopped. I got up with my daughter to run away. When we stood up a rebel called out to us. He spoke Kinyarwanda. He asked us where we were going and why we were running away. I trembled like a leaf. I thought that our last hour had come. The soldier let us go, showing us the road to follow to catch up with those who were going to be forcefully repatriated to Rwanda. During many days and nights I wandered in the forest with my daughter, looking for a path that would take us to the Bukavu-Kisangani road. Every time we heard a noise, we hid in the bushes because we thought that the rebels had found us. Often, we had to crawl for several hundred meters. Luckily we found some villagers. They helped us find the right road.

The march through the forest to reach Hombo was grueling for the survivors of Shanji. In addition to rough terrain, swollen rivers and streams crisscross this area during the rainy season. To get across the water, they had to build makeshift bridges with tree trunks they had felled with their machetes. In some spots they tied ropes to trees on both sides of the rivers and then wrapped women and children in sheeting that they slid from one end of the rope to the other. The men swam across. Sometimes the young men who could swim took others across on their backs for money. All of these obstacles slowed the march down considerably. Those who went quickly spent a week in the forest, while those who traveled more slowly took longer. And that is not counting the thousands of others who didn't make it through.

In addition, rebels often attacked the survivors of Shanji. Those who stayed in the forest more than two weeks were met at Hombo with machine guns. One day I happened to walk a while with a man who was with a little three-year-old boy. The boy took me into his confidence, probably because I reminded him of his mother. He told me that she had been killed along with his sister. He and his father had not suffered the same fate because they had hidden themselves. The father gave me more information about the killing of his wife and daughter. They had just arrived at Hombo when the first shots broke out. He ran to hide in the forest with his little boy. From their hiding place they could see what was happening on the road. That was how the little boy had seen his mother killed by a rebel bullet. She was carrying his little sister on her back. The father tried to help his son forget this horrific scene, but the little boy brought it up often. After Hombo they had to look for another road through the forest, which they were able to do thanks to help from the locals. In Walikale they were attacked again.

With every rebel attack, large numbers of refugees were killed and the survivors returned to the forest. The great majority of them did not survive the sickness, hunger, cold, and exhaustion. For fear of being seen by the rebels, they could not warm themselves with a fire, and in an area as mountainous as Shanji, the nights are very cold. Later, when a dozen people left the forest about sixty kilometers from Lubutu, they hardly looked human, they were so thin, dirty, and ragged. They explained that, along with many others, they had attempted to set up camp in the forest, but that they hadn't had anything to eat, there were no medical supplies, and they didn't even have matches to light a fire. They tried many times to get out of the forest, but every time they did, when they got to the road they found the decomposing bodies of people who had been killed by the rebels and retraced their steps. Those who left the forest knew that they were playing with their lives. When they arrived at the Losso River, in the area of Maniema, the Zairians helped them across in *pirogues*.[2]

After two days in Walikale, we left for Kisangani. Charles and a friend went the night before. Lily, Fauvette, Denise, and Shani stayed at Walikale waiting for a car that was supposed to take them, in exchange for payment, to Kisangani. They did indeed leave on a vehicle that had been seized by Zairian soldiers, but the soldiers took all the money they had. With the arrival of Marcelline and her four companions, my family group had grown appreciably, and we were now a dozen people. Immaculée, along with her three children and a young boy she had picked up along the way were with us. Margot and her two daughters stayed in Walikale to wait for Margot's sister, since some friends had told her that her sister had survived the massacres at Shanji. The Zairian soldiers had assured us that there was a camp about twelve kilometers away and that we would soon get help there. Our spirits rose. We ran the twelve kilometers, but we had been duped again. There had never even been a camp there. There was only forest, so we continued on our way, but very slowly. Our morale was at zero and our stomachs were empty.

The area between Walikale and Lubutu was relatively more populous and therefore richer than where we had just been. During the two hundred kilometers that separated the two places, we lived on cassava tubers that we stole from fields that belonged to Zairians. We had to go into the fields as a group, because if you went alone you risked being killed by the owners, who were never far off. When there was no sweet cassava, we ate the bitter, which contains a toxic substance when you eat it raw.[3] We ran a great risk of being poisoned. One evening we stopped in a village at

2. In its simplest form a *pirogue* is a dugout made from one log, but it can be larger and more elaborate.

3. Cassava, also known as manioc, yucca, and tapioca, is a member of the spurge family. Both sweet and bitter cassava contain cyanide, but bitter cassava contains more and is deadly poisonous. Whereas sweet cassava can be eaten raw, sun dried, kiln dried, or cooked, bitter cassava needs to be boiled for a long time to release the poison as a gas. It can also be pounded or soaked. Cassava roots are very high in starch, 30–35 percent, but have very little protein or fat. After planting, it does not need to be tended. Around three hundred million people, mostly the very poor, consume cassava on a daily basis. The leaves can also be eaten.

nightfall. An old man who had not run away from the Zairian soldiers sheltered the fifteen of us for the night. Our only meal of the day, eaten around two o'clock, had been bitter cassava, since we hadn't been able to find any sweet. We went to bed at about eight o'clock. We had hardly lain down when Nestor, one of the three unaccompanied children I had taken with me when I left Irangi, called me. During the time it took to light a match so I could see where to step, he began to vomit. A few minutes later Alphonse, Immaculée's youngest, began to moan and vomit. Jeanette, Immaculée's eldest, and finally Batiste joined in this concert of moans. His case was very serious. Not only did he vomit, but he also had diarrhea. Bakunda and Népo said they had horrible headaches and were nauseated but didn't vomit. We spent a sleepless night. In the morning they drank a little hot water and we continued on down the road.

We always tried to get up very early so that we could walk as far as possible before noon. In the afternoon the sun beat down, and the paved roads were so hot that those who were barefoot burned the soles of their feet. After a few kilometers they had to wrap their feet in rags. We walked an average of twenty-five kilometers a day, fifteen before lunch and ten more after the noonday rest. The boys walked faster, and we arrived at the meeting place an hour or more after they did.

One day the ten kilometers that we did after lunch ended up in the middle of the forest and night had already fallen. The boys continued on because the locals told them that the next village was only three kilometers away, but the information was bad and they would have done better to retrace their steps. The night was pitch dark. We began to sing at the top of our voices to keep our courage up. A storm broke. Lightning and thunder beat out a terrifying rhythm. We had to walk another six kilometers and were soaked to the skin.

As a result of the forced marches and the bad food, many refugees died of hunger and exhaustion. Some were abandoned by their families along the road. One day we got to a village that seemed bigger than the others and was occupied mostly by soldiers from FAZ and their families. There was a roadblock at the entrance to the village, and nearby soldiers were drinking *kanyanga*, an alcohol made from corn and cassava. Before getting to the roadblock we were stopped by a Zairian who asked us to take one of our sick countrymen with us. The woman was lying in the midday sun on the porch of a shop. The Zairians had given her some medicine, but she needed someone who could feed her and help her walk. Since our group was meeting in the village, I told the Zairian that we would first put our baggage down and then afterwards come back for the woman. He didn't want to believe us, since others before us had promised to come back and had not. Nevertheless we joined the others a few meters away. We put down our belongings and Marcelline and Virginie went to get the sick woman. She had malaria and was exhausted, and in her condition she couldn't chew cassava. Luckily, someone had a bit of corn meal and we made her some bouillie. When the rest of her family realized that she had not reached their meeting place, they sent a brother-in-law to look for her. When he arrived she had recuperated a little and was able to go with him. We caught up with them the next day, and she was doing better and could walk without help. This village was spacious and clean. The houses were occupied, and since it gave the impression of comfort, we decided to spend the night. Hardly had we decided to stay, though, when the soldiers began shooting. I thought I was back in INERA. We had to put our things back on our heads on the double and leave the village as quickly as possible.

Because of the Zairian soldiers and the refugees, some of whom were armed, the area was in a state of utter lawlessness. One evening we had just stopped in a village to spend the night when we heard several shots. I immediately thought that they came from rebels and began to run to the nearby forest, leaving what little I had in the room in the house where we were preparing to spend the night. I got to the first row of trees when the shots stopped. I waited a little and as it seemed calm, I returned toward the houses. Everyone was outside talking about what had happened. Only the women had fled. The men had wanted to know what was going on before following us. Later we slept, without knowing what really had happened.

The next morning we took our time getting up, since we had gone to bed very late. A friend woke us and urged us to leave the village. During the night a refugee had killed a woman to rob her, which explained the shots the previous evening, and he feared reprisals from the locals. We packed our belongings as quickly as possible and left. Ever since Bukavu, the killer, a young man of about twenty-five who liked to be called "sergeant," but who had never set foot in the army, assaulted people, locals as well as refugees, to steal their money. At Itebero I almost became one of his victims. I was sitting in front of the house where we were going to spend the night when he came by with another young man. Both were armed. He had a pistol and the other had a Kalashnikov. Someone whispered to me that the man with the pistol and smoke tinted glasses was called "sergeant" and that he was dangerous. The other was his "bodyguard." I didn't pay too much attention to this. I was too tired and all I wanted to do was sleep. Immaculée and I had walked fast all morning without taking a rest, and I was at the end of my rope. The "sergeant" looked in our direction and then left to entertain himself with one of the other people who were around. After a few minutes a man came to tell me that the "sergeant" wanted to talk to me. He was armed, so his word was law. When I got close to him he wanted to know who I was and see my identity card. He verified that I was Hutu and began to ask questions about Immaculée and her daughters. While I was being questioned, a former Rwandan soldier, who came from Byumba and was a real sergeant, arrived. He asked what was going on and why I was being questioned. The fake sergeant excused himself and left. But every time I saw him I was frightened. People said he would not hesitate to kill someone for a pair of shoes. Mine were still in good shape, and I told myself I could be his next victim. A while later he was executed, along with all of his band, on the orders of former officers from FAR. He was a danger to all of the refugees.

About twenty kilometers from Lubutu we began to run into refugees from the newly set up camp at Tingi-Tingi. They had already been there for a week. Zairian soldiers, who thought that the refugees promoted infiltration by the Banyamulenge rebels, blocked the road to Kisangani. For Zairians, all Rwandans looked alike, and it would have been difficult for the soldiers to know who was Banyamulenge and who wasn't.

This new camp was horrifying. Nothing had been set up, and the refugees were not yet organized. The scarcity of food forced many people to go back twenty kilometers to get a bundle of cassava leaves and a few cups of rice, since the price of these necessities at Tingi-Tingi was exorbitant. Zairian soldiers guarded the entrance to Lubutu, about eight kilometers from the camp, preventing the refugees from entering, even though the only market in the area was in the town. Humanitarian aid, expected since Walikale, was still unavailable; only displaced persons of Zairian nationality had access to it. Hunger was already claiming its first victims.

Knowing this, we decided to ask a Kumu family if we could stay with them about six kilometers from the camp and go to the camp when humanitarian aid arrived.[4] Since our group was mostly women and young boys, they agreed to take us in. Our hosts didn't want men to stay with them because they thought that they would bring trouble, so Bakunda, Népo, and Basita went to Tingi-Tingi to arrange for the places we would stay when we got to the camp. The whole house was made available for us, and we used our hosts' kitchen and their sanitary facilities. Even though these people sold cassava leaves, they gave them to us for free and even gave us firewood. They also gave us colocase leaves and sold rice to us at a reasonable price. After a few days we felt like part of the family. We didn't have much trouble communicating with them, because Swahili was spoken in all of this area and Assumpta, Jeanette, and Virginie had no difficulty speaking this language. This was a welcome exception.

For several reasons the Kumu were not happy to see the refugees: It was the first time they had had contact with Rwandans; we had arrived in the area by the hundreds of thousands, which made them feel invaded; and so many refugees in a thinly populated forest area that produced little food posed a very real danger to their survival. Since Walikale we had lived on cassava stolen from their fields because that was all we could do, and to protect their crops, the Kumu organized patrols. Several dozen refugees caught in the act of stealing were beaten to death.

After Walikale I had no more money. The seventy American dollars that I had in my pocket when I left Bukavu were spent in Irangi along with the fifty dollars from Egide. After Irangi we lived off of what we could find in the fields: cassava, colocases, and green papayas. That wasn't possible any more because the fields were off limits to us. A solution had to be found or else we would die. First I traded my pagnes for a few cups of rice. After that it was the T-shirts and the few clothes that the children had with them. Everyone kept just one set of clothes, often the one that the buyers didn't want. Everything else of value that we still had, like shoes, cooking pots, and blankets, was also sold. When we had nothing left to sell, we began a business selling cassava leaves in the camp and looked for work among the villagers. We ground rice, helped

4. The Kumu ethnic group live in the heavily forested area near Kisangani.

with the harvest, carried the cassava to be sold to the refugees, cleaned and weeded plots of land, helped lay bricks, and so forth. Nothing was too difficult or too dirty for us.

We were becoming accustomed to life in the Kumu village when our host's sons began to get too interested in the young girls in our group. Their little sisters warned us that they were prepared to resort to using black magic to get them for wives. Immaculée and I, the adults in the group, thought that if the magic didn't work, they would be tempted to use force, and we weren't big enough to defend the girls. This worried us a lot. We decided to join the other refugees in the camp, even though it wasn't yet well-equipped and humanitarian aid had not yet arrived. It was a painful decision.

At Tingi-Tingi I found my cousin André and his two eldest sons again. His wife and the two younger children had returned to Rwanda. The last time I had seen André and his family was a few days after President Habyarimana's assassination. They had fled toward Goma while I went toward Bukavu. They had miraculously survived the cholera at Goma, which in July and August of 1994 had killed eighty thousand people, sixty thousand in one week alone. Other members of our family, in particular my niece and my brother-in-law, died in this catastrophe. It was a great joy to see André and his sons and to hear news of the rest of the family. In my misery, I told myself that there was still someone in the family I could count on to see that I got a decent burial if I were to die at Tingi-Tingi.

8

The Death Camp
at Tingi-Tingi

I ARRIVED AT TINGI-TINGI during December 1996, with Bakunda,
Assumpta, Virginie, Marcelline, my nephew Gisimba, and my cousin
Mukunzi. We had nothing left to eat, but we had two sheetings, with
which we built two blindés, one for the three boys and another for the
three girls and me. The three unaccompanied children I had picked up
at Irangi decided to stay with the Kumu family because they could eat
there. Each child who came with me to Tingi-Tingi had his or her own
story.

Bakunda was the youngest. He was thirteen and came from Kivuye
in Byumba prefecture, where the guerillas began their incursion into
Rwandan territory in 1990. When war broke out, he was seven years old
and had just entered primary school. Following the massacres of the
civilian population that happened when the RPF passed through their
area, Bakunda and his family and their neighbors had to leave their
houses and all their belongings and find safety in areas not yet touched
by the rebellion. From 1990 until 1993, he had only known life in the
camps, first at Cyumba, and then in Miyove, Tumba, and Nyacyonga.
Since 1990 he had not set foot in a classroom. He and his friends spent
all their time running after the vehicles that belonged to the humanitarians and asking for money to buy beignets or peanuts.

I met Bakunda at a military checkpoint at Nyacyonga in February of
1993. After the fighting started again, the camp for displaced persons at
Tumba, where he had been with his parents since 1992, was destroyed.

The camp at Nyacyonga had just been set up, and most of the shelters were still made of branches. The "humanitarians" had not arrived, and the main food for the people was sugar cane. What struck me about Bakunda was his relative cleanliness in comparison to the other boys, and his sweet expression. We liked each other immediately. Every time that my car arrived at the roadblock, he would come running. He never asked me for money like the other urchins did, and as he himself did from the other drivers, and he never climbed on my spare tire, which was the favorite sport for the street children of Nyacyonga. When the other boys asked me for money, he told them to go away. He didn't want me to be bothered. Every time I saw him we spent five or ten minutes talking together about his life in the camp, his family, his interrupted schooling, and his plans. After a few weeks, we decided that it would be better for him to come live with me in Kigali where he could start school again and where he would have the comfort of a house and a real home. In short, he could learn to live like a normal boy of his age.

He had lost all trace of his mother after the RPF destroyed the camp at Tumba, and was living with his father in Nyacyonga. I therefore went to see his father and proposed taking Bakunda to live with me for a while. He wanted to know who I was and what I did, where I lived and what I wanted to do with his son. Apparently he was satisfied with the information that I gave him, because he decided to trust me with his care. That is how Bakunda became my adopted son. When the war reached Kigali, we fled first to Cyangugu and from there we went to Bukavu. Bakunda was a very intelligent boy, and despite the fact that his education had been interrupted by the war, he adapted to school right away. When we fled Bukavu, he had just finished primary school.

My first meeting with Assumpta dates from 1995 in the camp at ADI-Kivu. She was sixteen years old and had been taken in by my mother after having been sent away by the family with whom she had fled Rwanda in 1994. She was my younger sister's classmate, and they often came together to my mother's house in Byumba. When the war broke out in Byumba, Assumpta and my sister fled together. They wandered around the mountains for several days before being rescued by the people in charge of an agricultural project in North Kigali and were evacuated, along with other students from Byumba, to Butare. When my sister stopped to stay with a friend in Gitarama, Assumpta continued on with the others to Butare, where they lived in a secondary school building. She hoped to reach her family in Ntyazo, but the lawlessness in the area forced her to stay in Butare. From April until June 1994, the date that Butare fell to the RPF, Assumpta, who looked like a Tutsi, escaped death countless times. Every day she saw classmates being taken away. They didn't come back. One day they brought an old Tutsi woman whom she was supposed to kill with her own hands as proof of her truthfulness and ethnic purity. If she had refused, it would have been she whom they killed. It was a technique used to implicate people, to soften them up. By good luck students from Byumba who knew Assumpta came to her defense, and she was spared one more time. For several days she stayed under the beds in the dormitory to escape those who wanted to kill her.

When Butare was taken, Assumpta fled with the other students. At Gikongoro, which was then in the Turquoise Zone, she was taken in by a family of friends and traveled with them first to Cyangugu and then to the Rwandan refugee camp at Kashusha. After the family had been living there for several months, the husband began to make advances to her, even though she was barely fourteen years old. When he realized that he wasn't going to get what he wanted from her, he sent her away from the house. Kashusha camp was close to ADI-Kivu, where my family was, and Carmen, one of my little sisters who was up to date on Assumpta's problems, told my mother, who took her in. Bakunda and Assumpta first went with my mother to Kaziba, and when she left for Nairobi, they came to stay with me at Bukavu. I thought I would send them to my mother when I could afford it, but as I have already said, the war broke out in Bukavu before I had time to do this.

Virginie was twenty and like me was from Byumba. I had known her family since I was a child. My eldest sister was engaged to her uncle. Even though this marriage did not take place, our families had maintained strong ties. Once I spent my vacation with another of her uncles whose wife was my godmother. In 1992, she was a day student at Kabgayi in Gitarama prefecture and lived with me. Like my family, hers had fled Byumba in 1993, when the RPF arrived and began massacring the civilian population. After that she had to spend all her vacations in Kigali, either at her uncle's or with her brothers, who worked there. In April 1994, she fled Kigali with her uncle's family after he had been killed by the RPF.

Like so many others, her family tried to go to Burundi. At the border they were turned back by Rwandan border guards. Back in Butare they were present for the beginning of the Tutsi genocide there. They themselves were threatened with death every day. Since Butare had become too dangerous for them, and flight to Burundi was impossible, they retraced their steps. Virginie went with her uncle's wife and her cousins to Murama in Gitarama prefecture. At Murama, Virginie and her cousins could not walk around openly, because the peasants in this part of the country, which was far from the urban centers, were not used to seeing young women in pants, shorts, miniskirts, or braided hair. For these peasants, a young girl who dressed that way had to be Tutsi. According to them, young Hutu girls were too well brought up to dress like whores. When she was alone after her aunt and her cousins left, the persecution intensified because she was no longer protected. In a way she was saved by the RPF attack, which forced everyone to leave Murama. She went with her aunt's brothers and was with them until Gikongoro. At every roadblock they took her aside because she was wearing pants, didn't have an identity card, and came from Byumba, an area where the RPF had many adherents. For the peasants, who were badly informed about the situation in the country, Virginie had all of the characteristics of a rebel and had to be eliminated. I don't know how many times she was beaten before some better-informed person intervened to confirm that her student identity card was not a rebel identity card, so that she could be allowed to go.

After several agonizing days, Virginie and her group arrived in the Turquoise Zone. She stayed there at a small camp with her aunt's brother. Later his family went back to Murama, which in the meantime had come under the control of the RPF. Having heard that the new regime was mainly interested in killing people who were educated, he arranged for someone to go with Virginie as far as Gikongoro, more than one hundred kilometers from there. Since vehicles had become a scarce commodity in that area, Virginie and her companion had to cover the entire distance on foot in an area that they were unfamiliar with, risking being killed if they were suspected of being rebels. The first day passed without incident, and they were even able to find a room in a small hotel. Unfortunately her companion, who during the day had been pleasant and understanding, wanted to take advantage of the situation. Virginie was able to get away from him and spent the night with other refugees on the sidewalk. The next day she went as far as Gikongoro with them, where, in her unhappiness, she happened to find her aunt's nephew and his wife. It was with them that she arrived in Bukavu.

A few days after arriving in Bukavu, Virginie had problems with her aunt's family and had to go to the camp for unaccompanied children at Katana. In 1995, Katana was closed and she was transferred to the camp at Mudaka as "head of an artificial family." The organizations in charge of the camps had had the idea of making small groups called "artificial households." Virginie had charge of three other minor children. After 1994 she had no idea what had happened to her parents and three brothers. She had been looking for them for a long time and every week she sent out a search notice through the Red Cross. When Bukavu fell into the hands of the Banyamulenge rebels and the RPF, she left Mudaka with her small family and went to INERA. When INERA was destroyed, she miraculously escaped being killed. She was living at the edge of the woods that ran along the border of INERA camp, which was where the rebels hid during the night of Friday, October 31, 1996. Very early in the morning she was awakened by shooting. She left her sheeting at a run, taking a few pagnes wrapped in a cloth, which she wasn't strong enough to tie very well. Dragging this bundle behind her, she ran doubled up or lay face down. After a few hundred meters, a young man who was running by her side noticed that her bundle was not well tied and suggested that they stop for a moment so that he could help her tie it properly so she would not lose the few things she had left. When the shooting intensified and seemed to be getting closer, Virginie turned toward the young man to tell him to hurry. When she looked where he had been a couple of seconds before, all she saw was his head rolling several meters away from his body. He had just been decapitated by a STRIM shot by a rebel hiding in an avocado tree just above them.[1] When she looked up to see where the STRIM had come from, she saw the rebel take aim at her. She ran off leaving her bundle behind. The STRIM that had been meant for her cut a banana tree in half right where she had been a moment before. From INERA she traveled toward Bunyakiri, crossing Kahuzi-Biega National Park alone. The other

---

1. A STRIM is a rifle-mounted antitank grenade launcher of French manufacture. Most of these weapons were abandoned when Operation Turquoise left the area.

unaccompanied children she had been traveling with probably went toward Shanji. I found her at Irangi, and from this moment on she went with me everywhere in my wanderings.

Marcelline was twenty-five years old and came from Nyakizu in Butare prefecture. When the rebels arrived there, she fled with her sisters, one of whom was a student at the Université Nationale du Rwanda. At first they stayed in the camp for displaced persons at Gikongoro, earning their living by selling beignets. Later she continued her flight toward Zaire because she no longer felt safe in Rwanda. Her sisters chose to stay in the camps in the interior of the country and were still in the camp at Kibeho when it was razed in 1995. Ever since the destruction of the camps in the eastern part of Zaire, Marcelline had had no news of her family. I met her in 1994 when I moved into the camp at INERA. She was my nearest neighbor, and it was she who welcomed me and helped me start my life in the camp. Since she had no family, she very quickly joined mine. She became my "niece," just like my sister's children who lived with me.

Gisimba was the fourth among my sister's eight children. In 1992 he fled Miyove and went to Kigali. When President Habyarimana was killed, his mother and the two youngest children were visiting in Byumba. Gisimba fled with his three sisters and his cousin Mukunzi. Another of his sisters, Umulisa, was with me. His father, who stayed at Kigali, was killed by the RPF in 1994. Gisimba and his sisters stayed at Cyangugu until the French soldiers left the Turquoise Zone, and from there they went to the refugee camp at Kabila, on the Bukavu-Goma road. In 1996, after his sisters returned to Rwanda, Gisimba and his cousin Mukunzi rejoined my uncle Gashirabake at ADI-Kivu.

In short, there were seven of us who arrived at Tingi-Tingi. The camp was built on an unstable swamp, "tingi-tingi" in the Kumu language. When it rained, the ground swelled and let off a stifling heat. The climate was perfect for the proliferation of mosquitoes and every kind of microbe. The water was a dirty yellowish color. The first weeks at the camp, before humanitarian aid arrived, were Hell. People arrived exhausted and famished, with swollen feet, hoping to find food and care. They were welcomed by a blazing sun and disease. The health of the refugees was already compromised by the long march and malnutrition. In this filthy swamp, epidemics of malaria, dysentery, and cholera ravaged them. They died like flies. Every day we buried a good fifty people, mostly children and pregnant women.

We arrived before the camp was really set up. The first few days we had no tools to dig latrines, and everyone went to the bathroom wherever they felt like it. It was only later, after UNICEF gave us picks and shovels, that we were able to dig real WCs. There was no one in charge of educating those using the facilities, and the WCs were always a source of infection. To build our blindés, we had to clear the dense forest, running the risk of being bitten by snakes.

The plight of the children was particularly horrendous. Mothers had nothing to feed them. UNICEF, Doctors Without Borders, and Caritas distributed biscuits and bouillie, but it was insufficient. Infant formula was reserved for hospitalized children who were in critical condition. You can count the children under five who survived Tingi-Tingi on the fingers of your hand. Even those who arrived healthy died within a few weeks.

When we came to the camp, famine was in full swing. Those who had a little money, goods, or pagnes, could still buy a few cassava leaves or a little rice. Finding work with the Kumu was a matter of luck and only a few people succeeded. For a whole day's work they got barely enough cassava tubers to feed a family of three. The neighbors of anyone lucky enough to have a little cassava came to beg the peels, which were usually fed to pigs. They dried them and afterwards removed the outer part and boiled the rest in water. In the little market in the camp, there was almost nothing but some baskets of ground cassava leaves and a few kilos of rice and corn brought by the Zairian women. Each morning everyone came to the part of the camp where tents set up by the humanitarian organizations were located to glean what information they could about the hypothetical arrival of food aid. The people from the World Food Program (WFP) said that because of the poor condition of the roads and the danger presented by the Zairian soldiers stationed along the road between Kisangani and Lubutu, shipping food overland was difficult. The only possibility that remained was establishing an airlift. UNICEF was already chartering planes to bring medicines, biscuits, flour, and other food for children. They began at first with small carriers, and later they used a plane that carried several tons and made an average of two round trips daily between Kisangani and Tingi-Tingi.

Like many others, I left my sheeting at a run when I heard the drone of an airplane and took my place at the edge of the runway, but I had to be very careful, since I was dizzy from hunger. Along with the other refugees, I watched these planes land and take off, hoping to see a sack of corn or beans come out of the hold. After the plane took off I would return to my sheeting, my feet dragging and my eyes full of tears, and go back to bed. Others preferred to stay on the road, under the burning sun, until evening. The sight of cold fireplaces and empty pots was too much to bear. It was at times like these that I hated the international community, which had abandoned us at the moment that we most needed them. They knew that some of us had survived the rebels in the forest, but they seemed in no hurry to come to our aid. I had heard that some countries and international organizations had even declared that there were no more Rwandan refugees in the eastern part of Zaire, apart from some Interahamwe and their families who deserved, it seems, their fate. Nevertheless, there were more than a hundred thousand people at Tingi-Tingi. Every day when I succeeded in falling asleep, I had nightmares. I saw refugees falling like flies from an unknown sickness. I awoke with a start thinking about what would become of us if humanitarian aid didn't arrive within a few weeks. I sat in my bed and prayed. What else was left for us to do? In whom could we put our hope?

When I look back at this time, I cannot understand how we managed to survive in the weeks before the arrival of humanitarian aid. We had sold everything of value, and the little money we had gotten was already spent with the Kumu. When the situation became critical, we talked about what we each had to do to so that we would have some food to eat. Marcelline had to sell cassava leaves. She got up around five in the morning to be the first to arrive among the Kumu. The first few days Assumpta and Bakunda went with her to help her grind them. Later they returned to sell the ground cassava leaves in the camp. A small cupful sold for about fifteen thousand new Zaires. With the money we could buy two or three cups of rice. Rice and cassava leaves made up the only meal of the day, which we ate at around three o'clock. Since what Marcelline earned wasn't enough to guarantee our daily survival, Virginie looked for work among the Kumu. She helped build houses and weed and clean up fields. As payment she was given cassava tubers or sweet potatoes. Assumpta was hired by UNICEF to clean toilets in the health center. As compensation she got a packet of nine biscuits, which Bakunda sold separately. One day when our combined efforts had yielded nothing, I decided to sell my watch. My niece Sylvie had given it to me and it was the apple of my eye. But hunger was stronger, and I decided to sell it. I gave it to Charles so that he could go to Lubutu and exchange it for some rice. If Lily had not given me five dollars, I don't know what I would have done that day to feed my little family.

A few days later we once again had nothing to eat. Assumpta had not gotten her packet of biscuits, and Marcelline came home empty-handed from the Kumu. All the children looked to me to know what to do. I felt guilty for what had happened. The children must be asking themselves why I wasn't working with the humanitarians like the others so that I could bring home some flour or a packet of biscuits every day, since I also was educated. That day I painfully got up from my bed and went to Patricia, who worked at UNICEF, to see if she could help me. She gave me some small fish, enriched flour and peas, as well as two T-shirts and two pairs of pants. I had sold all my pagnes for rice. All that I had left was a faded black T-shirt and torn shorts.

One morning when we were beginning to despair of the arrival of food aid, I was awakened by shouting. The whole camp seemed to be meeting in front of the WFP. Cries of joy from thousands of throats parched by hunger and the sun of Tingi-Tingi accompanied the arrival of the first trucks. I got up and ran to join the others. Like them, I began to shout for joy, loudly thanking the good Lord. The hope that we wouldn't all die of hunger was reborn in our hearts. That day and the following days I spent hours in front of the stocks of the WFP, watching people unloading sacks of corn flour, peas, and containers of oil from the trucks. Just seeing these sacks stacked one atop the other made me feel less hungry than before.

As soon as the first trucks arrived, the WFP proceeded with the distribution. Even though the amounts of food were small in comparison with the masses at Tingi-Tingi, people were too hungry and couldn't wait any longer. Everyone received one and a half kilos of corn flour, between two hundred and five hundred grams of peas, and a few milliliters of oil to last seven days. This ration was hardly enough for a couple of days, but it was better than nothing. The distribution was not made equitably, though. The first to arrive at the camp had been the young men, and they took the initiative in organizing the camp into districts and subdistricts and allotted themselves the best jobs. When the food was distributed, they got the most while households with more people got less. In the second distribution, even though we saw some improvement, the inequities of the first distribution persisted.

It was in large part to try to find a solution to this problem that the women decided to organize and play a more important role in the distribution of food aid. We were convinced that if we were responsible for the distribution, there would be less cheating. Since I had experience in organizing women and was unemployed, I was put in charge. A committee of about a dozen women was set up to organize meetings and elect female representatives in the districts and subdistricts. It was proposed that the women's representative from the camp be part of the development committee so that the position of women in the camp could always be considered in decisions concerning the refugees. I was elected to be the vice-president of the organization. The presidency went to Thérèse, a member of the Girl Guides of Rwanda, who came from Goma.

Although food distribution was their primary concern, the women's organization looked into other problems encountered by the refugees in general and the women in particular, especially the problems of the invalids and women with small children who lived alone in the blindés and who could not eat or take care of themselves when they fell ill. There were many such cases at Tingi-Tingi. One of the most unfortunate was that of a young woman, a neighbor of Déo, the former financial administrator for the Collective, whom I found in this Hell and who told me the following story about a young woman who lived alone with two little boys, four and ten years old. Since the family had nothing to eat, the eldest decided to join the unaccompanied children, under the auspices of UNICEF. One day the young woman fell sick and stayed in bed in her blindé. No one noticed her absence. After several days, her neighbors were alerted by the smell of rotting flesh coming from her blindé. The woman was dead. As for her younger child, no one knew what had happened to him until the day he crawled out of the abandoned blindé a mere skeleton. He was taken to the hospital, but he only survived one or two days. To avoid such horrors, it was very important that the women in the districts know which people were living alone or had young children, so that they could keep track of them and help them if they needed it. In the case of sickness, for example, they could prepare food for them and inform the health authorities, who could help them get to the dispensary. The issue of hygiene also had to be addressed by the Women's Organization at Tingi-Tingi in order to lessen the risk of contamination, particularly from sicknesses such as diarrhea, which were causing dozens of deaths every day. Unfortunately, this organization was never fully functional because we had hardly started when we had to make a precipitous departure from the camp.

At Tingi-Tingi we paid close attention to the news of the Great Lakes Region that was broadcast on the international radio stations: Voice of America in Kinyarwanda, the BBC in Kinyarwanda and in Kirundi, and Radio France Internationale (RFI). I noticed with bitterness that what seemed to interest the international press were Kabila's rebel advance and the sudden counteroffensive announced by Mobutu. When they did mention the Rwandan refugees, when they finally accepted that we still existed, the journalists were only interested in the presence of members of the militia at Tingi-Tingi and in the recruitment of former members of FAR by FAZ. Of our daily life, of the Hell we had lived in since the destruction of the camps in eastern Zaire, of the horrifying death that awaited those lost in the forest, of the massacres perpetrated by the rebels, not one word. Only Emma Bonino, the European Commissioner for Humanitarian Action, dared to speak the truth. Unfortunately her calls for compassion toward the Rwandan refugees didn't awaken any echoes in the Western press. With other members of the League who had arrived at Tingi-Tingi, we began to ask ourselves what our role in the situation was. We had created this League to allow Rwandan women to express themselves on their suffering and on the events that had shaken Rwanda since 1990. Since the destruction of the camps in the east of Zaire, the situations in which we lived were untenable. We had to act and make our voices heard. Staying passive and mute was really no longer possible. What had happened to the thousands of people run out of the camps at Uvira, Goma, and Bukavu had to be spoken of. We had to talk about the people who were dying in the forest and in the camps every day. We had to talk about the women who gave birth in the forest without any help, without pagnes for their babies, without food or even water to wash them with. We had to talk about four-year-old children who had to run headlong for four hundred kilometers to escape the rebels who were pursuing them. We had no idea yet by what channel such a document, once we had written it, would arrive at the international human rights organizations and the media. We also didn't know how it would be received, but we told ourselves that the most important thing was to write it. We wanted to begin with concrete stories so that the reader could get an idea about what was happening in the East of Zaire, in sight of and with the knowledge of the international community. We hoped that with such a document our situation would stop being perceived as a just punishment for a group of genocidal people who did not want to go back to their own country for fear of reprisals. Not knowing how much time it would take us to finish our project, since the camp could be destroyed at any time by the rebels, we went right to work. By the time the camp was destroyed, we had begun to interview people, but nothing remains of the questionnaire that we drew up and the results of the first interviews. Sometime later I had to destroy all the documents that I had with me.

During the two months that I lived at Tingi-Tingi, I spent most of my time at meetings and funerals. Among the many friends, relatives, acquaintances, and co-workers buried at Tingi-Tingi, I particularly remember Jeanne. I met her for the first time in 1993 at the women's section of the Rwandan Association of Christian Workers. Jeanne was, along with her husband Damien, one of the first members of the Collective. When Caritas and UNICEF turned over the management of the camp for unaccompanied children to the Collective, Jeanne and Damien were the first administrators. Jeanne had, for many years, run an orphanage for young children in Butare and Damien took care of street children in Kigali under the auspices of the Rwandan Association of Christian Workers. Their little girl was named Delphine.

Jeanne was healthy when she arrived at the camp. Although she was eight months pregnant, she had survived the exhausting march through the forest relatively well. The doctors told her to rest, which was natural considering her state. I went by their blindé often to get news of her. When the time came for her to give birth, the doctors transferred her to the Zairian hospital at Lubutu for a cesarean section, since the camp hospital was not equipped for this sort of intervention. The operation was a success and Jeanne delivered a little boy. A few days later, Lubutu was looted. The civilian population, including the doctors and nurses, had to leave, abandoning the patients. Jeanne stayed for several days at Lubutu, alone, without food, without care, without medicine. It was impossible to take her back to the camp, because refugees were forbidden access to the town during the looting. Those who dared to go were badly beaten and even killed. When it was possible to get to the town, it was too late for Jeanne and her baby. We buried them at the same time as ten other people.

Among those whom we buried that day, there was an old woman I had known since INERA. She came from Gishamvu in Butare prefecture. The first time that she came to my house, I was away at the office of the Collective at Bukavu. When I came back at the end of the day, Marcelline told me that an old woman from her hometown had come by to ask for a little food because the ration from the WFP wasn't enough for her and her three children. Marcelline had given her some beans, corn, and lentils. The old woman left, promising to come back again and thank me personally for having brought up my children so well. She returned a few days later. She must have been between forty-five and fifty years old, but hunger, poverty, and despair had aged her prematurely. She wore a long skirt that was full of holes and a tattered pagne. Since she herself and her eldest son were often sick, she could not work regularly for the locals. When, once a month, she could do it, the little that she earned was used to supplement the ration from the WFP.

In my work with the women in the camp, I dealt with misery every day. But among all the cases that I encountered, the most painful to see were those of the middle-aged people who for years had worked hard to take care of themselves, keep a roof over their heads and prepare for a comfortable old age, and whom human stupidity now obliged to live like pariahs. The sight of this mother, dressed like someone insane, who had to beg from people that she didn't know in order to survive herself and allow her children to survive, made me think of my own mother. She also could be brought to this extremity some day. The old woman had had a house and a banana grove at Gishamvu, and maybe some livestock too. Her children had gone to school. Her son, a teacher, could buy her some beautiful pagnes and a beer from time to time. I gave her the only pagnes I had and a few kilos of beans and corn flour, and after that day we became friends. Later one of her daughters got a loan from the Collective and started a small sugar cane business. Little by little the family was able to get on its feet. The eldest son was able to get care and even to marry. But the four hundred kilometers that separated INERA and Tingi-Tingi were fatal to her. When she arrived at Tingi-Tingi, she was exhausted and sick. Bad food and dysentery did the rest.

It was also at Tingi-Tingi that Thérèse died, leaving her sixteen-year-old daughter in charge of two little boys. I had known Thérèse for twenty years. When we met for the first time, we were still teenagers. She was in primary school and I was at the Lycée. We walked together for an hour every day on our way to our respective schools. At noon we shared the meal that they brought to us at the school, because it was too far to go home. In the evening we walked the five kilometers back home. When we got there, we went together to get water from the spring. When Thérèse finished her studies, she married my brother's best friend, so we continued to see each other often. Life wasn't always kind to her. Only a few years after she married, her husband was killed when a car rolled over, and she was left with a little girl. After several years she decided to start a new life with another man. They had two boys together. This husband, who was Tutsi, was killed in the genocide. In Zaire, we met again at ADI-Kivu. When the camp was destroyed she fled to Shanji, and was among those who spent several weeks in the forest because they didn't know where to get out, either because the rebels already controlled the exits or because they didn't know what direction they were going in or what little path to take. When she arrived at Tingi-Tingi, I had trouble recognizing her. She, who had always been so plump, was now a walking skeleton. She couldn't have weighed more than forty kilos. Thérèse never recovered. When she died of dysentery, she only weighed twenty kilos.

Death was so close at Tingi-Tingi that we made jokes about it. When someone died, we wrapped him in a white pagne donated by Doctors Without Borders and took him to the cemetery, carried on the shoulders of four men. Every time that I came across a cortège, often limited to the four porters, I would glance at the body to see if it were a child or an adult that they were taking. Often the pagne didn't cover the feet of the dead person and you could see the toes and the soles of the feet. That is how you could see if the person they were carrying was rich, and had worn shoes during his life, or poor, and had gone barefoot. Jokingly, I used to tell the children and my friends to take a good look at my feet and toes, that way they could always recognize me if they ever came across my body on the way to the cemetery, so they wouldn't miss my burial.

When we arrived at Tingi-Tingi we didn't expect to stay long. We thought that the rebels and the RPF would catch up quickly. Even the most optimistic spoke of two or three weeks' respite. Around thirty elderly Zairian policemen had been sent to Walikale to stop the rebel advance, but a few days after they came through Tingi-Tingi we learned that Walikale had fallen. The refugees who were in the town when it was taken walked the distance from Walikale to Tingi-Tingi, a distance of about two hundred kilometers, in five days of walking day and night. They told us that the rebels had surprised them around six in the morning, when some among them were preparing to go to mass. The Zairian policemen were no help, and the rebels controlled Walikale after exchanging fire for only a few minutes. Some refugees who arrived in the town after it fell were stabbed to death and others hid in the forest. Among the victims was a businessman from Kashusha by the name of Nyiramubande. He originally came from Kibungo prefecture. Everyone was afraid of him because of the stories of sorcery that people told about him. Even the Zairian soldiers didn't dare ask him for money when he arrived at Bukavu. He was stabbed by the rebels, who had tricked him by speaking to him in Kinyarwanda.

After Walikale was taken, we expected that the rebels would fall on us at any moment. Between them and the camp at Tingi-Tingi there was nothing now that could slow their progress. In addition, the road was good, with one hundred kilometers of it paved, and they could drive. Less than a week afterwards, about fifty Zairian soldiers went through the camp toward Walikale. Rumor had it that the Zairian army had recruited former members of FAR to reinforce the eastern front. I had noticed that certain blindés in the camp were empty and asked a neighbor where the occupants were. He whispered into my ear that they had left for the front at the Losso River, about a hundred kilometers from Tingi-Tingi. They had left at night so as not to attract the attention of the other refugees. Even if I had not seen them leave myself, I was comforted to know that elements from FAR were fighting in the ranks of FAZ. I hoped that they could slow down the rebel advance. Nevertheless, I was still convinced that we had only a few weeks to stay at Tingi-Tingi. The Zairian army clearly did not intend to oppose the rebel advance, and a handful of former Rwandan soldiers would not change that. I began to consult a map of Zaire with my neighbors. We wanted to see the distances that separated us from various fronts. A second front had just been opened by Ugandan soldiers north of Kisangani in the area of Haut Zaire. We wanted to find a gap that we could sneak through when the camp was destroyed.

Hope revived when the international radio stations began to talk about President Mobutu's lightning counteroffensive. In fact, this "counteroffensive" consisted of two fighter planes we saw fly by doing aerobatics over the camp. In addition there were two combat helicopters piloted by whites, who were said to be mercenaries, two old tanks, and a few soldiers. These helicopters landed at the little airport at Amisi, where there was another, smaller, refugee camp only about twenty kilometers from the front. Neither these two planes nor the two tanks would keep the rebels from taking the bridge at Losso. When the fighting broke out there, rumors ran rampant in the camp. Some said that soldiers from FAZ had gotten around the rebel positions and that they were already at Walikale. Others maintained that Masisi and the mountains around Bukavu were under their control. It was rumored that the Zairian army would retake the areas of South and North Kivu and continue on to Kigali. To be sure, returning to Rwanda never seemed as close as it did then. People talked about where along the border they would reenter Rwanda, going back to the divinations of a certain Magayane who had, they said, predicted the war.[2] Speculations ran wild about the means of transport for a return. Some spoke of returning on foot, while others thought that the UNHCR would charter vehicles and planes as it had for refugees from other countries. Old women pretended to be seers, predicting a future return to Rwanda, and people clung to these predictions like a lifebuoy.

It was during this time that European Commissioner for Humanitarian Action, Emma Bonino, came to Tingi-Tingi. Since she was a

2. Magayane was a Rwandan seer who had dreams that predicted the future. Because he predicted future political events, including, allegedly, the 1990 war, he was considered a nuisance and was jailed by Security Chief Lizinde at the end of the 1970s. He died in prison.

woman, the women of the camp were asked to arrange a reception. We were very happy to do this, because everyone was aware of Emma Bonino's interventions on the part of the Rwandan refugees. Even the old women knew that the "mother of the refugees" was going to come and were pleased to welcome her. We knew that she was one of the rare people who still considered us to be human. In spite of the misery in which we lived and the alarming news from the front at Losso, we did everything in our power to welcome Emma Bonino as a mother. We didn't hide the misery of the refugees from her. She saw children in such terrible condition that they looked like old people, and children hospitalized with advanced malnutrition, so wasted that they hardly looked human. She saw women with cholera or dysentery who had become haggard old grandmothers even though they were scarcely thirty years old, and nursing and pregnant mothers who waited for a cup of bouillie under the blazing sun. They had lost all of their female attributes. You knew they were women only because they were taking care of children.

Alongside this misery we also wanted her to see the sweet smile of children, the toothless one of old women. We wanted nursing mothers to introduce her to her "grandchildren" and orphans to greet her. Her visit and her tears were a balm to our wounds. Thanks to her we knew that there were still people in the world who were concerned about our fate. This helped us to bear the inhumanity of the lives that the world had condemned us to live.

About two weeks after the visit from Emma Bonino, it was Madame Sadako Ogata's, the UN High Commissioner for Refugees, turn. When my neighbor informed me that he had heard about her impending visit on the international radio, I replied jokingly that it was time for us to pack our bags, because her visit would be followed by Kabila and the rebels. For two years, the UNHCR had seemed unmoved by the plight of the Rwandan refugees, and in certain situations it had blatantly acted against them, although theoretically their duty was to defend them.

All the initiatives attempted by NGOs like the Collective or the Jesuit Fathers Service for Refugees to educate and organize the refugees had repeatedly been thwarted by the UNHCR. It was because of the UNHCR that Ndagijimana Cyprien, a member of the Collective, had been taken to Kinshasa and charged with being an intimidator for having given a workshop on Active Non-Violence to the refugees.

After the destruction of the camps in the eastern part of Zaire, the UNHCR had even thanked the Banyamulenge rebels for having repatriated hundreds of thousands of refugees! When one knows that this repatriation was not voluntary, that many thousands of people died following this operation and that hundreds of thousands of others disappeared—at that time they estimated that five hundred thousand refugees were missing[3]—there is reason to ask oneself about the will and the capacity of the UNHCR to understand the problems they were confronted with.

A few days before the high commissioner's visit, the camp at Amisi, located about sixty kilometers from Tingi-Tingi, was destroyed. Tens of thousands of refugees came to swell the already large population at Tingi-Tingi. The camp continued to grow with the arrival of refugees from the camps at Kindu. When the camps in the area of Uvira were destroyed, a large number of the refugees were sent toward the camps in the Walungu zone, the most important of which were Nyamirangwe and Cimanga. When the camp at Nyamirangwe was in turn destroyed, some refugees went to INERA and Kashusha while others went to Cimanga. When the last camp was destroyed, the refugees split into two groups. Some took the direction of Shabunda and continued via Kalima, where ten Rwandan priests were killed by the rebels, and arrived in Angola by crossing Kasaï. Another group tried to get back on the Bukavu-Kisangani Road. When they got to Itebero, they had to retrace their steps, because the area was already under rebel control. The village of Itebero was strewn with rotting bodies when they arrived. From Itebero, they went via Kindu and Punia and arrived at Lubutu where the Zairians helped them across the rivers in pirogues.

Among the first refugees to arrive in Punia was Gabriel's brother. In Rwanda, Gabriel was the coordinator of an NGO and was known in the Rwandan NGO movement as someone who was dedicated body and soul to the cause of the peasants. In Zaire he had continued to work with the peasants in the valley of the Ruzizi. When, because of lack of funds, the Collective had not yet begun with its activities, Gabriel had

3. Author's note: The UNHCR later made this calculation: between the number of refugees who were counted in the camps at Kivu in October 1996 and those recounted in February of 1997, there were 230,000 missing!

begun to organize the women of Luvungi camp on his own time so that they could grow vegetables to supplement their food aid. He paid for the seeds and the tools out of his own pocket. To free himself of any encumbrance, he had taken his family to the village of Kaziba and had himself stayed in the camps at Uvira. Sometimes he had to go two weeks without saying hello to his wife and children, particularly when he had weekend meetings with the peasants.

The evening before the Banyamulenge rebels took Bukavu, Gabriel came to see me and tell me that he had finally found his family. He had spent the preceding week at Bukavu and in the meantime the road to Kaziba, where his family lived, had been cut. Gabriel found his wife and children in the camp at Izirangabo, a few kilometers from the administrative center of Walungu zone. From there they went toward Shabunda. They stayed several days in Kingurube. According to Gabriel's brother, many thousands were camping there waiting for intervention from the international community. He himself had decided to take the road to Kisangani, passing through Itebero and Walikale. Gabriel wanted to stay a few days longer with his wife and children. According to a Shi friend who had hidden with a Zairian family in the area, many of the refugees were killed at Kingurube when the rebels got there, whereas others, among them Gabriel and his family, were repatriated to Rwanda. He is now in prison, accused of having appropriated property from the NGO where he worked for his private use. The accusation has no basis in fact. These goods were given to the Collective of Rwandan NGOs.

We walked about four hundred kilometers to get to Tingi-Tingi; those who went via Punia covered more than five hundred in extremely difficult conditions. The first group arrived at Tingi-Tingi toward the end of January, whereas the third group arrived three days before the destruction of the camp on February 28, 1997. A young woman who was part of this last group told me that in the forest rebels often attacked them. They were most exposed when they had to cross the rivers. As there were so many refugees and so few pirogues, it took several days for everyone to cross. When the rebels arrived, they had to return to the forest to look for another place to cross. Several times former members of FAR, led by an officer named Nyamuhimba, saved them.

Madame Sadako Ogata arrived at Tingi-Tingi on a Sunday. The camp was destroyed the following Wednesday. I was therefore not completely wrong when I said that Kabila's rebels would follow soon after her visit. Amisi camp had been destroyed the day before. Four Zairian army helicopters preceded her helicopter. We thought that they were part of her security measures, but the truth was that Tingi-Tingi was the closest landing strip to the front after Amisi fell. When Sadako Ogata visited the camp, we were all upset to see a convoy of well-armed Zairian soldiers who were deserting the front pass by. They were returning to Kisangani on foot. A few hours later the two old tanks followed. Between the rebels and us no one remained. They could fall upon us at any moment.

The women had been mobilized to greet the high commissioner. We were present when she arrived, but our hearts were not. First of all we felt that her organization had, from the beginning, betrayed the refugees and that we could expect nothing good to come of her visit. We were also frightened. Since the night before, refugees from Amisi had been coming, swelling the numbers at Tingi-Tingi. We knew that only a few days remained to us in the camp and that its destruction would bring numerous deaths in its wake. We watched Sadako Ogata and her retinue walking around the camp, and everyone of us was worried about what lay ahead once the camp was destroyed. In such a situation, no one wants to smile. During her entire visit, Sadako Ogata met only closed faces. The governor of Maniema, who two weeks earlier had been present for Emma Bonino's visit, was shocked. In his speech, he asked the high commissioner to do everything in her power so that during her next visit she would be greeted more warmly. There were no more visits, and the unfolding events proved the most pessimistic people right regarding the loyalty of UNHCR to our cause.

We lived through the days following Sadako Ogata's visit in a climate of all-pervading fear. Every day we expected to be attacked. Rumors circulated constantly to the effect that the camp had already been infiltrated. Some refugees who had gone to look for cassava in the Kumu villages had been killed. In fact, there was good reason for this fear: strangers to the camp were intercepted in the nutrition centers and even in the hospital tents and, after being interrogated, admitted to being rebels.

The panic reached its apogee when the "humanitarians" left Lubutu to go to Kisangani. I was in the offices of Caritas when someone rushed in looking for Father Carlos and the nun who took care of the nutrition center. All the whites had quickly gotten on a small plane sent from Kisangani to evacuate them. It took off immediately. Hundreds of people were gathered all around the runway to help the humanitarians leave, but no one spoke. The impressive silence was only broken by the sound of the propellers of the little plane that had come to take the whites, leaving us alone to the mercy of the approaching rebels. We knew that since there had been an emergency evacuation of the humanitarians, it was only a matter of days until Tingi-Tingi would be taken. That night, like many others in the camp, I didn't shut my eyes. Around ten in the morning, the little plane from the day before returned with Father Carlos and the sister on board. She told us that Kisangani was also living in fear. The rebels had taken Bafwasende and were only a few kilometers away. The humanitarians were packing their bags everywhere.

From this moment on, no humanitarian spent the night near Tingi-Tingi. During the following days, those who dared came around ten in the morning and left around three in the afternoon. Watching them leave, we did not know if we would see them again the next day, and they didn't know if they would find the camp still there. This situation lasted about a week. Toward the end of February, rumor, or "sidewalk radio," held that the rebels who had been intercepted in the camp had said that the camp would be destroyed at the end of the month. We awaited the last day of the month with trepidation.

Wednesday, February 28, 1997, the camp awoke as usual. The little plane brought the humanitarians from Kisangani. There were even airplanes that had been chartered by Rwandans living in Nairobi to evacuate their families who were living in the camp.

As I did every morning, I went to the offices of Caritas to see if I could help and also to ask Father Carlos if he had received a message for me. A German NGO had invited me to participate in a seminar in Abidjan for the month of April and I was waiting for the ticket. The NGO had also agreed to pay for tickets from Tingi-Tingi to Nairobi for the children. It was out of the question for me to go and leave them at Tingi-Tingi in this deteriorating situation, and I planned to take them to Nairobi myself before going to Abidjan. Later, I learned that this much awaited message arrived, but too late.

At Caritas they had asked me to fill out identity cards for the unaccompanied children, who numbered in the thousands. Around two o'clock, when I got back from my noonday break, everyone was sitting around one of the people in charge of Caritas, who was informing them of the situation. He had just learned from a member of the development committee for the camp that we had to leave immediately because the rebels were only a few kilometers away. The Zairian soldiers had fled. There was no longer any obstacle on the road to stop the rebel advance. Father Carlos and the other humanitarians had rushed off. I ran to warn my family. In a few minutes everyone knew about the situation. All the people who usually loitered along the road waiting for planes to land had left. Only a few dozen unfortunates who were trying to force their way into the plane for Nairobi remained. After it took off, the road was deserted. It was about three o'clock. Everyone ran to the sheetings to pack. There were traffic jams in the little alleyways that snaked between the shelters. On the way I met Goretti and her husband Furaha. He was gravely ill and could hardly walk. Goretti had gone with him to the dispensary, but since everyone was preparing to leave, she couldn't get care for him. I had a little flour and powdered milk given to me by Caritas, so I suggested that they come by my place to get some. She needed it desperately.

When I arrived home, I found Assumpta, who had just run back from the hospital. There, too, it was a madhouse. The doctors had asked the invalids to return to their blindés. Those who had families had been taken away by them, while the others, including those who were unconscious, were left there. The camp authorities had promised to look for a way to evacuate them to Kisangani. In fact, due to the small number of trucks, only a few were evacuated. We had begun to pack our bags in an unbelievable hurry: sheeting, pots and pans, blankets, my little mattress that I had brought with me since INERA and that I was very fond of, jerry cans for water, glasses, plates, and provisions. Each of us wanted to take as much as possible, even though we knew that at the first mortar round we would drop everything trying to save our lives. When the baggage was ready, we had to decide who was going to leave with whom. We had to do something, because the children were in danger of being lost in the crowd if no one was paying attention. Normally the children would not have worried me so much, because Bakunda, the youngest child in my little family, was already thirteen years old. However, I was going to take three younger children with me: Zuzu, a little eight-year-old girl, her ten-year-old brother, and a little seven-year-old boy.

The brother and sister had moved to our district in the camp some three weeks earlier along with their maternal aunt's husband. After INERA they had lost their parents, who had disappeared in the forest like so many thousands of other refugees. Before finding their uncle, a neighbor cared for them, and it was with her that they traveled the four hundred kilometers from the camp at Kashusha to Tingi-Tingi. When the two children and their little sister arrived at Tingi-Tingi, Zuzu was in an advanced state of malnutrition and had to go twice a day to the nutrition center to get her ration of biscuit and bouillie. The camp was destroyed before she had completely recovered. When the first planes chartered by the Rwandan refugees in Nairobi began to land at Tingi-Tingi, the uncle left with the youngest girl, promising to do everything he could to have the other two children join him with the least possible delay. When we had to evacuate the camp, Zuzu and her brother were still there, and there were no other adults in the family to take care of them. I therefore decided to take them with me, along with a little boy who came from the camp for unaccompanied children at Kashusha.

The camp development committee had decided that the departure would be at night. According to them the presence of a hundred thousand refugees on the road in broad daylight would present an easy target for the rebel mortar shells. The first to leave the camp went at about six o'clock. Most of them had arrived from Amisi a few days earlier. I left the camp at about eight o'clock in the evening, holding Zuzu's hand while her brother went with Bakunda, Gisimba, and Mukunzi. Assumpta was in charge of the other little boy. We thought we would be among the first to leave the camp, but when we got to the road it was already crowded. Everyone wanted to leave at once, which made for a tremendous traffic jam. You had to really use your elbows. No one moved forward. It took us several hours to go the four kilometers to the village where we spent the night. Two hours after leaving we had not even passed the boundaries of the camp. Usually ten minutes were enough to go that distance. When we finally got out of the camp, a vehicle that had just overturned blocked us. Some of the victims were stretched out on the road still moaning, but no one could help them. It was very dark and you couldn't even see where you were stepping. We continued to advance, glued together, walking over the bodies of the wounded, pushed on by the thousands of people behind us. It was impossible to stop and help them, and they kept on moaning.

We had just covered two kilometers when we heard shots from automatic weapons. We thought that the rebels were attacking us from the front. Some people rushed into the forest and others turned on their heels. Turning around wasn't easy, because those behind us who had not heard the shots continued to advance. Finally I was able to get out of the crowd with the girls. By a miracle we found a place to sit down in front of some abandoned huts. That was when we were separated from the four boys. We found each other again two weeks later at Ubundu, but Zuzu's brother was not with them. He had met a paternal aunt on the road, and she offered to take him with her.

For more than an hour we waited for the flood of refugees to lessen so we could continue. We had just left when we once again had to turn back, pushed along by people in disarray because something, they didn't know what, had frightened them. Some spoke of a vehicle coming from Lubutu with all its lights off, perhaps rebels who wanted to block our way. In fact it was the sound of thousands of feet hammering the pavement, which in the silence of the night, people mistook for the sound of a vehicle. At that point I told the girls to find a corner where we could spend the night. I had decided to continue the next morning. This night march had not been a very good decision.

Many others had made the same decision as I had, because every square inch at the side of the road was full. Nevertheless, in spite of people swearing at us, we walked on the heads and feet of those who were stretched out in the courtyards of houses and the neighboring fields and were able to find a place in a ruined shed. Unfortunately the first refugees who came through there had used it as a latrine. When we left a few hours later, our bags and pagnes smelled like the shit we had slept in. We carried this odor until we could shower and wash the pagnes. When we left the shed, we hoped to get to Lubutu, eight kilometers from Tingi-Tingi, before the night was over, but about three kilometers from the Lubutu Bridge, we had to stop again. The Zairian soldiers didn't want us to enter the town in the dark, because they thought that rebels could be hidden among us. I spent that first night seated on my bags like everyone else. There was not enough room to let everyone stretch out. Not knowing what was in store for us, I dreaded the morning.

We got on the road to Lubutu very early. After walking a kilometer, we were stopped again. There was a bottleneck at the Lubutu Bridge, and there was such a crowd on the road that it was impossible to go forward. We stood for several hours in the hot sun without being able to make one step, leaning on each other with our bundles on our heads. You couldn't sit or even put your baggage down because there wasn't room. Finally, some former members of FAR, seeing the risk that we ran of being trapped by the rebels, had people make lines and little groups of fifty to a hundred people, leaving a few meters between themselves. But the flow was so great that after a few moments they had to start the whole operation over.

Around one o'clock, I finally got to the bridge with my little family. For fear of the rebels, everyone wanted to cross at the same time. We already heard the sound of shells, and people said that the rebels were destroying what was left of Tingi-Tingi. The panic that reigned made the work of those maintaining order at the bridge difficult.

I have no idea how much time I spent trapped in the middle of the crowd. I am rather small, and I had to use my elbows to make a little breathing room, or I would have fainted. Just as a small group of us neared the bridge, we heard shots. At first I wasn't alarmed, because I thought that soldiers from FAZ were shooting in the air to frighten the refugees so they could rob them. Later, the shots, which in the beginning had been sporadic, came more often. People scattered in every direction, abandoning most of their meager provisions. In this terrified mass, those who fell were trampled. There was such a crush of people attempting to cross the bridge that many of them were shoved into the river. Thousands of others threw themselves into the water, trying to swim to the far bank. Where the river was deep, children, the old and the sick drowned.

When people began to run in all directions, sweeping before them everyone who was in the way, I tried to keep my balance and held tight to Zuzu's hand, which was covered with scabies. She in turn tugged at my hand saying: "Auntie, let's run fast. If we don't, they will kill us." We ran on, pushed from behind by those who followed, and hid in the closest huts, but there was so much shooting that these were not safe either. We entered the forest by the first path we found. After running for about a kilometer, those in front stopped abruptly, as if there were something that had frightened them, and suddenly turned on their heels. We abandoned the path and entered the depths of the forest. The branches struck our heads, and thorns and brambles scratched our arms and faces. Happily, the other girls had followed me on this mad dash. Under the dense cover of the forest we stopped to figure out what to do. We couldn't stay hidden for too long, since we needed to eat and drink. Furthermore, the place where we were wasn't far from the road, and the rebels would find us during the first clean-up operation. Nor was it wise to continue deeper into the forest, since we were unfamiliar with the area. I decided to retrace our steps and try to find a shallow spot along the river where we could wade across. The water came up to my chest. I feel dizzy when I walk in water, and Marcelline held my hand so that I would not fall and drown. A man who was with us offered to carry Zuzu to the other side, since she was in danger of being swept away by the current, which was quite strong there.

When we finally reached Lubutu, we realized that two children were missing, a boy who left Tingi-Tingi with us and a four-year-old girl I had picked up the night before who had been separated from her mother in the confusion. I had entrusted her to Virginie. When we were running through the forest she let go of Virginie's hand and was lost in the crowd. As for the boy, Assumpta was the person responsible for him. She had succeeded in keeping him with her since Tingi-Tingi, in spite of the commotion. However, when the shooting broke out, Assumpta and the boy both fell, knocked down and trampled by the fleeing mass of people. When Assumpta finally was able to get up, she tried to find the boy, but in vain. Later we continued, unsuccessfully, to search for these two children. In light of the vast numbers of people who perished at Lubutu Bridge, I don't have much hope that they survived.

During the shooting we abandoned a large part of what we had carried from Tingi-Tingi so that we could run faster. We weren't the only ones who had to abandon part of our provisions. Mountains of peas, corn, flour, buckets, and blankets carpeted the road.

I found Goretti again in Lubutu. She was with her two children and one of her brothers. Her husband had stayed on the other side of the river.

9

Hunger on the Road

AT LUBUTU we had no time to grieve for the children we had just lost. We had to keep on running. The rebels were less than ten kilometers away. After traveling about ten kilometers, we decided to stop and make some bouillie, since we hadn't eaten since the night before. Assumpta went to look for firewood, Virginie went for water, and I found stones for the fireplace. The bouillie was almost ready when another group of refugees arrived in the village. They had run until they were out of breath. There was no more thought of eating bouillie. We poured it out on the ground and Virginie put the pot, unwashed and still hot, into her bundle. We ran frantically. Our hunger had to wait until the next day. I held Zuzu's hand so that I wouldn't lose her. We walked through the entire moonless night without stopping to sleep, one behind the other, Indian file, holding hands. At regular intervals I called out the name of each girl so that I would know that they were still there. Only the next day around noon were we able to stop, exhausted. Little Zuzu was at the end of her strength. We rested a little and continued on.

This relentless forced march sapped our strength and our morale. Marcelline was the first to break. We had gone about fifty kilometers when she became sick. The night before we had walked until nine o'clock stopping only long enough to make some food and rest a little. We spread out our sheeting on the ground in the courtyard of a house in a deserted village, in the middle of hundreds of other refugees. At two we got up to continue walking. We had just done two or three kilometers when Marcelline refused to walk any more. She was burning up with fever and couldn't take one more step. We couldn't stay there until she recovered, because the rebels were continually gaining ground, but there was also no question of abandoning her on the road like some did when their family members were too sick to walk. I divided up her baggage between Assumpta, Virginie, and me, which gave all of us about five kilos more to carry. We carried it on our backs, like the Zairian women. With this extra load, we walked doubled up, our eyes fixed on the road. Despite the fact that we had relieved her of her load, Marcelline was still unable to walk alone. I took her by the hand and she let herself be dragged more than she walked. How did my forty kilos succeed in pulling Marcelline's sixty kilos along? In situations like that you often have strength and courage that you wouldn't dream of in normal times. She wanted to drink frequently, and we had to stop every time and ask for water from people passing by. One only saw their shadows, because it was still night. When they didn't have any water, we had to wake people who were sleeping. Since we were walking day and night, many people simply spread out their sheeting on the road, leaving only a narrow passage for those who were still walking. That day we had to stop earlier to let Marcelline rest. As soon as she was able to put one foot in front of the other, we gave her a walking stick and continued our flight into the unknown. After Marcelline, it was my turn. I started to feel a sharp pain in my right knee. For several weeks I had been limping. If someone passing by hadn't given me a bandage to wrap around my ailing knee, I do not know how I could have continued.

Very few of the sick who were able to get across the bridge survived the effort it took to put a few dozen kilometers between themselves and the rebels. The third day after leaving Tingi-Tingi we began to pass the bodies of the dead and dying. When someone was too sick to keep on walking, he sat down by the side of the road and waited for death. The first and the last time that I dared to look at one of these unfortunates, my eye fell on a teenager hardly sixteen years old. Like the others, she was lying at the side of the road, her large eyes open. She watched, without seeing them, her companions in misery who abandoned her without giving her any help and who didn't wait for her to die before giving her a coffin. Her clothes were wrapped modestly around her, but I couldn't help noticing that they were soiled with the excrement that she could no longer hold back. A cloud of flies swarmed around her. Ants and other forest insects crawled around her mouth, nose, eyes, and ears. They began to devour her before she had taken her last breath. The death rattle that from time to time escaped her lips showed that she was not yet dead. All who passed by glanced at her and then took up their conversation where they had left off.

I stood in a daze in front of this sixteen-year-old girl, lying in agony by the side of the road in the middle of the equatorial forest more than five hundred kilometers from home. As in 1993, when I heard about the extermination of my mother's family, as in 1994, when I saw the burned houses, the fear in the eyes of the fleeing Tutsi, and the arrogance and the hate in the faces of their executioners, as in 1995 when I saw pictures of women and children assassinated by the RPF in the camp at Birava, I was overcome by revulsion. What crime had all of these victims committed to deserve such a death? Where was the international community that talked about human rights but withdrew when they should have prevented the genocide of the Tutsi by the Hutu militias and when they should have condemned the massacres of the Hutu by the RPF? Where was this international community that had applauded the destruction of the camps in eastern Zaire, which abandoned us once again and let us wander in the forest like wild beasts and which allowed this young girl of sixteen to collapse on the road like a dog, food for the ants of the equatorial forest? Even now, more than a year later, the image of this young girl haunts me and with it the feelings of futility and revulsion that I felt every time that I found myself faced with the death that lurked all around me and against which I was utterly powerless.

During the moments that followed this macabre discovery, I let my tears flow unchecked. I needed this flood of tears to ease my bitterness so that I could accept the fact that I had no power over the events that had poured into my life since 1990. We had to try to survive at any price. To do that we had to walk until we were exhausted. If the time came for one of us, she would lie down at the side of the road and await her death. The others would continue to walk. I just hoped that one of us would survive and be able to tell our families what had happened. After that day I no longer dared to look at the dead and dying by the side of the road. If I noticed the smell of rotting flesh, I asked one of the girls which side of the road the body was on. Afterwards I held my nose and looked to the other side until we had passed by. But even if I had not seen the body, I could not help thinking about the man, woman, or child who had ended their life there, alone, without any member of their family there to close their eyes and hold their hand during the last hours, to calm and comfort them. And every time I felt frustration when faced with my inability to do anything. Later, the girls and I tried to help the sick who were still able to walk, but without medicine, means of transport, or food, our efforts were often useless.

The only thing that temporarily made me forget the dozens of dead and dying, the crying of tired children, their little feet swollen by continual pounding on the burning pavement, the women and children with feet wrapped in bandages that made them look like lepers, and the countless other signs of our misery, was the humanity that some refugees still showed to their fellow sufferers. I am thinking particularly about the young men who stayed behind to cut trees so that they would fall across the road, hopefully slowing the rebel advance because they would have to stop and clear the road. The rebels were no longer on foot, since the road between Kisangani and Walikale was drivable. Today I still do not understand why they risked their lives by staying behind the others to let the women, children, and the sick put a few more kilometers between themselves and death. I also remember those who helped people they didn't know to carry the sick and thus accepted losing valuable minutes, which could make the difference between life and death. What do you say about those who, when the road narrowed, helped keep things moving? They stayed back for several hours trying to regulate the human flux until the problem was solved, risking their lives every time for the others. Many came to my aid, like the young man who gave me a bandage to tie up my knee when I could no longer walk. A hundred kilometers from Kisangani, when we were going to take the turn-off to Ubundu, someone gave me one million new Zaires, which allowed me to buy food for my family.[1]

Little Zuzu had suffered from malnutrition since Tingi-Tingi. To keep her strength up she needed a balanced diet. It was difficult for her to eat cassava, because it was too dry and hard. Often I had to grind it for her and feed her with a small spoon, like a baby, so that she would swallow it. I always carried a small cup with me, and when we got close to someone who was making bouillie I would ask for some for Zuzu. Few

---

1. At that time 120,000 new Zaires were the equivalent of one American dollar.

people refused. The Rwandan employees of Caritas and UNICEF did their best to help the refugees. One hundred kilometers from Kisangani a health clinic had been set up by UNICEF to give urgent care to the sick. It was there that we were able to get medicine for Marcelline. It was also there that I learned that Caritas had received the money from the German NGO for which I was doing consulting. This sum was supposed to allow me to evacuate my family to Nairobi. The person who had been sent to inform me had returned to Kisangani the night before. It was thus that my last hope of escaping from this Hell was extinguished.

We had left Tingi-Tingi hoping to go to Kisangani and from there to the Central African Republic. When we were one hundred kilometers from the city, the Zairian soldiers detoured us toward Ubundu, a little town on the Lualaba River where a new camp was going to be set up. The chances of establishing a humanitarian zone were almost nonexistent, and the creation of a new camp appeared to us to be a maneuver on the part of the international community to deliver us up into the hands of Kabila's rebels or the RPF.

Many among us thought that the only way to save our skins was to get out of Zaire. The Central African Republic had become our ultimate safe haven. But, as they say, "Man proposes and the Lord disposes." Not being able to break through the roadblock set up by the Zairian soldiers on the road to Kisangani, we resigned ourselves to the idea of entering the forest again, hoping that we would come out of it alive. We were apprehensive about the moment that we would, once again, trust our safety to the forest. Everyone still remembered the interminable, slippery descents in the Kahuzi-Biega National Park, where old women and young children slid down on their bottoms, the endless climbs, the pools of mud, and the nearly invisible trails where, given the large numbers of people, one had to wait for hours to get on the path. Who could forget rivers so deep that we had to wade with water up to our chests or cross walking on a slippery tree trunk at the risk of falling into emptiness, breaking our necks, or drowning?

The Belgians had built the road to Ubundu during the colonial period, and from lack of maintenance it had reverted to its natural state, but it was better than we thought it would be. From time to time we found old kilometer markers half hidden in the forest. We covered the fifty kilometers between the Tingi-Tingi–Kisangani road and Ubundu in three days. On the way we met people who had been to the town and said that the banks of the river were crowded and that food was becoming scarce. Many were forced to retrace their steps to find food. We were stopped four kilometers from the town by a roadblock set up by Zairian soldiers who demanded five hundred American dollars to let the group pass. This explained the crowding. It was only when the money was collected that we were allowed to pass. The negotiations with the commander of the garrison and collecting the money took three days.

We spent a restless night near Ubundu sleeping, as usual, in the square of an abandoned village. Around one in the morning I was awakened by screams. At first I thought that the rebels were arriving. Fortunately, it was only ants that had encircled the square and had begun to attack the sleepers from all sides. When they were chased off on one side they came back and attacked from the other. You would have thought that these little beasts had learned their strategy in a military academy. If they had been as well armed as the rebels, none of us would have come out of this attack alive. We spent the rest of the night trying to keep them away with fire. I had thought that I would wait in this village for the beginning of the Lualaba River crossing, but this nocturnal battle with the ants dissuaded me, and we went to stay in a camp near the Ubundu airport. A plane, chartered by the Red Cross, landed there two or three times a day with biscuits for the refugees. The day after our arrival they distributed corn flour, but we were not able to get any because we had left very early in the morning to go to the edge of the river to wait for pirogues to take us across. The negotiations with the commanding officer of FAZ at Ubundu had ended the night before and the crossing was beginning that very day. In addition to my four girls, I was with a family from Byumba prefecture. The couple had been on the run since 1990, and their two children had been born in exile. The parents had no idea where their eldest, who was four, was. The younger one, who was two, was with them. He was a beautiful chubby-cheeked boy and the mother carried him on her back. She had trouble keeping up with the other refugees because he was so heavy.

We had left the camp very early, but it took us until nine o'clock to get to the edge of the river, which was already swarming with people. The ones in front were in the water up to their waists trying to get the first pirogues. We found room for ourselves about five hundred meters from the banks of the river and moved closer as those in front left. The fare for one person was 50,000 new Zaires. It would cost at least 300,000 new Zaires for my little family to cross over. Of the one million new Zaires that a friend had given me the previous week, only 100,000 were left. The family from Byumba gave me five dollars for the trip, but as the hours passed by, the cost of the trip rose, first to 100,000 new Zaires, then to 200,000, and toward evening to 500,000. The following morning only payment in dollars or in kind was accepted. Those who had jeans, radios, or pots and pans in good condition could get across, whereas the others were condemned to stay there, jammed together under the blinding sun, awaiting the uncertain arrival of the promised boat sent by the humanitarians. Knowing that the rebels were about fifty kilometers away didn't do much to calm people's spirits. Fear and anguish could be read on every face. Everyone was prepared to give everything he owned just to find himself on the other side of the river with the mass of water between himself and the rebels. Sick of waiting, some people made improvised boats from bamboo and sheetings. Fifty of these boats were built and entire families got on them. Few of these boats, which were difficult to steer, reached their destination. Some, driven by the violent wind that came up in the late afternoon, capsized and their passengers drowned. Around thirty people were lost in this tragedy. In Ubundu, two days later, I met a young man who had narrowly escaped drowning. His parents, brothers, and sisters, a total of nine people, had perished. Three others had had more luck and had been miraculously saved by a rock, which they clung to as their boat sank. They had been fished out, chilled to the bone, by Zairian fishermen the morning after their shipwreck.

I spent the first night on the riverbank with the children, hoping that luck would smile on us the following day. Unfortunately, even the exorbitant prices of the previous day were no longer accepted. I ran from one boat to another, but none of them would accept my five dollars to take my family across. Some people were prepared to pay more than ten dollars just for one person. In the middle of the afternoon I returned to the village to get the latest news about the rebel advance and the arrival of the boat that had been talked about since the night before, which we had not seen yet. In the village square a man was stretched out on the ground. He had soiled his clothes. No one was paying attention to him. Seeing him lying there unconscious, the memory of the young girl by the side of the road came back to me. I asked Marcelline to help me, and, half dragging him we were able to put him in the shade of a veranda. It began to rain. Exactly what sickness did he have? I did not know. But even if I had known I wouldn't have done anything other than what I did do, which was to go get some bouillie for him. Obviously, this man was dying of hunger. As soon as he had had the bouillie, he stood and walked without help. He left telling me that he was going to go find his family. Did he really have a family, or was he ashamed, seeing the state we had found him in? Death prowled all around us, taking advantage of our least weakness. The only chance that we had of defeating it, at least temporarily, was solidarity.

The three boys I had been separated from after Tingi-Tingi had rejoined us the night before our departure from Ubundu. We spent the night together in a house in a village. I had given up hope of crossing the river in a pirogue. Our poor belongings and five dollars were insignificant before the growing appetite of the boatmen of Ubundu. The only chance that remained for us was the long-promised Red Cross boat. We had to pray that it would arrive before the rebels caught us. The third day I arrived at the edge of the river at the same time as a delegate from the Red Cross. He had just announced the arrival of the boat for that very day sometime during the morning, and indeed it arrived at about eleven. Not all of the refugees knew about this. We got on board among the first seven hundred passengers by elbowing our way through. I gave the five dollars to a Zairian soldier who helped get us aboard. There was no gangway. Those who fell were trampled. At least forty people drowned or were trampled to death that day.

Although we expected to get substantial help on the other side of the Lualaba River, the delegate from the Red Cross told us that food aid would be given to us at Obilo, about forty-eight kilometers from Ubundu, where the new camp would be built. We had to hold on. It took us two days to reach our destination. It rained heavily and the roads were slippery. We got to Obilo on a Sunday afternoon. Tens of thousands of refugees had preceded us. The camp was in the process of being set up and a clinic built by the Red Cross was already operating. Rumors that Kisangani had fallen to the rebels the night before were circulating. The promised aid had not yet arrived. The general climate was one of discouragement. I found Frieda and her family, Immaculée and her children, Damien and his little girl, and others I had not seen since Tingi-Tingi. Immaculée was horribly upset, because she had lost track of her eldest daughter.

This group, like all the other refugees at Obilo, was in a state of uncertainty. They did not know if they should continue on toward Mbandaka in Equateur Province, as some suggested, or if they should wait for the promised humanitarian intervention. Discussions were everywhere. Little groups formed around people who had hand drawn maps of Zaire. If Kisangani were really in rebel hands, the arrival of humanitarian aid was unlikely and the rebels could fall on us at any time. Going via Kisangani to the Central African Republic, about eight hundred kilometers to the north, was no longer possible. The only remaining way out was through Mbandaka, located more than fifteen hundred kilometers to the west on the border of Congo Brazzaville, and to get there you had to get through one hundred kilometers of trackless forest. The locals we consulted about this adventure tried to dissuade us. For them, going into this forest where there were no roads and no water was suicide.

When I went to bed, the discussions were still going on. Many were still undecided. Was it necessary to go as far as Mbandaka, risking everything crossing the equatorial forest? Many had already died of exhaustion and hunger between Bukavu and Tingi-Tingi after having gone only four hundred kilometers. Others had not been able to make the two hundred kilometers from Tingi-Tingi to Obilo. Could one hope to arrive alive at Congo Brazzaville after traveling fifteen hundred kilometers on foot? Where would we find the money to pay every time we had to cross one of the many rivers? How many days could we expect to survive in a forest that was said to be without water or food? These were the questions that every refugee asked himself and for which we had no answers. Most of us stayed there, our ears glued to some radio that still worked and that hadn't been bartered to get across the Lualaba River. Some still hoped for a military presence so that the humanitarians would be able to begin to help again. Others, tired out from walking since Bukavu, discouraged and not seeing any clear future, talked about waiting for the rebels, forgetting that ever since Bukavu the rebels had killed large numbers of refugees every time they caught up with us. Only a few of the bravest, mostly men, left that day.

When the fall of Kisangani had been confirmed, I decided to continue to flee, and God willing, I hoped to get out of Zaire, no matter how long it took. I was not resigned to waiting for the rebels to track me down in Obilo. Since 1993, I had been running away from the RPF and I knew that I could expect no clemency from Kabila's rebels, who were mainly made up of elements from the RPF. Since Byumba, I had heard the whistle of bullets around my ears, shells falling a few meters away, the sound of heavy artillery, and I had prayed to the good Lord to spare me this kind of music again. I didn't want to be afraid of getting a bullet in my head while I was running for the trees any more. I therefore decided to reenter the forest. If, as a result, I got to the point where I couldn't walk any more, I would lie down by the side of the road and await my death, as so many others had done before me and so many others would after me. Another reason that pushed me to leave Obilo as quickly as possible was the lack of food. In the absence of humanitarian assistance, the few provisions that we had brought from Tingi-Tingi were practically exhausted. For the last few days we had eaten cassava stolen from the fields of the locals. Even if the rebels decided to leave us in peace in Obilo, without humanitarian assistance we were condemned to die of hunger in the near future. Tension with the local population continued to grow. They feared that this mass of refugees that had descended on them would use up the reserves of cassava for the entire area.

To stay or to leave was a serious decision that everyone had to make for himself. A man could decide to leave, while his wife and children would decide to stay. Families were split apart. I wanted all of my children to know what was waiting for them in the forest so that they could make an informed decision. It was really a choice of two ways to die, rather than a choice between life and death. It appeared that, in a general sort of way, death was at the end of the road no matter which way one decided. No one was certain of living if they stayed or if they went. It was a question of probability. When a choice is so difficult, many prefer to leave it up to the will of the Lord. That is what happened at Obilo. At that time, not very many of us decided to go to Mbandaka.

I left Obilo on Monday, very early in the morning, with my whole family. Before I went, I sent one of the girls to tell Frieda and Immaculée that I was going. I wanted to know if I should wait so that we could travel together. Both told me that they would wait until the next day to see how the situation was developing. Frieda and her family joined me three weeks later. As for Immaculée and her children, I never saw them again. When I left the house I came across Damien. He was not yet reconciled to Jeanne's death, and was still very weak and walked with a cane. He asked me, smiling as usual, what decision to make in such a situation. I told him that I was leaving but that Frieda preferred to wait. I had always tried to boost the morale of my colleagues at the Collective when we encountered difficulties, but the situation at Obilo was so dreadful that I was incapable of saying more to Damien. I preferred to take my leave from him quickly, hoping from the bottom of my heart that he would take the road to Mbandaka and would one day join us. Since then I have had no news of him or of his little girl.

When I was leaving Obilo, I met Thérèse. I had known her when she was president of the women's organization at Tingi-Tingi. During the short time I knew her I admired her energy and her sensitivity to the poverty and misery in which the women of the camp lived. Since our departure from Tingi-Tingi her husband had suffered from gout and slowed them down a lot. In addition to her sick husband, Thérèse had a four-year-old daughter whom she had to carry since she couldn't walk very fast. For her and her family the trip from Tingi-Tingi to Obilo had been an ordeal. After crossing the Lualaba River, her husband was unable to walk any more. Thanks to help from friends, she was able to have him carried to Obilo. The fall of Kisangani had shaken her. Resting and taking care of her husband as she had hoped to do was no longer possible. She was there, seated by the side of the road, her husband lying in the grass by her side, protected from the sun by a sheeting stretched over four sticks. She watched the others go without knowing what to do. Had she and her family managed to escape the Hell of Goma only to die six hundred kilometers farther along the road? Why had they even tried? Why six hundred kilometers more? Why had they run so many risks? Why didn't they just die at Goma? It was all over! These were the words she used in response to my greeting. Like Thérèse, I was convinced that we had to leave Obilo as soon as possible, but what was she going to do with her sick husband? If she had been a man, such a crisis of conscience might not have occurred. She would have gone, abandoning wife and children, while trying to justify this action by the fact that men risked more than women if they were ever caught by the rebels, forgetting that when the camps were destroyed, the mortars and machine guns didn't distinguish between the age and sex of their victims. Thérèse was a woman, and it was unthinkable for her to abandon her sick husband.

All along the long six hundred kilometers from Bukavu to Obilo I observed the behavior of countless couples. To the same extent that the women were attached to their husbands, the husbands were irritated by the presence of the wives and children at their sides. When the situation deteriorated, many men went on alone rather than encumbering themselves with their families. They left the women to take care of themselves and their progeny. Examples of men who abandoned their wives on the other side of the Lualaba River are legion. On the other hand, Thérèse was not the only woman who chose to stay with her sick husband. At Irangi, Egide's mother stayed alone with her husband when all the refugees departed from the camp under the protection of former elements of FAR. Not having found any way to transport him, she chose to stay with him, even though she ran the risk of being treated badly by the Tiri when she was there alone before her son arrived and paid to have his father transported more than a hundred kilometers. The attitude of this old woman never ceased to amaze me during my two weeks at Irangi. He was a difficult patient. He only ate things that were hard to find in the forest and would only drink banana juice. Egide's mother needed a lot of ingenuity to satisfy this demanding man. She combed the entire area, indifferent to the danger posed by the Tiri, looking for bananas, which she later ripened under her clothes. At Walikale, rebels attacked Egide's parents. The mother, who had heart problems, fainted on the road trying to run away. When she woke up she was surrounded by locals and rebels who, luckily, let her leave. She rejoined her husband at Amisi, where he had gone.

When I left Obilo, Assumpta, Marcelline, Zuzu, Virginie, Bakundakize, Gisimba, and Mukunzi were with me. It was a large family that had to be fed and for whom passage across the numerous rivers of the area had to be paid. Even though I had decided to leave, I didn't feel very motivated because I was surrounded by discouragement at Obilo. Our first stop of the day was at a little village about five kilometers from the camp. I did not want to enter this inhospitable forest without provisions. I traded some plates and a pot for two bunches of bananas. Ten kilometers farther along we stopped to prepare the only meal of the day. The menu consisted of corn kernels. Because I didn't feel too well, one of the girls spread the sheeting on the veranda behind a house, so that I could lie down while the others prepared the meal. I had just dropped off when I heard shouts. The refugees who, like us, had taken their midday break in the village were packing their bags and leaving. The villagers yelled at us to leave. I didn't understand what was happening. These same villagers who were shouting at us and waving machetes were the ones who had welcomed us an hour earlier and let us use their courtyards and the verandas of their houses. It was only back on the road that I understood this change of heart. A dozen Zairian soldiers had arrived from Ubundu on their way to Kisangani. In all the villages they passed through, they put pressure on the refugees to make them return to Obilo. That was why they turned the villagers against us. They said they wanted us to return to Obilo to wait for humanitarian aid, but the reality was that the refugees were a kind of buffer between them and the rebels.

Since the threats of the villagers were serious, we left at a run. A few meters farther along we met a group of refugees coming from Obilo. They seemed determined to pass despite the threats of the locals and the soldiers. We turned around and mixed in with them. When we arrived at the village we had just left, the soldiers again made us go back. They shot in the air to frighten us, and again we ran toward Obilo. After about five hundred meters, we encountered another group of refugees. We turned around again, hoping that this time the soldiers would let us pass. But when they saw us in the distance, they began to shoot again. Once again we had to turn back. After the fourth time the boys lost hope and decided to return to Obilo. To them, a trip that had begun so badly could only lead to certain death.

I was close to sharing their point of view. All of these aborted attempts had tested my nerves. I decided to go back to the first village, where we had rested in the morning, to see how the situation evolved. After we had gone about a kilometer, we met friends who were resting and waiting for the road to open. They thought that the soldiers would leave after obtaining provisions for themselves at the expense of the villagers, and that then it would be possible for us to get safely back on the road. I decided to wait with my friends and go with them once the road was open. The boys were not convinced and wanted to return to Obilo. The three girls and Zuzu decided to stay with me. Since my family was splitting in two, it was also necessary to split the belongings and provisions that we still had with us: the sheetings, plates, pots, cups, and the two bunches of bananas we had bought that morning. It was particularly difficult for me to leave Bakundakize, but I couldn't force him to follow me. In the face of the uncertainty that lay ahead of us, he had the right to decide about his own life. After sad farewells, the boys left for Obilo. We waited almost an hour for the soldiers to take down the barrier. This first day we could only cover about twenty kilometers. We spent the night twelve kilometers from the place where we would enter the forest. I slept very little. The next day would be the moment of truth when I would see if I had been right in attempting this folly. Mosquitoes and other insects swarmed in the grass where we had spread our sheeting and the Zairian soldiers staying in the village were shooting in the air to frighten the villagers and make them give them more money, livestock, and porters. They even forced a young woman from the village to follow them. The villagers said they were going to rape her.

The next day our first break was in a village on the edge of the forest, fifty-two kilometers from Kisangani. All the villagers wore white headbands in their hair, a sign that they supported Kabila. They didn't look kindly on the refugees, who were supposedly enemies of their leader. Nevertheless, some among them sympathized with our plight and proposed that we stay there in their village rather than going into the forest, where we had little chance of getting out alive. Some Red Cross employees, who also wore white headbands, as well as some Zairian soldiers who wore Kabila's colors, discouraged us from going into the forest. They themselves were going to Kisangani, they said, to tell their superiors about the situation so that they could find a quick solution. The village was the last place where we could buy provisions before entering the forest. I bartered a blanket for two kilos of sweet potatoes. With the bananas bought the day before and two kilos of corn brought from Tingi-Tingi that we had kept for hard times, I hoped to sustain my family for a week and a half, if we ate sparingly and the Lord provided for the rest. With this food, a sheeting, two blankets, four plastic plates, four tin cups, a spoon, a fifteen-liter water bottle, and a few pitiful clothes I entered the forest with my "daughters," Assumpta, Virginie, Marcelline, and little Zuzu. I was the only one who had shoes. The others walked barefoot.

We went the first few kilometers without much trouble. The path was visible. The refugees who had left Obilo late Sunday afternoon had worn it down for us. When they had come to a crossroads, they had blocked the paths we shouldn't take with branches. To find their way on the little paths of the forest, the first group had hired a guide from the area. The paths, which according to the locals were used only by hunters, wound around and made detours depending on the presence or absence of game. We had gone about three kilometers when we met the first refugees to retrace their steps and return to Obilo. The forest was so dense and the roots from the trees and the fallen trunks made walking so difficult, that they had decided they would rather be shot than commit themselves to such a Hell. Actually, the walk was not as difficult as in Kahuzi-Biega National Park because it wasn't raining yet and the terrain was less rough. But many were already so discouraged when they went into the forest that the first obstacle broke the little spirit they still had.

We were in the forest for fourteen days. There really wasn't any food, but there was abundant water. In the forest the day begins late and night falls early. We started walking at six-thirty in the morning and stopped at around five-thirty in the afternoon. The rays of the sun never fell on us. To sleep we first had to pull up the biggest bushes and then we put our sheeting on the grass of the forest floor, but not too far from the path. One part of the sheeting was our mattress and the other our cover. Around noon we would stop and prepare the daily meal somewhere close to a stream. Our provisions were very limited and we sometimes had to content ourselves with a piece of banana or sweet potato or a few grains of corn that we chewed while we walked. One day we found ourselves about ten kilometers from Kisangani. Here the first group had left a message for the other refugees on a piece of paper stuck to a tree on the side of the path. They said to advance making no noise and to hide the sheetings. After another kilometer there were a lot of papers littering the ground, bits and pieces of diplomas, scholarly journals, passports, identity cards, and other documents that could compromise the owner. Since the message left by the first group had not mentioned ripping up our documents, we concluded that only those who wanted to had gotten rid of theirs.

The way through the forest was difficult, and we didn't go very fast. The young children, like Zuzu, slowed us down even more. Some people who had been undecided when we left Obilo, joined us later in the forest. They had been forced to flee again when the camp was attacked with mortars and machine guns, as the camps at Kivu had been. According to witnesses, the attack had begun the Wednesday that we left. That day tension with the locals had peaked. The villagers beat their drums the whole day and part of the night, and the refugees thought that they were calling for reinforcements from other villages so they could attack the camp. That night everyone lay awake. In addition to pressure exerted by the local population, hunger and exhaustion had begun to claim their victims, particularly among the children, women, and old people. Thursday morning a large number of refugees decided to leave the camp for Kisangani to turn themselves over to the rebels. Among them were many women and children. Most of the men had already left for Congo Brazzaville. Fifty-two kilometers from Kisangani the rebels stopped them. Saturday morning their camp was destroyed. Many were killed and others went into the forest. Some of them were able to find the road we had taken and joined us several days later, but the great majority stayed and hid themselves until the arrival of the humanitarian NGOs. The survivors I have been able to talk to estimate that several thousand people died at kilometer fifty-two and the neighboring forests. My friend Immaculée and her children were in the camp when it was destroyed and to this day I have not had news of them. I continue to hope that neither she nor her children were among the thousands of victims at Obilo.

We left the forest fifty kilometers to the west of Kisangani on the road to Opala. Most of those who did not have sufficient provisions and those who were sick or exhausted stayed there. The region of Opala produced a lot of rice, and there were stocks of newly harvested unhulled rice in the abandoned houses. It was a windfall after these days of fasting, but it would take a whole day or maybe even two to grind enough rice to feed oneself for a week. People who didn't want to lose so much time took the rice and mortars with them. They preferred carrying ten extra kilos to risking being attacked by rebels. With my daughters, I spent an entire day in a village grinding rice. Formerly, when I watched women working, I thought that it would be easy to grind ten kilos in a day. In fact, the work was not as easy as I had thought. At the end of the day we had only ground two kilos. At this rate we would have needed a whole week to grind enough rice.

Kisangani and the rebels were only a few days march away and those who had maps mentioned a road from Kisangani that the rebels could take to block our passage to Mbandaka. We had to hurry. We exchanged one of the cups we had left for a kilo of rice and we left.

When we were a few kilometers from the junction of our road and the road to Kisangani, we met many refugees who were coming back at a run. They were so frightened that they hardly answered our questions. From their hurried replies we found out that there was a rebel roadblock on the road coming from Kisangani. It seems that they were attacking the refugees and had already killed many of them. On hearing this news, we turned around and went back a few kilometers to wait and see what would happen. If the news were confirmed, we would have to find another way through the forest. We were only able to get back on the road at about four o'clock in the afternoon. The soldiers attacking the refugees were not rebels but members of FAZ. They had indeed killed two refugees, and they had taken clothes, buckets, pots and pans, and sheetings from the others. During their flight, many refugees had abandoned their stores of rice. We could hear shots. We ran through the village and then walked almost the entire night. We were in the habit of stopping wherever possible in villages so that we could find water. We got to the first village at about seven in the evening. Oddly, there was no fresh water. Those who got there before us and who were too tired to go on were using greenish stagnant water from holes on the side of the road to cook their food. We got to the second village after walking three hours along a dark road filled with tree roots and potholes and spent the night.

Before arriving in the area of Opala, the last large town in the province of Haut Zaire that lay on our route, we crossed another tributary of the Congo River, the Lomami, as well as a smaller river whose name I never knew. All I remember is the size of the pirogues that took us across. They were very long, deep, and wide and could hold twenty people without being overloaded. It was the only time I felt safe in a pirogue. The night before we arrived at the smaller river, we stayed with a young couple from the camps at Goma. The woman, who couldn't have been more than twenty, was pregnant and due to give birth any day. Her husband was very worried, because a year earlier she had almost died giving birth to stillborn twins and had survived only thanks to the doctors. However, in the forest there were no doctors or nurses or midwives or antibiotics and nothing to stop a possible hemorrhage. Once born, they had nothing with which to cover the baby during the cold nights. The husband had kept some corn flour aside so that the young mother could eat bouillie instead of the cassava tubers that were our only food. We met them again a few kilometers farther along. The woman had given birth to a little boy, and although she had some difficulty walking, she and her baby were doing relatively well. She carried him on her chest, wrapped in a pagne.

The day after we met the young couple we got up very early to try to be among the first across. The smartest ones had spent the night at the edge of the river. Thousands of people were jammed together over a distance of three or four kilometers. We made very slow progress because it was so crowded. The last to come refused to stand in line and went around the sides trying to join the line farther up. This created a complete bottleneck. Late in the morning former members of FAR who were fleeing Kisangani with FAZ once again intervened and brought some order to the situation and we advanced more quickly. The crossing cost 50,000 new Zaires each. I only had 100,000. Friends of Marcelline and Assumpta came to my rescue and paid their passage. After Tingi-Tingi, Zuzu had had infected sores all over her body. She couldn't bend her fingers or let her arms hang next to her body. While we were waiting to cross, a young woman who was watching her scratch suggested that I rub her body with boiled papaya leaves. She assured me that they worked better than antibiotics. I said I would try it that evening, but I didn't have much faith in it. The first few days of the treatment Zuzu cried so loudly that the other refugees thought we were mistreating her, but after several weeks the sores had completely disappeared and all that remained were the scars, black spots on her body.

After the nameless little river we crossed the Lomami, one of the principal tributaries of the Congo River. It wasn't as wide as the Lualaba. Thousands of refugees had gotten to the village of Yate, built on the banks of the Lomami, before us, and some had already waited there for

several days for the Zairian soldiers to give the green light. Since the
ferry that usually was the liaison between the two shores had been out
of commission for several months, we had to take pirogues. We stayed
in the village for two days with a Zairian family. Our host must have
been about sixty and was the only one in the family who could speak
French and Swahili. I would have liked to talk to his two wives, but they
only spoke Lingala, a language that we did not yet understand. All
through the day and most of the night the drums did not stop beating.
Since I was worried, our host explained that the villagers were calling
boatmen from the other villages to come urgently to Yate because there
was lots of work. The drums, used as a means of communication among
the forest people, were unknown in Rwanda and Kivu.

It was in Yate that I began to introduce myself as the mother of the
girls, so that I would be more respected. The day after our arrival in
Yate, Marcelline had a new attack of malaria. Her fever was up to 104
degrees. Since we didn't have enough money to have her treated, Virginie got the money from a friend. Fortunately there was a Zairian
nurse who agreed to treat her for the modest sum of 150,000 new Zaires.
By the end of the day her fever had dropped and we were able to take
our turn crossing the river. For five of us, we would have to pay 750,000
new Zaires. We didn't have a single penny left. The little that we had we
used up treating Marcelline. Luckily, in Zuzu's baggage there was one
of her father's suits. We sold it for 600,000 new Zaires. A boatman
agreed to take us for that price.

We weren't the only ones who had trouble paying to cross the rivers.
Many refugees were in the same fix we were. They had nothing left to
sell, not even their sheetings, and they had no friends to come to their
rescue, as we had. The only choice was to wait patiently until those who
could pay had crossed. Sometimes the boatmen took pity on them and
carried them for free. Sometimes they were caught by the rebels and
slaughtered on the riverbank.

Yate was the last town we went through in Haut Zaire before we got
to the province of Equateur, the birthplace of President Mobutu. We
hoped for a warmer welcome in this province, since it had not yet been
touched by the rebellion. In Haut Zaire the refugees had not been welcome. The population accused us of being Mobutu sympathizers and
they let us feel it. Ikela was the first town we came to in Equateur. Like

many other towns in the area, it is built on the banks of a tributary of the Congo River. We came across the first roadblocks set up by FAZ a dozen kilometers from the town. At each roadblock we were searched systematically right down to our underwear. While the men were searched at the roadblock, we were taken, along with the other women, into little huts at the side of the road. When we finally arrived at Ikela, our baggage was very light. The soldiers had taken our stores of rice and cassava, a piece of a mirror, the girls' sanitary napkins, Virginie's pants that were still wearable, my wallet, and the 150,000 new Zaires that friends had given us.

Ikela was reminiscent of Bukavu on the eve of the Banyamulenge attack. The soldiers who were running away from the war conducted a reign of terror. A large part of the population had deserted the place and were hiding in the villages in the forest. On entering the town we encountered former members of FAR who had fled Kisangani with their colleagues in FAZ. They helped us cross the town to the little square where we spent the night. Several hundred other people were there too. I didn't sleep a wink the entire night. The Zairian soldiers were shooting on all sides until morning. Luckily they were mostly shooting into the air or the town would have been in ruins by the time they left. We got on the road very early the next morning, still escorted by the former soldiers. The risk of being attacked by Zairian soldiers was too great. Those who went through the town a few days later, after the Rwandan soldiers had left, had horrible experiences. Many were robbed of everything they had. Women were raped. Others were cut down trying to run away.

From Tingi-Tingi to Ikela we had already traveled more than seven hundred kilometers in addition to the four hundred that we had walked from Bukavu to Tingi-Tingi. Signs of exhaustion were visible on our faces. Many fell by the side of the road and didn't get up again. Every time I passed by a man or a woman lying by the side of the road and did nothing I felt guilty for the rest of the day. In my heart I always told myself I could have done something and might have saved them. In order not have any more regrets, I promised myself that I would never pass someone on the road without at least trying to help.

The first person we tried to help was a man named Parti. We came upon him by chance while we were looking for a place to go to the bathroom. He was lying in a little hut in the forest. The closest village was more than ten kilometers away. He was shaking from fever and couldn't walk. Since we didn't have any medicine to give him, the best we could do was to carry his things and help him to walk at least to the next village where we hoped to find someone there who could give him a couple of aspirin. When we arrived at a place where some refugees were cooking, we stopped to make him some bouillie. There was still a little corn flour in his baggage. At the end of the day he felt well enough to continue on alone. We heard later from other refugees that Parti was a criminal, well known in the camp at Kashusha for having killed and robbed a priest there. I still didn't regret having helped him, because I remain convinced that every human being in need has the right to be helped.

After Parti there were two other young men. The first was lying beside the road and the second in the square in a village. Neither one had swallowed anything in several days. In their condition they couldn't go into the fields to find cassava and prepare it. Their companions had abandoned them when they hadn't been able to keep up. We stayed with them for several days. During the day the other refugees gave us a little food for them, and at night we shared our meal. When they were well enough to carry their things and go on alone, they left.

Later, we found a mother and her baby. She was lying on the ground at the side of the road, her baby still on her back and her bundle beside her. When I asked her what had happened, she told me that she had felt faint and had fallen. I was alone with Zuzu. The girls had stayed behind with the two other sick ones. First I helped her get up. Since she could no longer walk carrying her infant on her back and her small bundle on her head, I took the baby on my back and put my own bundle, which I usually carried on my back, on my head. The baby didn't like being separated from his mother, and he didn't stop crying the whole time I carried him. Happily, we found her husband a few kilometers down the road. He was waiting for his wife, not knowing what had happened to her. The next morning she felt better.

We were not always lucky enough to get there in time to save people. One day when, for the umpteenth time, we took a path through the forest to avoid crossing one of the many tributaries of the Congo, I heard a death rattle coming from a thicket about fifteen meters from the road.

At first I thought it was an animal. When we got closer I realized that it was a dying person, a girl of about eighteen, and she was unconscious. All our efforts to wake her were in vain. We had no way of carrying her to the next village. We couldn't even lift her off the ground. Accepting that we had to leave her there, prey to the ants and other insects that had begun to invade her, was difficult, but we had to face reality. We weren't equipped to help people who were already unconscious. With bitterness in our heart and tears in our eyes, we abandoned the young woman to her fate.

Another day it was a man, still young, dying by the side of the road a few kilometers from one of the many villages deserted by its inhabitants at the first sight of a group of refugees. He was lying on his side using his bundle as a pillow. He seemed to be asleep. Every time we tried to help him up, he was too weak and fell back down. Some young men who came by helped us and gave us some aspirin to bring the fever down. Even working together we could not pry his mouth open. After several tries I managed to slide two tablets into his mouth. He used his last bit of strength to spit them into my face. For him, death was probably welcome. At least he was going to rest, and forget the Hell he had been living in every day. I had to accept leaving him to die on the road. Every time I found myself unable to help, I was disgusted. How could the world accept that people were dying on the road, abandoned by everyone?

The third time it was a very young girl. She couldn't have been more than fifteen. She was all alone on the road in a forest with no villages for at least ten kilometers in any direction. She staggered along as if she were drunk. When I got close to her I could see that she was burning up with fever. It had to be above 104 degrees, and she was beginning to hallucinate. I took her by the arm to help her walk and keep her from falling. She couldn't tell me who she was or where her parents were. After two to three kilometers, refugees who passed us told me that I risked killing her by making her walk. I learned that her parents were behind us on the road and decided to leave her propped up under a tree. I couldn't stay long because the girls were waiting for me in the next village.

Before arriving in Boende we had to cross yet another of the many rivers that run through the area of Equateur. The crossing was assured by a few Zairians who were helped by refugees who came from Kibuye and Cyangugu near Lake Kivu and who were used to this kind of trans-portation. As usual we didn't have any money and we were counting on divine mercy to be able to pay the 250,000 new Zaires that they were asking to take all five of us across. Again there was a monstrous bottle-neck at the river, and again the presence of former members of FAR guaranteed order and prevented everyone from jumping on the few available pirogues at the same time. Once again luck was on our side and a friend of Virginie's paid our passage. Virginie and Assumpta were the first across. It was almost impossible to find five seats in the same pirogue. When it was our turn, the boat was so full that it almost cap-sized before leaving the shore. I had to get off with several other people, but Marcelline and Zuzu stayed on board. A few meters from the other side it capsized. Luckily the river wasn't deep there and everyone got out safe and sound. A few minutes later another boat sank and several people drowned. I was so frightened that I didn't dare get back into a boat. Virginie's friend found a little pirogue for me with just one seat. I decided to get in after the boatman, a young man from Cyangugu, assured me that he was an excellent swimmer and that he could save me if the pirogue tipped over.

We stopped to dry our clothes in a hut. A family with three men and a young boy of about twelve had gotten there first and were seated around a fire eating a blackened cassava pastry and some cassava leaves that they had boiled without first grinding them. It had been weeks since I had eaten any vegetables and I was dying to ask them for some. The young boy didn't seem to like them much, and when he saw that we coveted them, he offered to share. The three men didn't approve, but we threw ourselves on the food. The vegetables didn't have much taste and the pastry didn't look very appetizing, but it is true that when you are hungry you don't worry about how food looks. I was astonished that a cassava pastry could be so black when cassava is usually white. They told me afterwards that the pastry that I had just eaten was made from scraps of cassava that the Zairian women dry in a ball over the fire. They use these scraps to make a distilled alcohol all over East Africa. In Uganda they call it *waragi,* in Rwanda, Burundi, and at Kivu it is known as *kan-yanga,* and in Equateur it is called *lotoko.* That same evening I decided to prepare cassava leaves, now that I knew that you could eat them without grinding them or adding oil and salt. We ate them with bitter cassava. The next morning Virginie and Assumpta vomited and had diarrhea. We had to stop after walking for two or three kilometers and let them rest and couldn't get back on the road until late in the afternoon. It was the bitter cassava that made Virginie and Assumpta sick, and after that day we didn't dare to eat cassava leaves either. Later Frieda showed me how to use the juice from palm nuts instead of oil and we began to eat cassava leaves again. In the meantime some refugees came across some salt in an abandoned house. By begging from them, from time to time we were able to put salt on our food. This quest for salt had produced several victims among the refugees. One day some of them ate chemical fertilizer thinking it was salt. A few of them died but others lived after they were able to buy palm oil as an antidote.

Equateur abounds in fruits of all kinds. Some, like pineapple, oranges, lemons, and mangos were known to us. Many others, such as coconuts, safous, and flamboyants, would have helped us survive if we had been familiar with them.[2] Virginie always had her pockets full of mangos and lemons. Every time we were hungry or thirsty we could have some. She was the "boy" of the group and climbed the trees to get the best fruit. She and Assumpta were also in charge of getting cassava for the family. I helped them carry it because we had to take provisions for several days to avoid long stops every day and in case we crossed through an area where there was no food. Zuzu was too young to help, and Marcelline's illness kept her from carrying heavy loads. Our daily meal consisted of cooked sweet cassava and water. As for me, I ate a piece of grilled cassava washed down with hot water and peppers. When, from time to time, we found fresh corn, dried cassava for making flour, or fermented cassava for making *chikwanga*, it was a time to

---

2. The safou, *Dacryodes Eduliis,* is a tropical fruit-bearing tree that belongs to the Burseraceae family. The fruit has an oblong cylindrical shape and a bluish-black color. It is filled with a rich, oily pulp containing one large seed and is rich in protein, fat, fiber, minerals, and essential amino acids. In some places it provides a staple food for three or four months when other foods are out of season. Flamboyant, *Delonix Regia,* belongs to the Leguminosae family. Grown widely as an ornamental tree, it produces numerous long pods that are twenty-five to forty centimeters long. These pods contain large numbers of seeds of moderately high nutritional content. Although these seeds are widely available, they are not widely utilized as food at the present. Nutritional studies suggest that these could be put to far greater use.

celebrate.[3] The effort it took to find flour or chikwanga was nothing compared to the pleasure we felt eating something besides boiled cassava. Most of the time that was all we had to eat.

After several months of this diet, all the refugees were thin and exhausted. Women's menstrual cycles were irregular. I had no periods at all after Tingi-Tingi, though they returned several months later when our diet was more balanced.

Boende is about five hundred kilometers from Mbandaka, the capital of Equateur. It lies on the banks of the Tshuapa, a tributary of the Congo. It is possible to go from Boende to Mbandaka by boat, and rumor had it that the governor of Equateur had sent a boat to pick up the refugees. When we arrived in the area, a first group of refugees had just left, and the boat was expected to return any time. In spite of this, we decided to continue on foot, because it seemed safer than waiting for the boat's uncertain arrival. Unfortunately, we were right, and the refugees waiting for the boat were attacked by rebels who had come from Kisangani to take the town of Boende.

I learned what had happened from a young man who had escaped the massacres. He came from Buyoga and had been responsible for our subdistrict at Tingi-Tingi. According to him, the refugees were beside the river when they heard shooting. By the time they could figure out what was happening, the rebels were already there. Some, overcome with panic, threw themselves into the water even though they didn't know how to swim. Others ran, not knowing which way to go, because the bullets seemed to be coming from everywhere. Large numbers of them fell, cut down by bursts of machine gun fire or grenades that the rebels threw into the crowd. The young man ran away, sometimes crouching, other times crawling. He passed bodies that had been torn to bits and were soaked in their own blood. By some miracle he reached the forest. According to him, very few of the refugees had survived the massacre at Boende. Soldiers who spoke Kinyarwanda, probably members of the RPF, were responsible for these massacres. Among the victims there were women and children.

3. *Chikwanga* is a bread made from a fermented paste produced by pounding cassava root. It is then wrapped in forest leaves and boiled. It is also called "cassava bread."

Our decision to continue along the road on foot had been a good one. No boat would have been large enough to take all of the waiting refugees at one time, and besides a day spent waiting on the banks of the river was a day when the rebels could catch up with us. Since they were never very far off, staying in one place for several days raised the risk of being trapped and killed. In fact, danger was very near, even for those of us who had continued to run.

The rebels who were responsible for the massacres in Boende arrived from Kisangani by a different route than that taken by the hordes of refugees fleeing Ubundu. They came on trucks and Land Cruisers. If it had not been for a warning from a Zairian, they would have fallen on us. The route they had taken crossed ours about twenty kilometers from Boende toward Mbandaka. For several days we had not moved ahead too fast. When we saw the condition of the roads, we were sure that we had shaken off our pursuers. We thought that there was no other road fit for driving in the area, and that to follow us they would also have to go on foot. Since they would first have to "pacify" the area they went through, we hoped to have an appreciable lead over them. This confidence was misplaced and would cost the lives of many in our group. I am thinking particularly of Kabeza, a former mayor of Nyaruhengeri. We had gone five hundred kilometers together. Through having slept in the same village squares, alongside the same roads and in the same forests, we had become friends. His wife was Tutsi. She had preferred to suffer along with her husband and children rather than to return to Rwanda. She said that she could not go back to a country where they were not welcome.

The night before Kabeza was knifed, we had slept in the same house in an abandoned village. On waking we had, as always, spoken of the rebels. Kabeza figured that we had lost them for good. I maintained the contrary, not that I really believed it, but just for the pleasure of contradicting him. I have always loved to contradict and never let an opportunity to do so pass me by. Those who know me don't think it is excessive, but for others it can be annoying, and I think that that was the case for Kabeza. We didn't know that the rebels, who were getting us so hot under the collar, were only about forty kilometers away, and that many people in our group, Kabeza among them, would be killed by them two days later. We got on the road very early. Kabeza's family walked very quickly, but they often stopped to rest. That day we passed them about noon and we decided to see each other again in the evening. We had decided to rest at one o'clock, and had gone about four kilometers and were preparing to stop when a young Zairian man warned us that the rebels had arrived. He came from the opposite direction and was very agitated. He spoke very bad French mixed in with Lingala. All that we could understand was that the rebels were coming. They were riding in many trucks and jeeps and wore white headbands. They said they were going to Boende and were asking the local population about the refugees. They particularly wanted to know which roads the refugees had used. The young man urged us to leave as soon as possible so we could get past the point, about six kilometers from the village, where their road and ours crossed. We had some doubts about the truth of what he was saying, but the mere mention of the rebels put wings on our feet. Everyone began to run. Those who had begun to cook dumped their food on the ground and packed their pots while they were still hot. The most fearful abandoned their belongings right there. Less than an hour later we got to the junction of the two roads. Indeed there was a road that came from Kisangani, as the aging road sign said. It must have been at least thirty years old and the red paint was so faded by the daily rains that you could hardly read the word Kisangani. Even though we could not hear the sound of motors approaching, we did not linger. We continued to walk quickly to the next village, about twelve kilometers away. After a forced march of three hours, we could go no further and decided to spend the night so as to be rested the following day. If the arrival of the rebels were confirmed, the next days would be difficult. We needed to gather our strength to double, if necessary, the distance that we usually covered daily. That night Kabeza's family did not join us. During the whole night I expected to be awakened by refugees who had encountered the rebels, but it ended without incident.

The next morning we were on the road again. I began to think that the young Zairian had lied to us. But why? Some of the refugees thought that he had just wanted to frighten us and get us to leave the area quickly to protect their fields of cassava. Night fell again and Kabeza's family still had not caught up with us. We did not know that he was already dead.

Toward midnight I was awakened by the sound of footsteps. I woke the girls up and we went outside to see what was happening. Hundreds of people were passing through the village. They walked quickly and in total silence. Even four-year-old children trotting in front of their parents or being dragged along behind didn't utter a peep. Babies on their mothers backs, who usually cried incessantly from the heat, hunger, and thirst seemed to share their parents terror and were quiet. Without asking any questions, we knew that the rebels were there. Fear invaded our hearts again. Like the other refugees sleeping in the village, we packed our bags in a hurry and followed the others. In a matter of minutes the village was empty. We walked through the moonless night, not knowing where to put our feet down. All the villages we passed through emptied immediately. It was the following morning that I learned what had happened. For about twenty kilometers after Boende, the rebels shot the refugees that they came across or killed them with bayonets. Those who were able to escape fled to the forest.

The person who told me this was a former student at the Université Nationale du Rwanda whom I had known since Irangi. He had told me about his turbulent departure from Bukavu and swore that he would walk as far and as fast as possible so that he would never again have to encounter soldiers from the RPF. When Bukavu fell to the Banyamulenge and the RPF, he went out on the road to see what was going on. The first person he saw was a *kadogo* he knew.[4] The boy was armed to the teeth. He wanted to know what the former student was doing at Bukavu and why he didn't return to Rwanda. When he tried to answer, the young soldier began to slap his face and continued to interrogate him. He was saved by the arrival of another kadogo who had come to warn his companion that a group of fleeing refugees had arrived and they could go and have some fun with them. The first kadogo forgot the former student for a minute so that he could run play his favorite game, shooting his machine gun indiscriminately into a crowd of men, women, and children running away from the fighting.

After Tingi-Tingi, the former student usually was at the head of the group. He had found himself behind us because he had waited too long at Boende for the boat promised by the governor of Equateur. When he

4. *Kadogo* is a Swahili name for the child soldiers of the RPF.

saw that it was taking its time coming back, he decided to go on foot. A dozen kilometers farther along he heard about the possible arrival of a group of rebels by another road coming from Kisangani. Like many others he had thought that it was just one rumor among many others that were circulating among the refugees, and he continued on his way unafraid. When he reached the crossroads, he and about thirty others decided to stop and rest. To prove to everyone that the rebels were only a mirage, he took several steps down the road, which appeared to be empty and peaceful. He had just gone two or three hundred meters when he heard the sound of motors. He hardly had time to turn around and warn his companions before the rebels were there and opened fire on them. He didn't know how he had jumped into a thicket. From behind a tree he watched the carnage that followed. The people who were in houses getting ready to eat or resting had not heard the rebels arrive and only came out when the first shots were fired and it was already too late. How many were killed at this crossroads on the Kisangani-Boende road? The former student couldn't tell me. All that he knew was that when he came back out of the forest after the rebels had left, he had seen around a dozen corpses in front of the houses and on the village square. He didn't go into the houses to see if there were other bodies. He was in too much of a hurry to get away from that evil place. After that afternoon, he walked without stopping.

As for Kabeza, according to the story told by members of his family who arrived exhausted four or five days later, he was killed that afternoon. The group had just left the village where they had rested at noon when, at a turn in the road, they came upon the rebels. The vehicles were stopped. Kabeza, who was walking ahead, stopped in surprise as did the others. One of the rebels told him in Kinyarwanda to join him. Kabeza seems to have gone forward without a second thought. Maybe he thought that the soldier was a member of the CZSC who had learned a few words of Kinyarwanda. When he got close, the soldier pulled a knife and stabbed him. The others took this as a signal and began to shoot at the rest of the group. With bullets flying around them, the rest of the family fled to the forest to hide, leaving the lifeless body of their husband and father alone on the road. They wandered for several days not knowing what direction to take. Finally they found some villagers who helped them to find the road.

Many of those who fled to the forest after the repeated rebel attacks disappeared. That was what happened to the husband of a woman who represented Cyungo in the Tingi-Tingi women's organization. After Obilo, we were almost always in the same group, and we often spent the night in the same village. The young woman was with her husband and three children under ten. Zuzu called her "Auntie" because they were neighbors in the camp at Kashusha, and it was from her that I had heard the little girl's story. When the rebels attacked them, they were resting in the shade of the trees in a village square. Because of the noise that people were making getting ready to eat, and the shouts of the children, they didn't hear the vehicles drive up until they were in the village. The rebels began firing before they had even come to a stop. When the shooting broke out, this woman and her husband and children scattered into the forest to hide. When, with several other refugees, she found herself under cover of the forest, her children were still with her, but her husband was missing. She had no idea what direction he had taken off in and how to search for him, so she decided to stay with the other refugees, hoping to find him later. For many days she, like her companions in misfortune, wandered around lost in the forest without seeing a living soul. When, after a few hours, they thought that they had made some progress, they would find themselves back where they had started. They had just decided to stay in the forest for good, rather than wandering around exhausting their strength and their meager provisions uselessly when some Zairians discovered them and helped them find the road taken by the other refugees. When she rejoined us, she still had no news of her husband.

After the night that we learned that the rebels were hot on our heels we quickened our pace. Whereas we usually made an average of twenty-five kilometers a day, we now did more than thirty and sometimes forty. Zuzu was in terrible shape. She had been completely exhausted for days, and could hardly walk because of the huge blisters on the soles of her feet. She was still in an advanced state of malnutrition, and many of our friends predicted that she would not reach Mbandaka.

Zuzu had more and more trouble walking. The cold and the rain had aggravated her condition considerably. We had gotten to within less than five kilometers of the river when she decided to squat down by the side of the road and wait for death. She could do no more. Since she usually walked behind me, I didn't realize right away that she was no longer with me. Every time that I had tried to make her walk in front of me, she had refused. She said that it was easier for her to adapt her pace to mine when she walked behind. After having gone almost a kilometer, I turned around to see if she were having trouble following me. I saw to my horror that she wasn't there. I called her name over and over again and got no answer. If she had decided to go hide herself in the forest, how was I going to find her? What if she had fallen without my knowing and was dead? Thoughts of the most horrible possibilities crossed my mind. To my great relief I found her lying under a tree by the side of the road. She was soaked to the skin and trembling. Her teeth were chattering, but she was alive. It had begun to rain and the other girls had left with the sheeting. We had nothing to protect ourselves from the rain, and Zuzu couldn't take one more step. When I managed to get her upright, she fainted. I had to slap her several times to bring her to herself. In my distress I prayed loudly to the Virgin Mary for help. Zuzu, who from time to time regained consciousness, asked me who I was talking to, because there was no one else around. We were completely alone in the forest, it was raining, and I was cold. If I didn't find a solution quickly, both of us risked dying of exposure. Night had already fallen and the peasants would not find us until the following day when it would be too late. With a superhuman effort I was able to haul Zuzu up onto my back, and, with my bundle on my head, I joined the others at the edge of the river.

I arrived exhausted and sick at Ingende, which lay on the banks of the Tshuapa, a tributary of the Congo. Before we got there, we went about twenty kilometers through a forest without seeing a village. I thought that Ingende lay on both banks of the Tshuapa, but when, carrying Zuzu, I got to the edge of the river around eight o'clock, I was disappointed. There was only forest. The town was on the other side. Since it was still raining, we slept on the side of the road, in wet clothes, covered with wet sheeting. We crossed over the river the next day at the end of the afternoon. To pay for our passage, we had to sell part of our sheeting. The rest of the 250,000 new Zaires was paid by a friend whose wife also came from Buyoga. With the fatigue and the cold and the rain of the night before, my malaria flared up. I had been shivering since the morning and lay beside the road the whole time we were waiting our turn for the boat. While my back was turned, someone who must have needed money for the boat, robbed me of my shoes. Fortunately Assumpta gave me a pair of flip-flops that she didn't wear much. I wasn't used to walking long distances in flip-flops. A few days later my feet and legs began to swell. The thong between my toes cut at every step. The wounds that resulted took a long time to heal.

We stayed for two days in Ingende, waiting for permission from the military authorities so that we could continue on our way. Thousands of people slept on both banks of the Tshuapa. People had been so traumatized by the rebels that they thought they saw them in the bushes when the wind moved them, in passing pirogues, everywhere. Marcelline was almost beaten up because she did not want to turn off her flashlight going by the bushes. People said that her light would signal our whereabouts to the rebels. Authorization to go further was granted at the end of the next afternoon. Frieda and her family left right away, but I stayed at Ingende trying to recuperate a bit. We spent the second night with a young man who was dying. He was about twenty-five. His wife and son had been repatriated from Mugunga camp near Goma. When he was still able to walk and talk, he showed me photos taken in Rwanda with his wife and son. He looked younger and bigger. It was difficult to imagine that the man in the photo, so full of life, was the same who accompanied me in this misfortune. I often shared mangos with him. He was dying in this unknown house, in an unknown village, thousands of kilometers from his son and wife. Their absence weighed heavily on him.

The next morning we took the road to Mbandaka, which was only a few hundred kilometers away. The companions of the dying young man left him in the hands of the Zairian doctors in the hospital at Ingende, which was still functioning. A few days later the rebels entered the town. At the edge of the river they found thousands of refugees waiting to cross. According to the story told by a Zairian official of the International Red Cross who helped to bury them, rebels killed at least thirteen hundred people, among them women and children, at Ingende. Many bodies had been hacked to bits. Only by the size of the bones in the skull was it possible to tell children and adults apart.

10

My Life for Ten Dollars

AFTER TWO DAYS at Ingende I left, still sick and exhausted. I could no longer carry my bundle and I had to lean on a cane to walk. It took us three days to go from Ingende to the little town of Bonde. The day of our arrival we took our noonday rest in Bokatola, a village a dozen kilometers from there. After this pause, Assumpta and Zuzu left about fifteen minutes before the rest of us, walking slowly. They were deteriorating rapidly and Assumpta had pains in her feet. Around two o'clock, we caught up with Assumpta. Zuzu was not with her. Since we hadn't seen her anywhere on the road we thought that she had gone ahead, and we would find her traveling with other refugees. We didn't ask Assumpta right away. Zuzu's absence was completely understandable, and we economized with our strength and our words. After two kilometers we realized we had probably passed her at a time when she had left the road to go to the bathroom. I stopped to wait for her with Marcelline and Virginie. Because it was difficult for her to walk fast enough to keep up with us, Assumpta had gone on ahead. We thought that it wouldn't be long before we found Zuzu and were sure that we would catch up with Assumpta before nightfall, but we never saw her again. Around ten, when Zuzu still hadn't arrived, we had to leave without her to find a village where we could spend the night and not be at the mercy of the young thugs who assaulted isolated refugees and robbed them. That same day we had almost fallen into their hands. When we were going through one of the abandoned villages, we found ourselves surrounded by four young men armed with clubs. The looks on their faces didn't give us much hope that we would get out of it unharmed. They were beginning to close in on us, but when other refugees arrived, they disappeared into the forest like a bad dream.

It was while looking for a village to spend the night in that we came to Bonde, which is in the area of Bokatola, in Ingende zone in the province of Equateur. The Mongo are the main ethnic group inhabiting the area. Virginie devoted herself to finding a place to stay, since she spoke Swahili and French well. Lingala was spoken in the Bokatola area, but many men in the villages understood French. She had no trouble finding us a place to stay with a Zairian family whose eldest son, Cyprien, immediately declared his love for her. His family gave us a warm welcome. That night I took a hot shower with soap, my first real bath since Tingi-Tingi. The next day, since Zuzu hadn't turned up, Cyprien offered to go with Virginie to hunt for her. The little one hadn't left the village of Bokatola, where we had taken our midday rest the day before. When she left with Assumpta, she stopped to go to the bathroom a few houses farther along and felt too weak to walk any farther. That night she had shared supper and sheeting with a sympathetic refugee. Virginie and Cyprien found her at about one o'clock. She had spent the entire morning sitting by the side of the road. Even though many people had passed by, no one had offered to help her. Everyone knew that she was close to the end, and no one wanted to be burdened with a sick child who would slow them down. She was so exhausted that she refused to walk and kept repeating that she would rather die right away than take one more step. Cyprien and Virginie carried her to Bonde on their backs. I was very relieved to see her. They got to the village around four o'clock, and it was too late to travel farther.

Cyprien, whose nickname was Sipi, offered to take us by pirogue to Mbandaka the next week. I gratefully accepted his offer. Neither I nor Zuzu had enough strength to travel the one hundred and thirty kilometers that separated us from Mbandaka on foot. We needed to rest and I tried to take advantage of this providential stop to regain my strength. Sipi's family made it all possible. They gave us free oranges and cassava. Morning, noon, and night we ate oranges by the basketful. During this week we met many people who were going to play an important role in our lives several months later. There was Loyi, whose mother was from Bukavu and whose maternal grandmother was Rwandan; Musa, a Muslim from Kinshasa; Ma Mundimi, the village madwoman; and many others. The evening of the second day Sipi took us to a party at the neighbor's. The peasants were astonished to hear women speaking such good French, and they came and sat beside us to listen to us speak.

Sipi was counting on a friend who had a pirogue to help take us for free to Mbandaka, but the friend in question, citing the lack of security in the area, refused to go with him or even to lend him the pirogue. Tuesday, the day that we were to leave for Mbandaka, came and went. Wednesday evening, Sipi told us that it had been impossible for him to find a pirogue and offered to go with us to Mbandaka on foot to protect us. Our departure was set for very early the following morning. We were ready to go at six. Around ten Sipi came and told us that the lawlessness in the area was growing and that he didn't want to leave the village. Since he was the eldest son and had been responsible for the family since the death of his father, he didn't want to leave them alone in the present situation. He offered to let us stay with him and his family and promised to take us to a hiding place in the forest if the rebels came through the village.

In spite of this tempting offer, I decided to leave for Mbandaka. I hoped to get there and cross the Congo River before the rebels arrived. I was counting on divine mercy to provide us with the money for the fare. Loyi recommended that we go first to his mother's house in Bombenga, a village about eight kilometers from Bonde. He would have liked to go with us and introduce us himself, but he was busy, so Musa was put in charge. I left Bonde with Zuzu, Marcelline, and Virginie. Sipi's mother had at first wanted Zuzu to stay with her. Her health was so bad that everyone feared that she would die before we reached Mbandaka. She changed her mind at the last minute, probably because she was afraid that the little one would die at her house. It was obvious that Zuzu needed medical attention and a rich diet that this woman didn't have the means to provide.

We got to Ma Marie's house at the end of the afternoon. Since it was too late to travel further, she offered to have us spend the night. Ma Marie was overjoyed to welcome her countrywomen. Earlier she had taken in a young woman and her baby. The woman was sick, but with Ma Marie's care, and medicine from her husband, a medical assistant with the Zairian Red Cross, she recovered. She had left for Mbandaka the night before our arrival. Ma Marie would have liked to keep her there with her, but the young woman was so frightened of the rebels that she didn't want to stay in Zaire. The following morning we prepared to leave. Our hostess suggested that we stay a few days more and see how the situation developed, since the news from Mbandaka was not good. She said that all the refugees had been taken to the Zairian navy training camp at Irebu, which was not a good place for women. Since I hadn't completely recovered and Zuzu's health had not improved, I accepted the offer. Marcelline and Virginie were also too tired and hoped for a few days rest. At Ma Marie's I felt safer than at Sipi's, probably because she spoke a little Kinyarwanda and her husband had medicine. I told myself that if any of us fell sick, we would be cared for.

Early in the morning of the third day Ma Marie burst into our room to warn us that the rebels had arrived. She was in a state of extreme agitation. She had the information from refugees who were running through the village. According to them, the rebels were less than twenty kilometers away and were traveling in vehicles. She offered to hide us along with her family in the forest. Since her husband was a reserve soldier in FAZ, he was even more frightened than we were. We very quickly packed our bags and left. However, it was not without second thoughts that we followed our hosts into the forest. I could remember only too well what was waiting for us there. Crossing swollen rivers on slippery tree trunks, pools of mud so deep you practically had to swim, rotten tree trunks lying across the path that took every ounce of strength you had to climb over, tree roots that slowed you down, trails slick from rain. My worries were well founded, but we didn't have to go far. Some time earlier Ma Marie and her husband had outfitted a refuge less than a kilometer away.

It was a shed, and to get there, there was no visible trail. The going was hard, since in April there was water everywhere. The forest had turned into a huge swamp. In some places there was water up to our navels. The Mongo women, accustomed to moving around in this environment, pulled their skirts up to the tops of their thighs. Since we didn't dare imitate them, our clothes were completely soaked when we got where we were going. We stayed hidden for a week. The shed, which must have been five meters wide and four long was built on a little mound to keep it out of the water. There were twenty of us there. In addition to Ma Marie, her husband and three sons, one of whom had a wife and three children, there were also her husband's brother, his two wives and four of their children, not counting my three girls and me. The little shed was surrounded by water on all sides. We drank this water, which we also used to cook and bathe with. It was also into this water that we went to the bathroom and threw our garbage. The second day after our arrival in the shed I woke up with a little fever. Ma Marie's husband gave me a couple of Nivaquine and some aspirin, but it didn't do any good. At night the fever was so high that I could not sleep. Marcelline and Virginie took turns mopping my forehead with a damp cloth. The third day I was worse. My fever was 104 degrees and I couldn't swallow anything. When I ate medicine or food, I vomited. I also had diarrhea. When I had to go to the bathroom, Ma Marie's husband or one of their sons carried me on their back, because I could no longer walk. While I was relieving myself, crouched on a root sticking up above the water, whoever was with me held my arm so that I wouldn't tumble into the water.

I began to be dehydrated from the fever, diarrhea, and vomiting. My hosts were worried that I would slip through their fingers. Ma Marie's husband did everything he could to save me. He himself gave me several shots of antibiotics, an injection of quinine, and herbal baths. I sat on the tree roots and he poured water on me. The fever went down, but I still couldn't swallow anything. In the meantime, Ma Marie's son went around to the other refugees in the forest and came back with bad news. The rebels had begun to search the villages and forests for Rwandan refugees. Even though I was gravely ill, I wanted to leave right away. I didn't want to expose our hosts in case the rebels found our hideaway, but they wanted to wait until the next day to make a decision. The fear that I felt at the thought of being discovered by the rebels made me delirious. The fever had gone down considerably, but in my weakened state, the worry was unbearable. Ma Marie's husband gave me Valium so that I could sleep. The whole family prayed all night for my recovery. When I was at death's door, the two people I thought about were my mother and Frans, a Dutch friend. I took advantage of the rare moments when I was conscious to tell Virginie and Marcelline my last wishes: once they were out of the forest they should rip up any papers that could identify them as Rwandan and they should do everything to get in contact with Frans, who could help them get out of Zaire. Another thing dear to my heart was for my mother to know where I was buried. I hoped that one day she could come visit my grave and maybe even take my remains to Rwanda. The fever and diarrhea had weakened me to the point that uttering a few words took several hours. I tired very easily. When I started a sentence, I had to stop after two words. I began again several minutes later. Since I often forgot what it was I had wanted to say, I went on to something else.

Virginie told me later that I was delirious for more than a week. In the meantime, we learned that the rebels had taken another road, and our hosts decided to go home. We followed them. I got back to the village on the back of the eldest son. I have no memory of the warm herbal baths that they gave me every day after we got back from the forest, the salt that they went to buy from a village deep in the forest to season the food so that I could eat, and all the efforts Ma Marie made to keep me alive during the days and nights when my life was hanging by a thread. I began to notice what was going on around me five or six days after we returned from the forest. I was still very weak. Virginie had to hold on to my arm to take me to the bathroom, and she bathed me and fed me with a spoon because I was incapable of doing it myself.

Ever since I arrived at Ma Marie's house, her husband had been making advances to me, but I didn't take it seriously. I was in such a depleted physical state that I thought I had lost any appeal for a man, even an old Mongo villager. I was only skin and bones and was wrinkled like an old woman. My breasts had disappeared. My clothes were dirty and threadbare. I was covered with lice. Apparently Ma Marie's husband didn't look at things the way I did. He still found some feminine charm behind all this misery. He even offered to take me to live with him in another village where he proposed to open a dispensary to take care of my needs. When we were in the forest he did not bring up the subject, given the crowding and my sickness. After I regained consciousness, he suggested that we take a walk behind the house. He said I wouldn't get well if I stayed in bed all the time. The idea seemed sensible to me and without a second thought I said I would walk a few steps with him. Still being too weak to walk alone, I leaned on him. I wasn't worried. It didn't occur to me that someone would want to take advantage of me in the state that I was in. Once in the forest, he began to explain to me that if I wanted to get well soon, I would have to make love to him. I was speechless. On the contrary, it would be the best way to kill me. But he seemed determined to have his way. He backed me up to a tree in order to be able to undress at his leisure. I couldn't stand up alone. When he began to undress, I realized that he wanted to go through with it. I had to do something if I didn't want to die in this adventure. In spite of his sixty years, Ma Marie's husband was still strong and must have weighed more than eighty kilos. I don't know where I got the strength that let me turn around and go back to the house by myself.

The shock that I had suffered caused the fever to return. I immediately became delirious. In spite of the entreaties of Ma Marie and Virginie, the man refused to give me any aspirin to bring the fever down, saying he had no more medicine. He told Virginie that I had rejected him and he couldn't do anything more for me. He was so angry about his failure that a few days later he chased us out of the house. He said he couldn't risk his life and the life of his family by keeping Rwandan refugees there. Rumors were circulating that the rebels were searching the villages, killing refugees along with those who gave them shelter. Since I had rebuffed his advances, I had to take care of myself. Faced with this situation, Ma Marie behaved like a true mother to us. Not being able to prevent her husband from sending us away, she did everything possible to make the trip easier for us. She prepared a week's worth of provisions and gave us 100,000 new Zaires to buy salt and oil.[1]

At first Ma Marie wanted to keep Zuzu, but changed her mind at the last minute, no doubt because her husband opposed the idea. During our whole stay, she had never stopped caring for the little girl. She gave her a very rich diet, which she said would let her recover quickly, and her husband gave her vitamins and antibiotics.

We left Bombenga early in the morning. Virginie and Marcelline were in charge of the luggage, except for the sheeting, which Ma Marie's husband had kept as compensation for the care he had given us. Zuzu, very sick and completely exhausted, had decided not to move. In spite of my pleas she refused to follow us. I did my best to explain to her that the villagers of Bombenga didn't want anything to do with us, but it

1. Author's note: At that time 100,000 new Zaires was less than a dollar. For Ma Marie, the sum was nevertheless enormous. She had earned this money making and selling chikwanga. One chikwanga was worth 5,000 new Zaires.

did no good. She decided to stay even if she died of mistreatment. Neither I nor Virginie was strong enough to carry her on our backs as we had always done when she couldn't walk. In spite of the pain that I felt leaving her among people whose animosity was so obvious, I decided to go. To console myself I told myself that she had a small chance of surviving with a Zairian family, whereas she had none with us on the road. We had no more sheeting to protect us from the rain, no medicine for her, and not enough food. Zuzu only survived three more days after we left. I was only told of her death two weeks later. As for myself, the only thing that sustained me was my unshakeable faith in God. No matter what, I remained convinced that somewhere else along the road to Mbandaka, another welcoming home was waiting for us where I could regain my strength.

Since the area was under Kabila's control, the villagers had advised us to disguise ourselves as Mongo women and wear a white headband in our hair. They did the same thing when they traveled even for a few kilometers, in case they encountered Kabila's rebels. We had exchanged our sacks for baskets, and dressed in pagnes with Mongo baskets on our backs and white headbands in our hair, we took to the road. Who would have thought that one day I would wear Kabila's colors, after everything that the rebels had done to us? The only thing I carried was the cane I leaned on. Marcelline had to support me from the other side so that I wouldn't fall. I often asked them to stop so that I could rest. There were very few people in the villages that we passed through, since many were still hiding in the forest. Some villagers refused to let us sit down to rest in their villages. Others, by contrast, were very sympathetic to our situation and gave us cooked cassava or fruit to refresh us along the road. After walking for four kilometers we got to Batsina. I was at the end of my strength and very thirsty. I asked Virginie to go ask for water for me in a nearby house. She returned along with a villager. He helped Marcelline and Virginie to take me to the house and suggested that we wait there until the sun was less fierce. He brought us to a shed in the courtyard and had us sit on the bench that ran around the interior. Some men were already there, sitting around a large fire. He gave us water and grilled corn, and since I couldn't sit upright without falling over, he went to get a camp bed from the house so that I could stretch out. Women from the village who were on their way to the spring to get water stopped by when they heard the news. They glanced at me quickly and turned away wiping away tears. Everyone was convinced that I would die. In the end we stayed in this village for a long time, and during the first week these women would come every day to ask about my health. They were happy to see that I was recovering.

After we had been in the courtyard for about an hour, a young man named Shako arrived on his bicycle. He had just come from Mbandaka, 122 kilometers away. He told us that the rebels were slaughtering Rwandan refugees between the village of Kalamba, less than fifty kilometers from Batsina, and Mbandaka. He said he had never seen such savagery. No one was spared. Women and children were butchered without pity. At first he spoke in Lingala and then repeated everything in French to be sure that we had understood. According to him, continuing to travel toward Mbandaka was certain death. Our white headbands, pagnes, and baskets would be no help at all. They didn't fool anyone. The Rwandan soldiers fighting in the rebel ranks would recognize us right away. He offered to hide us for several weeks, until the end of the killing, in an unoccupied house in his compound. It would have been suicidal on our part to overlook Shako's offer. We gratefully accepted it.

At any rate, we were in no physical state to continue. I managed to stay alive with cassava and pondu à la mosaka, but I was not well.[2] When I left Bukavu, I weighed fifty-five kilos. By Batsina I weighed around thirty. My skin was like wrinkled parchment and so elastic that you could stretch it several centimeters. My bones and backbone stuck out. My eyes were sunk into their sockets. I slept with my legs spread wide apart, because putting one leg on top on another was horribly painful. I had infected sores all over my body. Only my face had been spared. Every scratch became infected right away. With sores on my buttocks, I could not sit for long. Marcelline was not in any better shape. She had walked up until then, but her health was more than fragile. After Tingi-Tingi she was constantly sick. As for Virginie, she held up by force of will and because she had no choice, but she too was extremely weak.

The owner of the house and his wife were away working in the fields. The decision to stay in the village under Shako's protection had just

---

2. *Pondu* is a vegetable dish based on cassava leaves. Mosaka is a sauce made from the pulp of palm nuts.

been made when they returned. The man showed no astonishment at seeing refugees in his house and welcomed us like any other visitors. He told us to call him Ya Pepe. When Shako told him how the rebels were treating the refugees that they caught, he agreed with the others. We had to stay in the village until the end of the slaughter, and he proposed to keep us at his house. Since we were women alone, it would not be proper to live alone in a house, as Shako had proposed. We risked being disturbed by the men of the village.

On the following morning Ya Pepe got a room ready for us in his own house, but his wife was not enthusiastic. She did not want women around who could have conversations with her husband in French, a language that she could not follow. In a society in which marriages are as unstable as they are among the Mongo, she was worried that one of us would take her husband, and she threatened to leave if he didn't turn us away immediately. However, he was a Christian in the true sense of the word. Convinced that he was doing the right thing, he refused to give in to his wife or to the entire extended family when they came to the rescue of the endangered spouse. She put her threat into action, and we spent the first two weeks without her. Faced with her husband's stubbornness, though, she finally had to come home.

During the three months that we lived with him, Ya Pepe behaved like a true father to us. In spite of his poverty he made sure that we had cassava and pondu à la mosaka every day. The first few days the food was given to us already cooked. After his wife's return, Ya Pepe thought we would be more comfortable cooking our own food. The job fell to Virginie, since Marcelline was sick and I was still too weak to help her. Virginie got up early to get water from the spring. When she returned, she helped me wash and then went out to look for something to eat during the day. We got cassava and palm nuts from Ya Pepe's family, but it was not enough, and we made up the difference with what people gave Virginie: some corn, grilled cassava, a little pondu. Preparing pondu was difficult, especially for someone like Virginie who had no experience with it, and she finished cooking two hours after the others. Afterward she fell exhausted into bed. Her exhaustion kept her from feeling the bites of the bugs of every type and color that infested our bed.

Nevertheless, little by little we got used to our situation, and I began to improve. The first thing that interested me when I became fully conscious of what was going on around me was the daily life of the women. Like many African women, the Mongo women did a tremendous amount of work. I admired them for their courage, but I asked myself if I would have been able to adapt myself to this kind of life. Certain Mongo customs interested me too. For a few days I dreamed of doing an in-depth study on subjects like their funeral ceremonies. Time passed and the hope of getting out of this forest diminished. Survival became my only concern and I forgot about everything else.

After we had been in Batsina for a month, it was Virginie's turn to get sick. Ever since Bombenga she had had untreated malaria. For several weeks she was unable to get out of bed. I had no money for treatment, which would have cost at least 350,000 new Zaires. Ya Pepe didn't have any money either, so we treated her with leaves. I have never believed in the efficacy of this treatment, but I had no choice. Every morning I went to get papaya, lemon, and mango leaves and ground them before boiling them in a little water. I gave this mixture to her three times a day. Her illness forced me to recover so that I could take care of the household, something I had no experience in. Until that time I had used all my energy for my professional life and there were always people around me who took care of the cooking and the household work.

I started to get up early like the Mongo women. I began by sweeping our room and then I took a little five-liter jerry can, which was all that I could carry, and went to get water. I had to make several trips to the spring to have enough bath water for Marcelline and Virginie. The villagers had told me that hot herbal baths, applied daily, helped cure malaria. Then I went to gather cassava leaves for pondu. The first day I went around the whole cassava field without finding enough to feed one person. It was the first time in my life that I had done that kind of work. Byumba, where I came from, was too cold for cassava. Grinding cassava leaves is the most exhausting part of making pondu. For a beginner like me it was even harder. My first grinding session took two or three hours and I ended up with less than a kilo of pondu. Then I had to grind the palm nuts. Every time I dropped the pestle into the mortar, all the palm nuts scattered onto the floor. To console me, Ya Pepe's children told me that all beginners had the same difficulty.

Finding firewood wasn't easy either. The Mongo, like many forest people, practice slash and burn agriculture. At the beginning of the dry season, the men prepare the fields by cutting all the trees, even ones with trunks more than a meter across, with machetes. When the felled trees are dry enough, they burn them. In reality only the grass, branches, leaves, and twigs burn. The trunks lie in the fields for years until they rot completely. The branches that are left after the fire are an important source of firewood. Every morning the women go into the fields with baskets on their backs and machetes. After working in the fields, they cut the branches into smaller pieces and put them into their baskets. These trees are very useful, but to pick cassava you have to climb over them or crawl under them every time. With a heavy basket on your back, it isn't easy.

When I had to gather firewood for the family and use a machete, I was completely at a loss. As a child I didn't dare use a machete. I used a kitchen knife to cut banana leaves for covering the cooking pots. Machetes frightened me. When I had one in my hand, I imagined what would happen if I suddenly went crazy and hurt someone or hurt myself. Then I put it down right away. After the genocide, when I met someone with a machete, I wanted to run away, even if he didn't show any hostility toward me. I tried to convince myself that all these fears were infantile, without any logical basis, but in spite of everything I kept my fear of machetes. I preferred to pick up dead wood from the ground, even if it wasn't dry enough. After piling it in the basket, I had to put it on my back. Seeing how quickly even the littlest Mongo girls got the baskets up on their backs, I decided that it must be a reasonably easy operation. At the first try, the basket tipped over and all the wood fell on me, opening the sores on my feet. When I saw the blood running out of them I started to cry. Then I began to complain out loud about my fate. I thought about all the people who had been killed by the rebels and who continued to die in the streets of Mbandaka. I thought about Jeanne and other young women and children dead at Tingi-Tingi and those we passed dying by the side of the road. I thought about little Zuzu and all the other children abandoned dying in the forests and village squares. I thought about the thousands of other refugees forced to live hidden in the forest, at the mercy of all kinds of bad weather, and I was ashamed of my weakness. Did I have the right to complain when I was still alive, when I ate every day, when I had been cared for when I was sick, and when I had a roof over my head? This little sermon gave me courage.

After many more attempts I managed to put the recalcitrant basket on my back and I returned home to prepare the evening pondu.

Ya Pepe kept us with him against his family's will. He had to stand up to enormous pressure from them and from a large number of the villagers who wanted him to send us away, but he remained firm in his decision. When they told him that Kabila's rebels would come and kill him and his refugees, he replied that he was not afraid to die. He would rather be killed while trying to save a human life than to fail in his charitable duty. The rumors among the villagers about rebels hunting for Rwandan refugees kept us in a state of perpetual fear. When a plane flew overhead it was enough for someone to say that the rebels were arriving to make us run for the forest, which happily was only ten meters from the house. Even if we didn't have to go far to hide, the situation was traumatic. The massacre of the refugees lasted from April until the beginning of June. It was only after the arrival of humanitarian organizations and their denunciation of this new genocide in the international press that the rebels stopped killing people indiscriminately.

Starting in June 1997 another type of hunt for Rwandan refugees unfolded. At the origin of this manhunt was the repatriation program of the UNHCR. When this organization, which was responsible for the safety of the refugees, arrived at Mbandaka, it immediately began to repatriate refugees to Rwanda. A transit camp was set up at the airport at Mbandaka, and all those who were hidden in the forest or had been staying in the area with Zairian families and who presented themselves at the camp to get some help, were repatriated whether they wanted to be or not. On top of that, the UNHCR went to outlying villages as far away as Batsina to look for refugees to repatriate. When someone refused to get into their car, employees of the UNHCR used force or threatened to come back the next day with Kabila's soldiers.

The delegation from the UNHCR arrived in the village of Batsina during the first two weeks of June. It was the time when, after being sick, I got up and walked a little in the courtyard. It was noon. Ya Pepe was still in the fields. The members of the delegation went first to get a young woman and her baby who were staying with a family a few houses away. She also had been dying when she arrived in the village. A Zairian family sheltered her and her baby and took care of her. Little by little she got better and her baby did well. When the delegation proposed to take her and her baby to Mbandaka to repatriate them to Rwanda, she refused categorically. She said she had no family left there and that she didn't believe that she would be safe. In Batsina she had found a new family and was happy with her life. Since she refused to go with them in spite of the threats that Kabila's soldiers would come, one of the men in the delegation, who was called "Doctor," picked her up and threw her into the vehicle like a common sack of corn. Before arriving at Ya Pepe's they picked up two children that Zairian families had saved from dying. These children had lost their parents in Zaire. In Rwanda they risked ending up in an orphanage. Their host families begged the delegation from UNHCR to leave them in their keeping, but to no avail. They had spent all their savings on caring for the children and already considered them to be their own.

When the delegation arrived at Ya Pepe's, the whole village was already there. Two men came inside the house while the others stayed outside and talked to the villagers. The two men tried everything to convince me to accompany them to Mbandaka to be repatriated. They said that my safety in the village could not be guaranteed. Kabila's soldiers could come any day and no one would be there to keep them from killing me if they wanted to. According to them, in Rwanda I risked nothing; the situation had returned to normal. I wanted to ask them if I had walked two thousand kilometers just for the pleasure of it or out of the simple desire to visit Zaire. But I knew that it was no use getting into a discussion with them. The UNHCR had only one goal: repatriate the Rwandan refugees either willingly or by force. The measure of success was simply the number of people repatriated, and not the welcome that was reserved for them once they got there or whether or not they wanted to go. I had to find something else to convince them to leave without me. I justified my refusal to go by the fact that I had been a resident of Zaire since 1992. It was a lie, but in that situation I didn't have a choice. If I had resident status, my fate was no business of the UNHCR. I had the right to refuse to be repatriated to a country that I had left of my own free will two years before Rwandans were forced en masse to flee for their lives. Then they proposed taking me to the Red Cross to be returned to Bukavu, as they were doing with others who had been displaced by the war. I refused, since I had decided not to leave Batsina. As a resident of Zaire, I had the right to live anywhere I wanted in the country.

When they saw that I would not come along of my own free will, they opted for force and went to get reinforcements among their colleagues outside. The "Doctor" himself came to their rescue. When I saw how big he was, I was afraid. If he had decided to take me by force to the vehicle as he had done with the young woman and her baby, I could not have defended myself. In spite of my trembling hands and my voice, broken by privation, I tried to appear calm. I didn't want my interrogators to see that I was frightened. The "Doctor," in a very authoritarian tone of voice, ordered me to pack my bags and follow him without a lot of excuses. I patiently explained to him, as I had done with his colleagues, that I was a resident of Zaire, that I was no concern of the UNHCR and I would go back to Bukavu in my own way the day I decided that I wanted to. He wanted to know what I was doing in Bukavu. To show my importance, I cited several regional and international organizations for whom I was a consultant. Since it was a question of saving my life, I talked quickly and volubly not letting him get a word in edgewise. I hardly recognized myself.

Even though he had come specially to force me to follow him, the "Doctor" didn't dare to be rough with me. Ya Pepe, who in the meantime had come back from the fields, opposed the use of force to make us leave. Despite pressure from the villagers and the delegation from the UNHCR, he maintained that we would not leave his house until the day we wanted to go. When the men from the UNHCR threatened that they would send Kabila's soldiers, he replied that they should send them the next day and that he was not afraid to die. Since the discussion was dragging on, the head of the delegation, who came from Benin, joined us. When he learned that I worked for the Council of the NGOs at Bukavu, he wanted to know if I knew a Burundian married to a woman from Benin who worked for the same organization. He gave me an unexpected opportunity to show that everything I had said up to then was the truth. The Burundian in question had been a fellow worker in the Centre de Services Coopératives at Gitarama. He was one of the first people with whom we had set up the Collective in 1994. After 1995, he worked in the Information and Communication section of the Collective. I enjoyed talking to him, and it was with great relief that I heard the head of the delegation say to his team members that he had actually seen me in the offices of the Regional Council of the NGOs in Bukavu and that I really was not the concern of the repatriation program of the UNHCR.

I heaved a sigh of relief when I heard their vehicle start up and leave the village. The encounter with the UNHCR had morally and physically exhausted me. When I wanted to get up and go lie on the bed, I had to sit back down again, my legs were shaking so badly. Ya Pepe was as relieved as we were. His wife, on the other hand, was disappointed that we had not left with the UNHCR. For many days she grumblingly gave us our cassava and palm nuts. Some days she simply refused and we had to eat only pondu without mosaka and salt. I accepted this situation philosophically. I would have experienced worse if the people from UNHCR had succeeded in repatriating us to Rwanda.

The efforts of the UNHCR to find refugees wherever they were hidden didn't stop there. Not being able to get to all the places where refugees had hidden, the UNHCR initiated a system of paid compensation for any Zairian who brought them in. The bounty was ten American dollars for each refugee. Hunting Rwandan refugees became one of the most lucrative activities in the area. Bands of bounty hunters sprang up. They arrived in the villages with flyers from the UNHCR and demanded that the local authorities help them in their work. When a villager didn't want to listen to them and deliver up the refugees he had sheltered, they threatened that they would get Kabila's soldiers, who would come and kill him and all his family. In addition they offered to pay anyone who brought them refugees. Many villagers decided to deliver up the children and young men and women they had taken in after April 1997. Between money and Kabila's bullets, it was an easy choice. Only people like Ya Pepe, in whom humanity or Christian faith were so strong that they could accept the sacrifice of their lives in order to protect the lives of others, refused to enter into this human commerce.

In the villages of Batsina and the surrounding area, around fifteen refugees, the majority of whom were women and children, were handed over to the bounty hunters. Among them was a young girl from my district. Musa, our friend in Bonde, had taken her in along with two other young girls. Under pressure from the bounty hunters, who said they were envoys from the UNHCR, Musa had to let them go. The three girls and two boys who were with them told us that they would rather go than continue to live in fear of one day falling into the hands of Kabila's soldiers. They also thought that if they refused to leave while there was still time, one day the villagers would run them out of town with machetes. Watching the situation evolve, I was not far from sharing their point of view. Every time that a bounty hunter passed through the village, he arrived at our house with half the village. If it had not been for Ya Pepe's active intervention, they would have thrown us out on the road long since. The women were the noisiest. Among the ones who shouted loudest I recognized those who had wept with pity when we arrived. What had happened in the meantime? That the bounty hunters had stirred up public opinion was without doubt the most important factor in this about-face. The villagers, particularly Ya Pepe's family, feared reprisals from Kabila's soldiers.

In the end we were able to stay, but Marcelline left. She was sick. She hadn't gotten used to the food. She couldn't swallow the pondu without salt, and it was the only source of vitamins in the area. Her morale was equally low. She had become so sensitive that she cried over nothing. Any remark from me provoked a flood of tears. She became morbidly jealous of Virginie, which made living together a nightmare. We not only had to share a room but also a bed. Every night she cried when one of Virginie's legs touched hers. Her fits of crying woke up the whole household and Ya Pepe often had to intervene before she would quiet down. The situation got progressively worse. Finally she refused to feed herself or get up and walk. She also did not want to get up at night. When I forced her to get up, she would fall down like someone having a seizure, and it would take several people to get her back in the room. She fell down everywhere, in the toilet, in the shed, and in the kitchen. For my part, I didn't try to understand her or to surround her with the tenderness that she needed. I was too preoccupied with our daily survival to give much importance to something that I thought was childish. Looking back later, I realized that she was probably having a serious bout of depression and needed to be lovingly taken care of. The fact that she had had no news of her family since 1994 must have weighed on her, and the completely miserable conditions in which we had been living since October 1996 hadn't made things any better. Her refusal to eat, her incessant weeping, her bedwetting, her excessive attachment to me, and her migraines were symptoms of an illness that I did not recognize at the time and that physically and mentally depleted her. When we got to Batsina, even though she had already lost weight, she still weighed around seventy kilos. Two months later, she hardly weighed fifty. Her malnutrition showed itself outwardly. Her feet and cheeks were swollen. Her hair was limp. Her skin was pale. Infected sores began to appear all over her body. To recover, she needed not only medicine, but a more balanced diet. I had no money for food, and Ya Pepe, who was the only person in the village I could count on, was as broke as I was. The only solution left for me was to take Marcelline to the Red Cross hospital at Mbandaka, where she could get the treatment that she needed for free; but by going to Mbandaka, she risked being taken to the transit camp and repatriated to Rwanda. Making the right decision was not easy. Could I make a child who had found a new mother in me return to Rwanda, where there might not be anyone to take her in and where her safety could not be assured? On the other hand, keeping her with me would be condemning her to a speedy death. After several days of discussions, Marcelline left for Mbandaka with Ya Pepe.

After Marcelline left, I was a little depressed. I felt like a tree without branches. During our long walk through the forest, I had told myself that the worst thing that could happen to me was to find myself alone. So I easily accepted privation thanks to the presence of the children at my side. I asked myself what would become of me if something happened to Virginie, the only one left of the ten children who had been with me when I left Tingi-Tingi. I had lost the first two on the bridge at the Lubutu River. I did not know if they were alive or dead. Zuzu's brother had found a maternal aunt. I was not too worried about him. Bakunda, Gisimba, and Mukunzi had stayed at Obilo. Did they fall, like so many other countrymen, to the bullets of the Banyamulenge rebels? Assumpta had gone on alone to Mbandaka while we were waiting for Zuzu in Bonde. Was she able to leave the town before the rebels massacred all the refugees who were waiting for the boat to take them to Congo Brazzaville? As for Zuzu, she died of exhaustion and malnutrition in Bombenga.

Following Ya Pepe and Marcelline's departure for Mbandaka, our relations with his family deteriorated even more. His wife cut our daily rations of cassava drastically, and several times she refused to give us the palm nuts that were so important for the preparation of pondu à la mosaka. In this critical situation, prayer helped once again. I left Bukavu with a Bible, and in Irangi someone gave me a rosary. Every time I felt ready to crack, I read the Bible or recited the rosary. When it was impossible for me to do that, I sang. At Tingi-Tingi, my daughters taught me religious songs that I sang often, even on the road or when I was fetching water. The songs that I loved the most were: Nyir'ibambe ndaje unyakire (Lord I come to you, welcome me) and Ni wowe rutare rwanjye (You are my rock). After praying I felt restored. Thanks to my faith, I was able to bear the daily humiliations, deprivation, sickness, and misery better.

While Ya Pepe was still in Mbandaka, his family came to throw us out. It was early in the morning, and we were still in bed. His mother, wife, and children burst into our room armed with machetes. Ya Pepe's mother spoke in a loud, threatening voice. She seemed to be very angry with us. Since I didn't understand Lingala, the language she was speaking, I asked Virginie what she wanted and why she had come into our room so early in the morning. I tried to remember everything we had done since the night before that could have caused such wrath, and could think of nothing. The last few days we had been alone at Ya Pepe's. The rest of the family had gone to his mother's for the week-long wake in memory of his aunt, who had died the previous week. We had not gone because Ya Pepe had told us that our presence there would not be appreciated. Not knowing the customs of the area, we had not insisted. We were waiting for the end of the ceremony to go pay our respects to the old woman. She took our not having gone to the wake as a pretext for sending us away from her son's house. Ya Pepe's absence was an opportunity not to be missed. Convincing the old woman to throw us out must not have been difficult. The threat of reprisals from the bounty hunters was still hanging over the families who continued to shelter Rwandan refugees, and this was reason enough to lead Ya Pepe's mother to act against the wishes of her son. In a few seconds our possessions were taken from the house and thrown into the street. A crowd formed, made up mainly of women and children, to watch us leave the house accompanied by the shouts of Ya Pepe's family. Some showed their compassion, while others snickered and made no effort to hide their pleasure at seeing us thrown out like thieves.

Among those who had pity on us was a sister of Shako's, the young man on a bicycle who had been the first to offer us his protection when we arrived at Batsina. Since then, his family had never stopped bringing us his help. After our relations with Ya Pepe's family became strained and his wife refused to give us anything to eat, the help from Shako's family increased. They regularly sent us flamboyants, cassava, and fish. Shako's older brother showed us great solicitude. Since he was a hunter, from time to time he brought us game: a moorhen, a turtle, or a haunch of antelope. He was a little bit in love with me and wanted to marry me and even made an official offer. In spite of how kind he was, I was not ready to accept a life as a Mongo peasant with no future for my children. In spite of my refusal, he held no bitterness toward me and we remained good friends.

Shako's sister was passing by on the road when, seeing a small crowd in front of the house, she came over to see what was happening. She was as upset as we were when she learned the reason. She could hardly hold back her tears when she saw our distress, and she immediately offered to take us to her house until Ya Pepe's return. She had to talk it over first with her mother, since her brothers had gone to Mbandaka to sell cassava, so Virginie left with her to explain the situation to the old lady. I sat alone in the ruins of a former health center at the side of the road, waiting for her to return. I asked myself what would become of us if the old woman refused to take us in. Like all the villagers, she must still have been afraid of Kabila's soldiers. To raise my morale, I picked up my rosary and began to pray. By the time Virginie came back to tell me that Shako's mother was willing to take us in until Ya Pepe's return, I was calm again. She didn't even know that I had been crying. I had to maintain a calm and serene manner in order not to worry her unduly. We stayed two days with Shako's family, during which time we were treated like princesses. We had all the cassava, pondu, flamboyants, and fish we wanted. People who came by to say hello gave us food and firewood. This warm welcome reconciled us with the village of Batsina for forty-eight hours. But as the old saying goes, it was too good to last. The third morning, Shako's mother asked us to leave. Ya Pepe's family was threatening to write to Kabila's soldiers stationed at Ingende and tell them that we were staying with her. She could not continue to keep us. The idea that the soldiers could descend on them and kill the whole family terrified her and her daughters, because, in the absence of the two sons, there was no one to defend them.

Shako's mother's decision caught us unaware. It was a heavy blow, but once again prayer calmed me down. After much thought, I decided to return to Bonde, the village that we had left in April. We needed a roof over our heads and food, and only Sipi was prepared to offer that to us without asking for anything in exchange. For a while, after hearing about the difficult conditions we were living under in Batsina, he had been sending message after message asking us to return to Bonde. Sipi even came by to see us a few weeks earlier at Ya Pepe's and repeated his family's invitation. The only difficulty that could arise at Bonde was Sipi's opposition to our plan to go to the Central African Republic. Shako's neighbors, soldiers in FAZ, told us that it was possible to go from Batsina to Ngemena, a town on the border of the Central African Republic, by pirogue. One of them was planning to go in the next few days and offered to take us with him. But this plan soon proved unrealistic. Once we were settled again in Bonde, we went back to see our old neighbors to discuss the practicalities of the trip. As it turned out, no one had ever intended to go to Ngemena. It was a strategy to get close to us and force himself on Virginie.

We left for Bonde without taking our belongings, because we were skeptical about the reaction of the people in the villages we would be going through. With the campaign of intimidation led by the bounty hunters, the villagers had developed a phobia about refugees and wanted them all out of the area. We were afraid of being attacked if they saw us coming back with our luggage, so we only took a blanket and some clothes that we wrapped in a pagne. Bonde is about a dozen kilometers from Batsina. The villages along the way had changed. When we first went through them, they were almost completely deserted. Weeds grew up to the doorways of the houses, some of which were already beginning to crumble. The courtyards were full of cassava peels and the stones and bricks that different waves of refugees had used to make their fires. When we went back through the same villages, they were swarming with people. We knew that we were approaching a village by the smoke rising from the thatched roofs, the shouts of children and the high-pitched voices of the women. I entered a village with a knot in my stomach because I did not know how we would be welcomed, but we went through the five villages that lay between us and Bonde without incident. I had had this feeling for several months when I saw a crowd. During our long walk through the forest, I was afraid every time we went through a village that was still inhabited. When we were alone, I asked the girls to stop and wait until other refugees arrived.

We arrived in Bonde at nightfall. Only Ma Eyenga, Sipi's older sister was at the house. The rest of the family had gone to the forest to gather fish. During the fishing season, which is from June to August and from January to February, the majority of the villagers go to camp on the shores of the numerous rivers and streams in the area to gather fish. Gathering fish in the dried up rivers and streams is child's play. A child of six can gather up enough fish in a day to feed a family of ten. From morning until evening we had eaten nothing, and our stomachs were aching from hunger. One of Sipi's neighbors, Fox, brought us smoked fish and two chikwanga to calm our hunger. That evening he brought fresh fish from the forest. It was a celebration. After eating we took a warm bath with toilette soap. It had been almost three months since we had washed with soap. I felt like we had finally come home when we lay down to sleep. Sipi's welcome made us forget the way we had had to leave Batsina.

The day following our return to the fold, we went around the village saying hello to our old friends. It was with real joy that we saw Musa, Roy, and Ma Mundimi, the village madwoman. All of them had helped us with their understanding and friendship the last time we stayed in Bonde. We were happy to see the village adventurer who claimed to have visited all the countries of Central and West Africa and who had promised to help us leave Zaire for another country. He disappointed us a month later by distributing fliers from the UNHCR asking the local authorities to help him take us to Mbandaka. By then he saw us as an opportunity to earn an easy twenty dollars.

We spent our first week in Bonde with Sipi, Ma Eyenga, and her baby. The villagers had nicknamed her Kabila because she was born at the precise moment when he had taken power. Thanks to the joint care of the brother and sister we looked human again when the rest of the family came back from the forest. Ma Eyenga busied herself with feeding us and took it very much to heart. When we didn't succeed in finishing all the fish, cassava, and pondu that she had served us, she was angry. She never stopped reminding us that we had to eat a lot to regain the weight that we had lost. As for Sipi, he took charge of our cleanliness. He made sure that not only could we take a bath every day, but that we could also wash our clothes with soap, something else we had not been able to do for three months. Sipi had a large family. In addition to his mother, he had four daughters, a son-in-law, and four grandchildren. All of the family lived, somehow or other, in one four by six meter room. Only Sipi and his married daughter lived outside of this room. Everyone gathered in this room when it was too hot outside, and it was also where the family ate and received visitors. When Fox, Jérôme, and others came to pay court to me, we were in this room, and the whole family participated in our conversation.

Ma Ndumba, Sipi's mother, welcomed us warmly. She was between fifty-five and sixty years old and had been a widow for many years. After we left she had never stopped asking for news of us and had asked us to come back to live with her at Bonde many times. She had told me often that I should think of her as a mother and that we would have nothing to fear when we were under her roof. She kept her word. When the bounty hunters came to Bonde to terrorize her, the same way they terrorized all the villagers in Bonde who sheltered refugees, she sent them away. To her children, who pressured her to give us up, she replied that she would rather be killed by the soldiers than turn us out. For her, we were children sent by the Holy Spirit and she owed us protection. Ma Ndumba was very devout. They had nicknamed her Maman Miyeke (Mother Castanet) for the musical instrument that she accompanied herself with when she sang in religious ceremonies. The chapel of the Episcopal Church was built on her property. She took charge of our health and practically force-fed us. She was happy that we had begun to put on weight. In less than a month, Virginie had gained more than ten kilos. Ma Ndumba's presence was very reassuring, and we felt truly at home. I felt so grateful to her that I promised myself to do everything to come back and see her once I was out of Zaire. And if one day I ever had a job again, I promised myself to dress her like the town women who from time to time passed through the village, and to buy all the things that she needed but didn't have the money to buy herself, like meat, sugar, corn flour, and coffee.

Our first month at Bonde passed by like a dream. All we did was eat and sleep. Sipi's family took care of the rest. We recovered so quickly that everyone who had seen us when we arrived a month earlier, thin and covered with infected sores all over our bodies, spoke of a miracle. This state of grace had its day, and then things returned to normal. After a month we began to be an irritation. When we returned to Bonde, the family presented Virginie as Sipi's fiancée. In Mongo culture fiancés can begin to live with each other but they have to wait for the whole dowry to be presented before the young man can take her to his house. In the meantime, the man can go to live with his future wife or visit her regularly. The whole time that the visit lasts, the fiancé spends the night with his fiancée in a house given to them by the neighbors. More often than not, children are born of these regular visits. Ma Eyenga's engagement lasted more than ten years, for example, and she had already had three children with her fiancé. Two other of Sipi's younger sisters each had a child by their respective fiancés.

Two weeks after our return to Bonde, all the visitors wanted to know if Virginie and Sipi's engagement had been consummated. When the family replied in the negative, they began to whisper that the marriage would never take place and that we only wanted to use Sipi. Since his mother was on our side, their bad will didn't frighten us. Sipi also, in spite of pressure from his friends, respected Virginie's wishes to put the marriage off until later. He understood that the most important thing for us was go get in contact with my colleagues in Zaire and in Europe so that they could help us get out of the country. Even though he expressed doubts about the probability of marrying Virginie once we were no longer in Bonde, he did not oppose the idea that we would one day leave. His sisters did not share his and his mother's point of view. Since Virginie had refused to sleep with their brother, they saw no reason to keep us there. They decided to reduce our daily ration of cassava and pondu. By starving us like that, they hoped to force us to leave by ourselves, because Sipi and his mother refused to throw us out. This treatment did not have the desired result, because other people in the village, particularly Ma Mundimi and to a lesser extent Fox, made up for this new shortage with their help.

Fox was a traditional healer known in all the villages throughout the area. He became interested in us the first day we returned to Bonde. We met him on the road when we arrived from Batsina and from that moment we were friends. Every day he brought us fish and from time to time bananas, palm nuts, avocados, and other fruits. When the season for fish was over, he brought caterpillars and game especially for us. He regularly made palm oil to sell, and he never failed to save some for us. At the beginning I thought that his friendship was disinterested, and I had trouble understanding how someone who knew us so little, and who on top of it was not rich, could spend so much on us. It was only when he began to make advances to me that I understood that he hoped to profit from his investment. I rejected Fox's advances very politely because Musa had warned us about the young men in the village. He accused them of sorcery and advised us to be charming with all those who came to pay us court. If we rejected them rudely, we risked becoming the victims of bad spells, which they would not hesitate to cast on us.

I relied on the religious beliefs of the villagers to make Fox wait. At Batsina as well as Bonde I had introduced myself as Virginie's mother. When they asked me about my husband, I said he had died at Bukavu. By presenting myself as a married woman, a mother of grown children, I hoped to get more respect from the villagers. I asked Fox to wait for the end of my mourning, which, according to our customs had to last a year, during which time I was forbidden to know another man. This little lie worked, and even though from time to time he couldn't help reviving his suit, Fox accepted that he had to wait for the end of my presumed mourning before he could seriously court me. While waiting, he continued to help us. Up until our departure from Bonde, Fox remained one of the few people I could always count on. More than the muscular proposals of Ma Marie's husband, Fox reminded me of the precariousness of our situation. Would we one day have to give ourselves to men we didn't love so that we could survive? I remembered that in Bukavu I had met young girls from the university, teachers and elementary students who, during the genocide and even in the camps, had been forced to marry soldiers in order to be fed and protected. From time to time I lacked understanding for some of them because I didn't really ask myself about the deeper reasons that had pushed them to this extreme. Now that Fox reminded me that his help did not come without a price, and that I would have to give my body in repayment, I understood all these women who before me had found themselves faced with this alternative and who had chosen to give themselves rather than die.

In addition to Fox, others whom we had not known during our first stay in Bonde were interested in us. Many of them had never seen a refugee close up and they were curious to hear women speak good French. Among our new acquaintances was Jérôme. He lived in Bokenge, about six kilometers from Bonde. He was university educated and had been a teacher and prefect at a secondary school in Mbandaka. Like many other educated Zairians, he had gone back to agriculture because he couldn't feed himself on a teacher's salary. People thought he was a madman. He was angry and violent, and young women feared meeting him when they were in the forest. He had been married several times, but all his wives left him because he beat them. The villagers said they had seen him running through the streets of the village behind his naked wives, beating them on the buttocks. He had wanted to marry one of the three Rwandan girls living with Musa before they were taken to Mbandaka by the bounty hunters, but Musa was against it. All of the villagers had advised the young girls to refuse his advances. Jérôme had fallen back on refugees because none of the girls in the Bokatola area wanted anything to do with him.

Sipi introduced us to Jérôme. He was about fifty and spoke very good French. He came to Bonde to see us at least three times a week, and often brought us corn, coffee beans, caterpillars, and sometimes brought fish. With his corn we prepared tshisekedi, named for one of the leaders of the opposition to Mobutu who had, at that time, become prime minister. Under his mandate, the region had experienced a period of such scarcity that people survived by eating a sort of cornmeal porridge seasoned with palm oil. They gave this new dish the name tshisekedi, since, according to them, he was responsible for their misery. It wasn't only in Equateur that the name Tshisekedi was used this way. In Maniema, for example, children with kwashiorkor were called "the children of Tshisekedi."[3] When Jérôme brought the corn, he got into the habit of grinding it and making tshisekedi himself. In an area where food preparation was women's work, it was considered bizarre behavior, but Jérôme didn't mind. Nevertheless, one noticed that the other villagers disapproved of

---

3. *Kwashiorkor* is a condition that results from inadequate protein intake. It can be corrected by improving calorie and protein intake if treatment is not started too late, but full growth and height will never be achieved. If treatment is delayed, kwashiorkor can be fatal. Severe kwashiorkor may result in permanent mental and physical impairment.

his behavior. They showed it in different ways. The women, for example, refused to give him their mortars and Sipi's sisters would not loan him their pans. Toward the end of our stay in Bonde, he prepared the tshisekedi at his house and brought it already cooked.

Jérôme made all these efforts because he hoped to make me his wife. That was all he talked about when he came to see me. He never stopped reminding me that the hospitality at Sipi's house would not last forever and that no other family in the village could take over our food and lodging for free. Since we didn't have the money to pay for the services that people rendered, we had no other choice than to take a husband, preferably him, for several reasons: He was educated. He had many hectares of palms, coffee, cocoa trees, and cassava. He had a big house. At the end of the coffee season, he would have money to buy us clothes. Later he would help us go to Mbandaka and Kinshasa to make contact with our families and friends. He had a family in Kinshasa that was very well off. And I couldn't find a better match! If, from time to time, I hadn't seen a glimmer of something in his eyes that made me doubt his sanity, I might have been tempted to believe these speeches and follow the example of some of his wives who had left comfortable families in Mbandaka to follow him to the village, and bitterly regretted it later.

In the Mongo villages help didn't only come from available men interested in single women. Ya Pepe was one exception and Ma Mundimi was a real salvation. We got to know her during our first stay in Bonde. At that time she had offered us pondu à la mosaka, as she did for all the refugees who passed by. She lived with her son, Itsinge. In addition to him, she had two other sons who lived in the village, one of whom was a trader. Her youngest daughter was married in a neighboring village, and her other children lived in Kinshasa. From our first day back in Bonde, Ma Mundimi took us under her wing and came to see us very early every morning and again in the afternoon. She always had all sorts of books with her: ancient history, instruction books for learning Lingala, books on French and calculus. Where did these books come from? I never knew. She called them her Bible and read the word of God in them. I was the only one in the villages to whom she would lend her "Bible." She often brought us something to eat, palm nuts, or fish. As long as Sipi's family took care of us, Ma Mundimi's interest in us was limited to these visits and little presents. Later, when she realized, as did many others in the village, that our hosts were not giving us enough to eat, she began to invite us for dinner. Toward the end of our time in Bonde, we took all of our meals at her house.

Ma Mundimi lived on the charity of the villagers. Every day she went to the surrounding villages to beg. She had, in addition to her own children, people who regularly gave her cassava, palm nuts, and from time to time, fish or caterpillars. Rare were the days when she returned empty-handed. When she wanted money for chikwanga or tobacco, she stood by the road and asked for money from all the men who went by. Many gave it to her so that they wouldn't have to listen to her shouts and insults. When she decided to take us under her protection, she had to travel farther and ask more people to get enough to feed two extra mouths. No matter what time it was when she returned from her "tours," she cooked for us, and when the food was ready, she came to call us. One day when she got back later than usual, she was so tired that she wanted to go straight to bed, but she remembered that we had probably not had anything to eat that day and she prepared food for us first. She came to get us up at ten so that we could eat, which was a pleasant surprise, since we had gone to bed with empty stomachs. A real mother could not have done more. Some people from the village had tried to dissuade Ma Mundimi from helping us, telling her that by helping Rwandan women, she exposed herself to being killed by Kabila's soldiers. Each time she got so angry with them and shouted so many insults at them that they didn't dare talk to her any more.

She was so worried about us that she stopped smoking so she could use the money that she normally spent for tobacco on food for us. Everyone who gave us something to eat became her friend. She could even accept my speaking French with Jérôme when he brought us fish, chikwanga, or tshisekedi. Usually she didn't like to hear me speaking French because, according to her, everyone would know right away that I was a foreigner, and that wasn't good for us. According to her, since I still couldn't speak Lingala, it was better to keep quiet. And in addition, the people who came to listen to me speak were not all well-intentioned. Fox was also allowed to come see me at her house if he brought some meat or fish. When her son Itsinge came back from the forest with cassava and caterpillars, we could talk together all day long in French without her complaining, though some days she was irritated when we talked longer than half an hour.

She was very sad when, at first, we didn't want to eat caterpillars. In the Bokatola area caterpillars begin to fall out of the trees at the beginning of the rainy season in September. The villagers go from collecting fish to collecting caterpillars. Since our arrival people had bragged about their nutritional value. They told us that they were as delicious as fish and just as rich in protein. The Sisters at the Health Center at Boteka bought them to grind into a powder for babies. Finally they convinced us that they were delicious, and we waited for September when we could enjoy them. But when they began to fall, we realized that they looked and moved just like the caterpillars that we knew in Rwanda. Every time that they suggested that we eat them, I gagged.

It was Itsinge, Ma Mundimi's son, who got us to eat them the first time. That day we had come as usual to Ma Mundimi's. Itsinge was alone at the house, his mother having gone to another village. He had gathered a whole basket of spiny orange caterpillars in the forest. When we arrived, he was busy preparing them, à la mosaka. At first we turned down his invitation to share his meal, because, even cooked, they looked like living caterpillars. Itsinge was not discouraged by our looks of disgust and categorical refusal. He succeeded in convincing us to taste one after remembering that as educated people, we were not allowed to reject something without tasting it first. Also, given the state of our health, refusing to eat caterpillars was a luxury we could not afford. It was mostly to prove to him that we were educated that we agreed to try his dish. The most difficult part was just taking the caterpillar and moving it toward our mouths. Once the first bite was swallowed, the rest followed easily. It was good that we reconsidered. Ma Mundimi jumped for joy when, at her return, she heard the good news. From that time on we had caterpillars at almost every meal.

Our relationship with Itsinge had not always been that good. When we first were in Bonde he had made a bad impression on us. Perhaps it was because he told us that the best thing that could happen to the refugees was for them to be repatriated. After walking almost two thousand kilometers through the forest, after having miraculously escaped the slaughter of the refugees by the Banyamulenge rebels, among whom were Rwandan soldiers, we found it difficult to accept a speech like that. After we realized that people in Western Zaire were not well informed about what was happening in the eastern part of their country, we didn't hold Itsinge's original opinions against him. In fact the villagers had been informed in bits and pieces and believed that the rebels only hated Mobutu and that the Banyamulenge guerillas were an internal problem in Zaire. They refused to believe that, over as great a distance as that which separated Bukavu and Goma, they would relentlessly follow and kill us. Like most of his countrymen, Itsinge was unaware of the tragedy that had shaken Rwanda since 1990. He had never heard of the Hutu/ Tutsi issue before refugees came through his village. In fact there were only two people who understood why, as a person in charge of an NGO, I could not return to Rwanda without running certain risks: Ya Pepe, to whom I had explained my situation thoroughly, and a retired employee of the Airport Authority. This old man had a radio and from time to time followed what was happening in Rwanda. One day he even sent someone to tell me that eight employees of an NGO had been killed in Rwanda. That showed me that it was too soon to return there. The other villagers began to believe what we were telling them after seeing the rebels at work in Mbandaka and the surrounding villages.

By visiting his mother, we got to know Itsinge better and appreciate him. He had done three years of postprimary education and spoke French very well. We spent hours talking and discussing various things. His mind was more open than most of the men in the village, even those who had their humanities diplomas. He no doubt owed that to the fact that in his youth he had been head of a traditional dance troupe. He had traveled extensively in the province and met many people from different walks of life. It was during one of these trips that he met his first wife. He encouraged us to learn Lingala, because, he said, we did not know how much longer we would be in the village and we should try to integrate ourselves as quickly as possible. With his large size and eyes that sparkled when he smiled, Itsinge was not without charm. I think that if I had stayed at Bonde and if I had had to marry there, I would have chosen him for a husband. His first wife, who had grown up in Kinshasa, and their three children lived in her village of origin, about ten kilometers from Mbandaka, where they had a lot of land. Itsinge wanted to marry a second wife who would stay with his mother at Bonde, and Ma Mundimi clearly saw her son's interest in me. That, however, did not prevent her from mocking him because of his interest in lazy women.

With Ma Mundimi we had a kind of relationship that we had never been able to have with mentally healthy people, except perhaps Ya Pepe. For her we were not poor refugees to whom one gives food out of charity, or women with whom you could sleep for a few bags of fish or caterpillars. She was among those rare individuals who, behind the mask of misery, saw the women we had once been and respected us. From time to time she was angry with us when we did something she didn't like. Her anger was like what she showed her son when he did not give her money for food or when he came back from the forest without bringing cassava or palm nuts. She also often made us laugh. When speaking of our suitors, for example, she said: "How can these men, who are from Mwanda, hope to marry you, who are from Rome?" For her, Mwanda represented Hell and Rome was Paradise. In Mwanda they ate cassava and pondu without salt, whereas in Rome they ate rice, fish, and meat.

Ma Mundimi was very funny, which few of the villagers appreciated, because she alone dared to tell people the truth. For example she loved to make fun of my weak arms and legs. She loved to tell me "The men who want to marry you are idiots. How could anyone want to marry a woman like you with limp legs, who doesn't know how to do anything? Would you know how to bring a basketful of firewood, cassava, and pondu back from the forest like the women of Bokatola do?" Although everyone in the village told Virginie, who had put on a lot of weight, that she was beautiful, Ma Mundimi said that she looked like a big fat fish. She compared her to one of her sons who was too fat but whom she loved a lot because he gave her money for tobacco. We didn't take offense at her teasing, because she accompanied it with a tender smile. She loved to go to religious ceremonies organized by the Brothers of Christ, where one of her sons was a member. When she got back she made us all laugh by imitating the way everyone prayed. Another thing that amused us was her habit of talking to animals. She spoke to them as if they were human. One day Itsinge came back from the forest with caterpillars. Since they were still alive, some got out of the basket and wandered around the house. When Ma Mundimi would come across one, she would pick it up and put it in the basket saying: "You are really stupid to think about escaping when I want to cook you for dinner." Sometimes, when we came to her house, we would find her deep in conversation with Ma Ndumba, Itsinge's goat. She talked to us about her as if she were an old friend.

When we wanted to annoy her, we talked about Mobutu. Already when we came through the village the first time, she attacked anyone who said anything good about Mobutu. She said she was the wife of Kabila, Lumumba, Tshisekedi, or Isidore Bakanja. Where did this animosity against Mobutu come from? I never knew. Her mind had been fragile for about ten years. Her children had done everything to have her cared for, but in vain. The nearest psychiatric center was in Kinshasa, 930 kilometers away and you had to have a lot of money to get help in Zaire. Had her mental deterioration been the result of the socioeconomic situation in Zaire, which had begun a breakneck downhill slide that forced many Zairians to leave their work in the cities and return to the villages and go back to agriculture? Did Ma Mundimi still remember this period? While people with sound minds quickly forget and want to put their misfortunes behind them, had Ma Mundimi's mind hung onto the time when only Mobutu was guilty? While the other villagers saw Tshisekedi as the one responsible for the current crisis, Ma Mundimi thought of him as a liberator since he opposed Mobutu. In the same way, when Kabila came to power, she accepted him since he fought Mobutu. In this she proved herself to be more consistent than the rest of the villagers.

Ma Mundimi's crises came most often when something annoyed her or someone went against her wishes. When she had a crisis, she took a little drum that she always kept on her bed and began weeping and beating it with both hands. While she wept she often repeated the name of Isidore Bakanja. At first I thought that it was her husband's name, but later I learned that it was a martyred Congolese priest. Her crises could come when she was preparing a meal. She didn't stop, but instead continued to cook while singing and weeping. When we arrived for the meal, she would stop crying and beating her drum while she served us and then, excusing herself for not being able to eat with us, she would begin again. At these times we didn't stay long. Seeing her in this state was very depressing.

After we had been in Bonde a little over a month, Sipi's grandmother had some serious health problems. For many years she had suffered from a strangulated hernia, which was getting worse from year to year. When the latest attack came, the family decided she should have an operation, but because they did not have enough money, they could only take her to the little clinic operated by a medical assistant, which was not equipped to treat her. After a week in the hospital, her condition did not improve, and on top of it she got dysentery. The children took her out of the clinic, because with this new illness, the medical expenses were too high and they couldn't afford it. The old woman could not go back to her own house, since she needed constant care, so the children decided to take her to Sipi's mother's house. To make room they moved us to a room in the house that Sipi was building beside his mother's. At the same time Ma Eyenga's fiancé came to visit his in-laws. For Sipi's sisters and all those who wanted us to leave, this visit came just at the right time, and Ma Eyenga's fiancé became their ally. He came from a village close to Ingende, where Kabila's soldiers were stationed. Whenever anyone came from the outside, the villagers thought that he had good information and that what he said was the word of God.

Our relations with Sipi's sisters were at their worst. For several days they had tried to convince their mother to send us away, but she wouldn't listen to them. As usual, she told them that she would rather be killed by Kabila's soldiers than show us the door.

While Sipi's mother was at the clinic at her mother's bedside, the rest of the family came up with a plan. A credible story to tell Sipi's mother to convince her to send us away had been found. Her daughters and son-in-law told her, in the presence of the whole family, that her name was on a list at Mbandaka because she sheltered refugees. She could expect a visit from Kabila's soldiers any day. A heated discussion followed. One part of the family wanted us thrown out right away and the other was against it. The final decision was in Sipi's mother's hands, but her family and the neighbors put so much pressure on her that she had to ask us to leave. Sipi remained opposed to this decision, but after they harassed her for three days, Ma Ndumba gave in. She took our belongings out of the house and put them in the road. An argument broke out between mother and son. She wavered when they called out from the house that the grandmother had died. Those who were there interpreted it as a punishment from God for throwing us out. The night before, the old woman's health had been considerably better and her children had begun to return to their own homes because they thought she was out of danger.

The decision to send us away was put off during the seven days of mourning. The grandmother's death was followed by that of her sister, who also died of dysentery, which they called "red diarrhea." This gave us another seven days of respite. After her death I then got red diarrhea.

Ever since I had arrived in the area of Bokatola in April I had had diarrhea at least once a month. In the absence of medicine, I treated myself with coffee and grilled cassava and didn't eat fish or pondu. The last time that I had had diarrhea was during August. Coffee and grilled cassava didn't help and I chewed medicinal herbs that Fox and Jérôme gave me. This time I again resorted to Fox's herbs, but without results. I didn't have the money to buy antibiotics, and there was no one else in the village who could help me.

The friends I still had didn't dare come visit me for fear of being contaminated. I have to admit that the death of the two old women from the same disease did not put my mind at ease either. Only Musa and Ma Mundimi loved me enough to run the risk. A traveling trader who came through the village gave Virginie a few anti-inflammatory tablets and vitamins. Even though neither of these was indicated for red diarrhea, I was in such a critical situation that simply the sight of them revived my spirits. As was to be expected, they had no effect at all, and I continued to have more and more bloody diarrhea. The only thing left to do was wait for death. Musa, who had gone to another village, hurried back when he heard I was ill. He made me drink juice made from orange tree roots. This medicine, which I did not believe in, worked miracles. Two days of treatment was enough to stop the diarrhea. I was completely cured by the time that the funeral wake for the second grandmother had ended. During the seven days that it lasted, Sipi's family had had time to discuss our situation again and had convinced his mother that it would be better for the whole family to send us away. Why risk the lives of the entire family for people they didn't even know? Sipi allowed himself to give in. Our game was up.

Since it would have been stupid to let us go without recovering part of the expense of having kept us for the last two months, they decided to deliver us up to the UNHCR and collect the bounty. For someone from Bonde, twenty American dollars was a small fortune. Sipi decided to take advantage of his uncle's return to Mbandaka by pirogue and send us with him. To convince us to go with him without asking too many questions, Sipi explained that village life didn't suit us, and that the best thing for us would be to go to Mbandaka, where it would be easier for us to contact our families and friends. The uncle was happy to take us. Since at first we didn't know that Sipi had had a change of heart, we did not see the plan behind his solicitude and quickly began to prepare for our trip to Mbandaka. People from the village came to tell us goodbye. Ma Marie, who had heard that we were leaving soon, came from Bombenga to wish us a safe trip. The day came when we were supposed to go, but Sipi's uncle left without us. The pirogue was too full to take two extra people on board, since the night before he had had a chance to buy several tons of corn that he could resell in Kinshasa, and he had opted for that plan. By mistake, one of Sipi's aunts told us they had decided to deliver us to the UNHCR and that it was Sipi who would get the bounty.

Sipi returned from Mbandaka a week later. He learned that we knew about his plan to turn us over to the UNHCR and knew that we would not let him do it, so he decided to ask us to leave. The reason he gave was that Virginie had refused to sleep with him and that I had supported her refusal. Under the circumstances he could no longer risk his life for us. Before throwing us out, knowing our fear of going to Mbandaka because of Kabila's soldiers and the bounty hunters, Sipi had taken the precaution of telling Jérôme what was happening so that he could come and try his luck. Both of them no doubt thought that Sipi's decision would put us in such a predicament that we would be happy to accept any offer of hospitality, even if it came from Jérôme. For us, going to his house or any other house in the village was out of the question. Itsinge and his brother had already offered us their hospitality if we ever were sent away from Sipi's family, but I had had enough of Bonde and its intrigues, daily humiliations, and advances from young men who could have been my sons. It was too much. We would go to Mbandaka. I hoped to see Ya Pepe at Batsina to ask his advice. But even if he wanted us to, I had decided not to stay.

Jérôme, who had come running when Sipi told him, did not appreciate either my decision to leave for Mbandaka the following morning or my refusal to go live with him. He started to insult me and call me names. In spite of my pleas, he refused to leave the room where we were living. He said he didn't take orders from foreigners and that he would spend the night in the room if he wanted to. Seeing the predicament that Jérôme had put us in and wanting to put an end to the scene he was making, Sipi's mother offered to let us spend the night in her house. We left our belongings in the room, taking only the clothes we were wearing and a blanket. The next morning I got up early to get ready to go. When I saw that the door to our room was already open, I was astonished that Jérôme had gotten up so early and, on a hunch, I went and took a look. The room was completely empty. Of the basket in which we kept our things, the blanket we had loaned him for the night, the dirty pots and pans, which had been on the floor, nothing remained. Jérôme had left with everything he had found in the room. All I had left to wear were threadbare shorts whose original color was completely unrecognizable, a long-sleeved T-shirt ripped at the neck, shoulders, and sleeves that belonged to Virginie, and a torn and faded pagne that was full of stains that Marcelline had given me before she left. Virginie wore jeans, a red sweater that was too hot for the equatorial climate and too small for her and a jacket that had once been olive green and was now dirty-white and stained.

When the family heard about the robbery, there was pandemonium and the situation reversed itself. Sipi's mother, one of her daughters and her son-in-law each took a machete and asked us to go with them to Jérôme's village to reclaim our belongings. Musa, Ma Mundimi and a few other young men from the neighboring villages came along too. Once there, Jérôme, in spite of pleas and threats, refused to give our belongings back to us. He considered them payment for the tshisekedi that he had made for us and other presents he had given us. After a day of discussion about everything he had taken, I only succeeded in getting him to return my Bible, which for me was the most important. I stayed calm. The people who were there were astonished at my attitude. However, for us, keeping calm had become a survival reflex, and it was a consequence of the divine will that had allowed us to survive all of our ordeals. We hoped to meet charitable souls on the road to Mbandaka who would give us what we needed, as had been the case at Bukavu and Tingi-Tingi.

After Jérôme's low blow, I didn't want to stay a day longer in Bonde. Overcome with pity, Sipi's mother offered to let us stay a few days more in the village so that we could prepare better for our departure, but I decided to go very early the next morning. That evening we went around the village to say goodbye to our friends. Some were sincerely touched by our departure, while others could hardly conceal their relief. Some villagers we didn't even know gave us food for the road. Up until that time I had avoided telling Ma Mundimi that we were going. I was a little afraid of provoking the tears that so often were the result of her not having gotten her way, and I was worried that she would refuse to let us go. On the other hand, I did not want to cause her pain by leaving without her blessing, after everything she had done for us. For a week she had been talking about our leaving, but she said that all three of us should go together by pirogue to Mpama. Once there we would leave for Kinshasa by boat. I don't know where this idea came from, but these words would come true in the near future. At that time it seemed like an impossible scenario. I decided to tell her Tuesday morning, the day we were leaving. I hoped that, faced with a fait accompli, she would accept our decision without too much discussion. I didn't know Ma Mundimi. She received the announcement of our precipitous departure badly and became really angry when she learned that we were going without provisions, without money, and without anyone to accompany us, at least to Mpama. Since I didn't want to hurt her, I decided to put our leaving off until the next day so that she could prepare some provisions for us. We spent this last night with Sipi's family and tried to forget the tensions of the last few days during our farewells.

11

The End of the Ordeal

WE LEFT BONDE the next morning with Ma Mundimi and Musa, to the complete indifference of the entire village. Musa went with us to the edge of town. Only Ma Mundimi wanted to go with us to Batsina, where she would leave us in the hands of Ya Pepe, whom she greatly respected. She was convinced that he would accompany us to Mpama and help us find a pirogue to take us to Mbandaka. Ma Mundimi was very insistent that we have reliable people with us. Since we were women and also refugees, she was afraid that we would be attacked. Four kilometers from Bonde, in Ikenge, she asked if we could rest for a while in a shed. She wanted to talk to us for the last time. While she was beginning to give us her parting advice on the attitude to adopt toward the people we would meet on the road, the pastor of the Episcopal Church in Bonde, who was coming back from a pastoral visit in Batsina, joined us. After another ten minutes a young man named Aigle came by. He had hurried on his bicycle from Bonde and was sweating profusely after having ridden so fast. He said he had heard from a family member who had just returned from Mbandaka that the hunt for refugees had begun again, and he came at the insistence of his father, who offered to take us in, to ask us to return to Bonde until the roads were safer.

Ma Mundimi looked like she had just been relieved of a great burden, but I was confused by this information from Aigle. In the past few days, many people had come from Mbandaka, and none of them had said anything about this resumption of the slaughter. Seeing my hesitation, Aigle suggested that I come back to the village to talk to his father myself. In the meantime Fox, who was back from Mpama, where he had gone to care for the sick, joined us. He supported Ma Mundimi and the others who were trying to convince me to accept Aigle's compromise. I was nervous about possible tension between Sipi's family, who had just thrown us out, and Aigle's family, who were prepared to let us stay with them. As it turned out, when his family had found out about the situation in Mbandaka, Aigle had gone to see Sipi to ask him to take us back for a few days. Sipi had replied that he wanted nothing to do with us, but if someone else wanted to take us in, he had no objections. After thinking about it, I decided to return to Bonde to talk to the young man and find out what he had to say. I also suggested that Virginie should go the next day to Batsina to ask Ya Pepe for his advice. I was so confused that I needed someone wise to help me sort out the situation and make a decision.

Aigle's father and the entire family were waiting for us. Even though they welcomed us warmly, I didn't feel as comfortable as I had when we had returned to Sipi's family two months earlier. Their smiles and consideration toward us were not enough to erase the deceptions and blows of the last few days. Ma Mundimi wanted to take us to her house, but Aigle managed to convince her that it was better for us to stay with him. She nevertheless had to see for herself that we would be well housed and fed, so she visited the house where we were going to spend the night and questioned the women about what they had cooked for lunch and what they were going to prepare for dinner. She apparently was satisfied by what she had seen and heard, because she told us goodbye with a smile. As soon as we arrived at Aigle's house I asked about the young man from Mbandaka. His father told me that he had gone to a neighboring village and would return the following morning. I never did see this young man. When we left Bonde for the last time, early the following afternoon, he still had not come back. Today I doubt his existence. Had this perhaps been a trick on the part of Aigle's father to get us to come back to the village?

Thursday morning Ya Pepe was away and Virginie did not go to Batsina as we had planned. In the late morning we went to Ma Mundimi's for our daily visit. She was waiting impatiently for us and had planned to feed us tshisekedi and pondu à la mosaka. Virginie had begun to grind the corn when I heard the sound of a motorcycle and a voice shouting: "They are over there." I jumped. I tried to banish a frightening thought from my mind: Had the hunt for refugees that the young man was talking about reached Bonde? Two or three minutes after the motorcycle went by, Ma Mundimi's eldest son came looking for us. He said that some whites, Americans, were looking for us but that we didn't have to be afraid because there were no soldiers with them and we could just tell them that we didn't want to leave the village. They could not force us to go with them. His words were reassuring, but I was far from calm. Bonde was not Batsina, and at the time of the first UNHCR visit, Ya Pepe had been there to defend us. At Bonde I could not hope for any such intervention. The people, for the most part, feared authority too much. Only Ma Mundimi would shout, but how seriously would they take the ravings of a madwoman?

The visitor, who was neither American nor white, was waiting for us in the courtyard of the compound that belonged to the village chief, surrounded by almost the entire village. When we got there, he stood up and greeted us warmly, which reassured me a little. In my heart I felt that someone so calm, so smiling and so polite would not take me by force to Mbandaka. There would always be a way to negotiate with him. After a short pause, which seemed like an eternity, he asked me if I were indeed Béatrice and showed me a photograph of myself, taken during my last stay in Belgium in 1995. I was a little worried. How could this man whom I had never seen know my name and have a photograph of me? I could not imagine that my suffering was almost at an end. Our visitor was named Mathieu and had been sent by an NGO in Mbandaka. When he told me this, I stood there dazed for several seconds. I cannot describe the joy that I felt when, after several seconds of uncertainty, I understood that my friends had finally found me. What I remember is hugging Virginie and laughing until I was out of breath. Ma Mundimi watched everything that was happening closely, and even calmly, contrary to what was normal for her. When she saw our joy, she understood that Mathieu was a friend and she began to dance around and insult the villagers who had behaved so badly toward us.

Mathieu had saved another big surprise for me. When I had calmed down and was sitting on a chair that the village chief had pulled up for me, he told me that Frans was with him. Even though I only knew one person with that name, I didn't understand right away whom Mathieu was talking about. I could not imagine that my friend Frans, who should have been tens of thousands of kilometers from Bonde, could be the same one Mathieu was telling me about. For once in my life, what happened to me surpassed my wildest dreams.

Frans had been my friend for a long time. Our friendship had begun in Gitarama in 1988 when I started my work at the Centre de Services Coopératives and it was based on a common belief in the African peasantry and a joint search for what our role would be as development workers.

In Bonde, I often dreamed of Frans. Once I had dreamed that he came to see me in the village and gave me a million new Zaires. Another time, he came back and gave me dollars. Since Irangi, Virginie and I had paid close attention to our dreams. Most of the time they came true or else announced events that would happen in the near future. On the other hand we didn't give much credence to dreams dealing with Frans's arrival in the village. We didn't want to be disappointed. To be sure, we enjoyed this idea, but we rejected it quickly so we could think about things that were more likely to happen. I mainly thought about looking for work teaching in a primary school or going to Mbandaka and teaching in a secondary school. One of Sipi's cousins, who was a student in Mbandaka, had suggested that we go live with him, because his parents had a house there. Virginie would sell the bread that the young man made and I would look for work outside the house. Like many other promises we had been given, this one did not amount to anything. Sipi's cousin went back to Mbandaka without telling us. Anyway, living in Mbandaka and looking for work there would not have been possible until after all the Rwandan soldiers had left the area and after we had gotten official papers from Zaire. We had begun the process to obtain citizenship.

Frans's arrival in Bonde was the best thing that had happened to me since October 1996. During the two days that we were together I never stopped talking. I didn't let him get a word in edgewise, I had so much to talk about. I wanted to tell him everything that had happened to me in the last two years, and two days seemed too short to me. I told him pell-mell about Ma Mundimi, Ya Pepe, Tata Nsambe, Ngengeri, the Kumu family who had sheltered us at Tingi-Tingi, and Irangi, not caring about chronology. I told him about my sickness, Zuzu's death, Marcelline, hunger, being pursued by the rebels, the slaughter of refugees from

Bukavu to Mbandaka, the assassination of the former mayor of Nyaruhengeri and the conversation I had with him the evening before his death. I told him about the young girl who was dying, unnoticed by the other refugees, by the side of the road; the man who spit the pills back in my face because he was sick of suffering and wanted to die; the bandaged feet of four-year-old children on the burning pavement of the road; and about Jeanne and the other young women who died in child-birth in the camps and forests. I wanted to show how strong I was, to continue playing the role of the woman who was bothered by nothing, but at the same time I could not keep my voice from trembling a little when I recalled all the tragedy I had been through.

The village of Bonde gave us a farewell worthy of the highest dignitaries of the land. Mathieu and Frans's arrival had increased our prestige. The night before, they had thought we were good-for-nothing, dirty refugees, women who risked drawing reprisals from Kabila's soldiers down on the village, unsubmissive women who didn't even want to sleep with their men. Suddenly they understood that we were honorable women before the war and that a few months in the forest did not make us into the ragged beggars we seemed when we first entered their village. I understood them a little because it really was hard to believe that this gaunt old woman who wore an old pagne and a filthy T-shirt, who was losing her hair and whose body was covered with wounds and black spots was in charge of an NGO and had traveled throughout Africa and Europe. Sipi was the first to regret not having taken my word, because the few hundred dollars that Mathieu and Frans had to give to the people who had helped us would all have gone to him, if he had decided to keep us a few days longer.

The villagers formed an honor guard until the end of the village. Everyone seemed sorry to see us leave and tried to shake our hands and wish us bon voyage. I was enraged by these wonderful manners coming from people who the day before had let us leave with complete indifference. Ma Mundimi danced along with us for a few meters, but I saw sadness in her face. I said goodbye to her with a little tug at my heart. I felt considerable regret at leaving her like that, without knowing if I would ever see her again. Crazy or not, she had been a true mother to us. I will always thank the good Lord for having chosen her to be our protector during the two months we were in Bonde. Her insanity did not diminish her humanity. Musa and Fox were away when we left, and I was sorry to leave Bonde without thanking them one more time for all that they had done for us.

After leaving Bonde, we went to Bombenga to say goodbye to Ma Marie. Unfortunately we could not talk to her for as long as I would have liked, because she was seriously ill with dysentery. I hope that Musa's medicine, juice from orange tree roots, which I suggested that she take, had the same effect on her that it did on me. With her inimitable accent, she tried to say a few words in Kinyarwanda to Frans, after I told her that he spoke this language. Her husband wanted to be reimbursed for the care he had given me when I had malaria, but he didn't insist. He no doubt remembered that he had thrown us out in the middle of the night five months earlier. From Bombenga, we went to Batsina. I wanted to see Ya Pepe again. We had seen him only once since his family had turned us out. I had tried to see him, but all my attempts had failed, usually because he had gone to Mbandaka to sell cassava. Once again, he wasn't there. He had gone to Mbandaka a week earlier. It was with great sadness that I finally left without having seen the person who had been like a father to me, even though he was hardly older than I was. I could not forget that Ya Pepe had endured the absence of his wife for two weeks as well as the discontent of his entire family and all of his friends rather than put us out of his house. I also remembered the day that he had butted heads with the delegation from the UNHCR that wanted to force us to go to Mbandaka.

We spent the first night of our "return to life" in the village of Mpama. The motorized pirogue that had brought Frans and Mathieu from Mbandaka was waiting for us along with some new clothes. I was so happy to be wearing underclothes again, since our last underpants were either worn out or eaten by mites months ago. During dinner I let Frans talk for a while and tell me how he had found me in that little village at the end of the world. It hadn't been easy. The last news that he'd had of me dated from the February when I was still in the camp at Tingi-Tingi. After the destruction of the camp he had continued to follow the news of the refugees through information he got from watching television or on the radio or in the paper. These news broadcasts were always appalling, and he didn't hold out much hope of ever seeing me alive again. In May, Frieda, who had arrived in Congo-Brazzaville, had written to the European partners of the Collective. It was through her that he learned that I had arrived in Ingende. Frieda told them that she had left me at death's door. Since then, as there had been no other news of me, many of my friends thought that I had died. Some even had masses said for the repose of my soul. Others among them, who, contrary to all logic, continued to believe that I was still alive, prayed for me and sent me positive thoughts.

In July, Marcelline was repatriated to Rwanda and was able to go to my mother's house in Byumba. She gave her a complete rundown about the state of my health and exact information about the family that was sheltering me in Batsina. My mother knew where to find Frans, who at that time was on mission in Rwanda, and she brought him up to date. Frans was relieved to hear news of me, and he immediately sent the message to my Belgian friends who, since July, had unsuccessfully done everything possible to find me. Together they set everything in motion to locate me through their contacts in Zaire.

Difficulties with communication and safety interfered. Finally an opportunity presented itself when Frans had to participate at the General Assembly of Zairian NGOs in Lubumbashi in September. In early October he decided to make a detour into the Mbandaka area to try to find me. This decision was not without danger, since there was no guarantee of safety in the area, but Frans was not afraid to run risks, even big ones, when his friends' lives were in danger. In May 1994 he had come to a Rwanda torn by war and genocide. It was a big risk to take, because one died easily in those days.

At Mbandaka, Frans contacted the NGOs in the area. Helped by one of their staff, Mathieu, he began to search. Around Mbandaka, there were two villages named Batsina, but they did not know this. The first day, they went to the other Batsina, where they learned that no refugees had come through the village. Discouraged, they thought that Marcelline's information was inaccurate and were going to abandon the search, until they were informed by the villagers that there was another Batsina in Bokatola zone and that the Rwandan refugees had gone through there. That was how they arrived in the right Batsina the night before Frans had to go back to Kinshasa. It was their last attempt, and it was crowned with success. The first people they spoke to led them to Ya Pepe's house. His wife told them that we had left for Bonde. Four kilometers from Bonde they met the village chief. He confirmed the presence of two Rwandan women in the village, one of whom resembled the person they were searching for, and offered to serve as their guide. This is how the Lord arranges things. If, the night before, we had left for Mbandaka, if Aigle had not come to ask us to return to Batsina because the refugee hunt had begun again, which apparently was untrue, maybe we would have missed Frans and Mathieu! Frans was leaving the next day for Kinshasa, and could not have made another try. Since news travels fast in the villages, I would no doubt have learned that the so-called Americans were looking for me, and every time I heard the sound of a motor, I would have run to the forest to hide until the Americans who were hot on my heels would have disappeared. Would we have finally fallen into the hands of bounty hunters and been forcefully repatriated to Rwanda? Would we have stayed hidden in a village until Providence came to our aid? I think that the chances of our getting out would have been slimmer every day. Maybe we would have decided to marry a villager somewhere between Bonde and Mbandaka.

We finally got to Mbandaka on Friday, September 29, 1997, about a year after I left Bukavu. I arrived gaunt and weak, but healthy in body and mind. Virginie and I had just walked at least two thousand kilometers on foot. Frans left the same day for Kinshasa. We stayed in Mbandaka during the entire month of October. We needed to get Congolese identity cards and we had to find a boat that would agree to take us to Kinshasa. The idea of traveling by plane had been abandoned because of the presence of Rwandan soldiers at the airports at Mbandaka and Kinshasa. They would certainly have caused us problems. Even if we had Congolese identity cards and Congolese clothing, it would not have been difficult for a Rwandan to recognize our facial features.

Our stay in Mbandaka gave us a chance to see Ya Pepe. When he was already on the river going back to Batsina, the boatmen who brought us from Mpama told him we were there. Our reunion was warm. Along with Ma Mundimi, Ya Pepe was the only one who was truly happy that our troubles were over. When I was still in Batsina, he had insisted that I write my sisters who were in Europe to tell them about my situation. He devoted his first trip to Mbandaka to trying to find people who could send my letters, either by fax or regular mail. Unfortunately, all the people he contacted told him that it was too soon, that all the means of communication were still in the hands of Kabila's army. No one dared send a fax from a Rwandan. At that time you could be killed for less. Fear ruled Mbandaka, and many people did not dare to resume their normal activities. When we had to let Marcelline go because she was sick, Ya Pepe had insisted that she memorize all our co-ordinates. He said that my family could find me easily that way. I think he was as happy as we were to see that his tactic had worked.

When he came to see us at Mbandaka, I gave him two hundred American dollars to thank him for his hospitality. I knew very well that the money could never be enough to make up for everything he had done for us, but I wanted to make the gesture. He spent most of the money on sugar and tobacco. Seeing how much he had bought, we thought that he was going to open a little store in the village. We couldn't have been more mistaken. On his second visit, he told me what he had done with it. Ya Pepe had never forgiven his family for having taken advantage of his absence to send us away from Batsina and was looking for a way to make them pay for their treachery. When he arrived in Batsina with his provisions, many people came to see him to get the news. Ma Mundimi, Sipi, and other people from Bonde were there too. We weren't a danger for them any more, and the inhabitants of Batsina and Bonde were sorry we had gone and were interested in what had happened to us. Ya Pepe made them generous gifts from the sugar and tobacco that he had bought in Mbandaka. He told me later that in making this distribution he wanted to give a lesson in charity to every-one who had, not long ago, considered us to be no more than good-for-nothings, poor refugees from whom nothing could be expected. In doing so he hoped he could teach them to respect every person who came their way. The members of his family got nothing. He even gave the 350,000 new Zaires that I had given him for his wife to the young men in the village so that they could buy beer.

A week after his first visit, Ya Pepe rented a motorbike and came to see us again in Mbandaka. He brought us game and sweet potatoes, since we had told him that that was what one ate in Rwanda. He stayed three days with us and I took advantage of this to see the town with him, something I would not have dared to do alone. I went to the market and bought some pagnes so that I could turn myself into a real Congolese. He showed me the fort, where Kabila's rebels had killed thousands of refugees when they took the town the previous April. Virginie and I had been saved, but the horror continued to surround us. Many people in Mbandaka told us about these massacres, which they described as horrifying. Even women and children were killed without pity. The rebels, we were told, took babies by their feet and smashed their skulls on the walls of houses or put a bullet in their heads. Those who survived these acts of genocide had hidden with the local population or had been able to reach the surrounding forests.

In a friend's house, where a room had been prepared for us, our neighbors were a Zairian family who had been displaced by the rebels. Around ten soldiers had entered their house during the night when the husband was away in Kinshasa. They first tied the wife's hands behind her back as if she were a criminal. Then they aimed their guns at her six children to force her to tell them where the money was hidden. When she was slow to answer a question, one of the soldiers took her youngest son, who was barely a year old, by his feet. The child's head was hanging down. The soldier put a pistol to the child's temple and threatened to put a bullet in his head if she didn't answer quickly. The mother couldn't stand what she was seeing and fainted. The soldiers let her lie there and left with everything they could carry: her clothes as well her husband's and children's, kitchen utensils, pots and pans, furniture, and money. Before they went they put bullets in the ceiling, doors and windows, making the house uninhabitable.

Two weeks after we got to Mbandaka, we fell ill. Virginie had malaria, intestinal parasites, and sinusitis. As for me, the diarrhea that I had had since Batsina came back. This time it wasn't bloody, but it looked very much like cholera. Orange tree root juice did not help and I had to go to the dispensary. Luckily they had medicine, and a few days of treatment were enough to put me back on my feet. We left Mbandaka at the end of October. Mathieu accompanied us and took care of all the formalities so that we would not be seen. Although Virginie could easily pass as a Congolese, at least to the Congolese, I was more easily identifiable as a Rwandan. Before embarking, we got a lemonade at the hangar of the Office National des Transports (ONATRA), where the Rwandan refugees had tried to hide when the town fell to the rebels seven months earlier. The exterior signs of this tragedy had been erased, but people still spoke of it.

We left Mbandaka in late October and covered the eight hundred kilometers between Mbandaka and Kinshasa in a week, on board a boat transporting merchandise. Thanks to Mathieu we were able to find room in a little cubbyhole, which we shared with four other women, their children and their baskets of salted, smoked fish. In addition to the characteristic odor emanating from the fish, maggots crawled out of them by the hundreds. They climbed up the walls and fell down on us. Others got under the covers with us, and we found them in the most unexpected places, like our buttocks, thighs, and chests. They were so invasive I was afraid they would enter my most private places. The smell of fish mingled with the odor of the excrement of the pigs and goats tied to our door.

On the river, our boat was stopped often at military checkpoints or by soldiers who simply wanted money and shot at boats that they wanted to pull alongside and rob. Every time that the boat was stopped, we pulled our covers up over our heads and pretended to be sick, quietly praying that the soldiers wouldn't search until they found us. The boat could end up at a checkpoint for several hours, depending on the nego- tiations between the soldiers and the crew over the amount to be paid for the right to pass. Kabila's soldiers were just as interested as Mobutu's had been in easy money, and they robbed good citizens with as much enthusiasm as their predecessors. Once we had to wait for the arrival of the mistress of the commanding officer so that we could take her to the next stop. If, sick of waiting, a captain of a boat decided to weigh anchor and leave, the soldiers pursued him in their launch. When they caught up, they would subject the entire boat to a beating and demand a huge bribe. The number of checkpoints on the river had tripled since Kabila had come to power, and it took five or six days to make a trip that should have lasted three or four. All the passengers complained about Kabila's regime. At least during Mobutu's time you paid, but you were rarely beaten, they said. In the whole province of Equateur, Ma Mundimi must have been the only person who liked Kabila.

We arrived in Kinshasa at the beginning of November. I will never forget our entrance into the harbor, which was filled with pirogues, water lilies, barges, and boats. A crowd was waiting for our boat to dock. Mostly they were traders who had come to buy fish at a good price, but the wives of the sailors had also come to welcome their spouses. During the trip I was struck by the attitude of the crew toward their wives. They were very kind to them and some of them even helped with the cooking. They exchanged smiles and little pats on the bottom. For Africans, as I knew them, such an attitude was strange. When I mentioned this to Mathieu, he told me that most of these men had wives and children in Kinshasa and were traveling with their mistresses. Since the wives were often waiting when the boat docked, battles between wives and mistresses were common. Mathieu laughed so much when he told me this story that I thought it was just one more joke, but it wasn't. Our boat had just docked when the wives of the crew burst on board. The smartest mistresses just had time to lock themselves in the toilets and the cabins. One who was still on the bridge was grabbed by dozens of hands, which began to tear out her hair and rip her clothes. They bit her ears. She defended herself as well as she could but she would have succumbed to her adversaries if it had not been for the intervention of the other passengers, who interceded to shield her from the betrayed wife and all of her friends and sisters who took part in the melee. The husband had watched the whole scene without lifting a finger. He must have been used to it.

At Kinshasa we stayed with friends from Bukavu for five months, the time it took to get the necessary exit papers. As long as we were on Congolese soil we could not feel safe, since there still were Rwandan soldiers in the streets of Kinshasa. After Mbandaka, we avoided speaking Kinyarwanda, even when we were alone, so that we would not be spotted. When we left the house we put on pagnes and wigs and the style of makeup worn by women in Kinshasha at that time, but even with this disguise I dreaded being recognized. One day I had to go to the hospital. When I was waiting to see the doctor, a woman asked me if I were Rwandan. Luckily I had dark skin, otherwise she would have noticed my distress. My heart beat wildly and I suddenly felt feverish. I responded that I was a Shi from Bukavu, but I didn't look at her for fear that she would see the terror in my eyes. I spent the five months in Kinshasa in our room or in the living room when there were no visitors. Even my friends from Bukavu couldn't come see me for fear that the intelligence services would find out I was there. To pass the time, I watched television for twelve to fourteen hours a day. The rest of the time I slept. On the rare occasions when I left the house to go to the hospital or to mass, I was terrified by the thought of running into Rwandan soldiers. The sight of a man in uniform, even several dozen meters away, made me break out in a heavy sweat. If possible I crossed to the other side of the street so I wouldn't meet him.

I left Kinshasa for Belgium at the beginning of April. We had to pass through the last checkpoint, the one at the airport, which was always manned by Rwandan soldiers. Our friends had thought of everything, and had used every possible artifice to transform us into real *kinoises*.[1] We wore pagnes, stylish braids, and makeup. Even the way we walked had not been forgotten. Our friends went with us as far as the waiting room and took care of all the formalities. I made myself very small to avoid being noticed. It was, surprisingly, Virginie who was caught by the dreaded Rwandan soldiers. There were three of them who intercepted her after she had left the waiting room and was already on the tarmac walking toward the airplane. They asked for her passport. One of the three soldiers told the others in Kinyarwanda that she was Rwandan, not Congolese, and that he recognized her from Gitarama. Since many Tutsi students from her school had joined the RPF between 1992 and 1993, it is possible that this soldier was an old schoolmate and that he had actually recognized her. No matter how hard she tried to get her passport back by speaking loudly in Swahili and Lingala, her hands on her hips, just like a real Congolese, it didn't work. Luckily one of our friends who worked in security at Ndjili Airport came to see if she had gotten on board. The three soldiers gave the passport back when he asked for it, and he walked with Virginie to the plane to prevent further incidents.

I arrived in Belgium the day after I left Kinshasa. It was with unmitigated joy that I saw my friends and my sister and her little eight-month-old girl, born while I was still in the forest. I tasted the pleasure of hugging them to my chest the way we do in Rwanda, without having to fear that I would be recognized. Starting to speak Kinyarwanda freely again was the most difficult. Every time I spoke a word in Kinyarwanda, I looked left and right to see if there were any soldiers in the wings. Only when I noticed that we were surrounded by whites did I remember that I had arrived in Belgium and that I did not need to be afraid any more. During the first few days, it happened from time to time that I

---

1. A *kinoise* is an inhabitant of Kinshasa.

trembled at the sight of a man in uniform, but afterwards I remembered that I was in a law-abiding country and calmed down. Now, I no longer fear speaking Kinyarwanda, and I can even ask a policeman for directions. Even if I still dream from time to time about soldiers from the RPF, the fear I feel is less intense. Is this the end of the nightmare?

◆

ACRONYMS

PERSONAL CHRONOLOGY

CHRONOLOGY OF POLITICAL EVENTS
IN RWANDA

Acronyms

ADI-Kivu	Action de Développement Intégré du Kivu
ANV	Active Non-Violence (Non-Violence Active)
ARNR	L'Action pour la Réconciliation Nationale au Rwanda (Action for National Reconciliation in Rwanda)
CCOAIB	Conseil de Concertation des Organisations d'Appui aux Initiatives de Base
CSC	Centre de Services aux Coopératives (Service Center for Cooperatives)
CZSC	Contingent Zaïrois Chargé de la Sécurité dans les Camps (Zairian Contingent in Charge of Security in the Camps)
FAR	Forces Armées Rwandaises (Rwandan Armed Forces)
FAZ	Forces Armées Zaïroises (Zairian Armed Forces)
GOMN	Groupement des Observateurs Militaires Neutres (Neutral Military Observers Group)
IAMSEA	L'Institut Africain et Mauricien des Statistiques et de l'Économie Appliquée (African and Mauritian Institute of Statistics and Applied Economics)
ICTR	International Criminal Tribunal of Rwanda
INERA	Institut National d'Études et de Recherches Agronomiques (National Agronomic Institute for Research and Study)
INGABO	Ishyirahamwe Nyarwanda riGira inama Abahinzi Borozi (Advisory Association of Agriculturists and Stockbreeders of Rwanda)
JRS	Jesuit Refugee Services
MDR	Mouvement Démocratique Républicain (Democratic Republican Movement)
MRND	Mouvement Républicain National pour la Démocratie et le Développement, formerly Mouvement Révolutionnaire National pour le Développement (National Republican Movement for Development and Democracy)
NGO	Nongovernmental Organization
NRA	National Resistance Army

ONATRA	Office National des Transports (National Transport Office)
PL	Parti Libéral (Liberal Party)
PSD	Parti Social Démocrate (Social Democratic Party)
RFI	Radio France Internationale
RPF	Rwandan Patriotic Front
SCR	Service Central de Renseigements (Central Intelligence Service)
UNAMIR	United Nations Assistance Mission in Rwanda
UNHCR	United Nations High Commissioner for Refugees
WFP	World Food Program

Personal Chronology

5.19.1959	Born in Byumba
1964–71	Primary school in Miyove
1971–74	First three years of secondary education at Groupe Scolaire de Byumba. The student uprising erupts in 1973 during my second year.
1974–78	Studied economics at the Lycée Notre Dame de Cîteaux in Kigali. I meet Esther and Spéciose.
1978–81	Baccalaureate degree from the Université Nationale du Rwanda. I meet Marie.
1981–83	Civil servant working at the l'Office Nationale de la Population (National Population Office)
1982–85	Degree in sociology from the Université catholique de Louvain, Belgium
8.1.1986	Death of my father. I have to leave the Ministry of the Interior, where I had worked for six months, to look for a job with a better salary.
11.1986	I am hired by the Banque Continentale Africaine du Rwanda (African Continental Bank of Rwanda). I meet Goretti.
11.1988	I am named director of the CSC. I move to Gitarama. I meet Frans.
12.1992	I leave CSC. Spéciose replaces me.
1.1993	I launch a support program for the women's associations in Byumba. I move back to Kigali.
2.1993	Widespread attacks by RPF rebels. My family flees the fighting and twenty-five people come to live with me. Bakunda leaves Nyacyonga camp and comes to live with me.
8.4.1993	Signing of the Arusha Accords. Some of my family members return to their homes. My mother and a dozen others stay with me. There are sixteen children and adults sharing the house.
4.6.1994	Assassination of Habyarimana.
4.8.1994	My family and I flee the fighting. We find shelter in Gahanga.

4.9.1994	We again flee and find refuge in the neighborhood of Kabeza. A week later we return to my house.
5.1994	I succeed in evacuating my family to Gikongoro and Gitarama. My mother, youngest sister, a niece and her baby, and I stay with Spéciose at Gitarama.
6.1.1994	Gitarama is attacked by the RPF. We flee to Cyangugu with Spéciose's family and arrive a week later. At Gikongoro I escape being killed.
6.1994	Members of the Rwandan development NGOs create the Collective of Rwandan NGOs in order to help those who had been displaced by the war.
7.1994	I move with my family to the refugee camp at ADI-Kivu in Zaire (now the Democratic Republic of the Congo). My brothers and sisters, from whom I had been separated since May, join us. We begin activities in support of the refuges under the auspices of the Collective of Rwandan NGOs. Belgian, French, and Dutch NGOs agree to finance the programs of the Collective.
8.1994	I am chosen to head the self-organization program for the women in the camps. I move to INERA camp in order to be near the groups with whom the Collective is working.
8.1995	Forced repatriation of the Rwandan and Burundian refugees from the camps in eastern Zaire. Many members of the Collective leave Zaire for safer countries. I am named head of the Collective in Bukavu.
2.1996	I move to a house in Bukavu in order to be closer to my work.
10.28.1996	Bukavu falls to the Banyamulenge rebels. I go to stay with Frieda, a colleague from work, at INERA camp.
11.1.1996	The camp at INERA is destroyed. I flee in the direction of Kisangani through Kahuzi-Biega National Park with Bakunda and Assumpta.
11.1996	We are prisoners of the Tiri militia for two weeks in the village of Irangi, one hundred kilometers from Bukavu. I find Virginie again. Ex-FAR soldiers from Goma who are passing through the area come to our rescue and free us. Marcelline, Mukunzi, and Gisimba join us again in Walikale.
12.1996	About four hundred kilometers from Bukavu, at Tingi-Tingi, soldiers from the Zairian army force us to stop. We stay there for two months. Zuzu joins us. Thérèse and Jeanne both die.
2.28.1997	The camp at Tingi-Tingi is destroyed. We flee at night. I pick up two other children who have been separated from their families.

3.1.1997	We cross the Lubutu River. Shooting breaks out and in the confusion I lose the two children I had picked up the night before.
3.1997	I arrive at the village of Obilo, located eighty-two kilometers south of Kisangani, where the Red Cross plans to set up a new camp for the Rwandan refugees. I learn that Kisangani has fallen into rebel hands. I decide to leave for Congo Brazzaville via Mbandaka, the capital of Equateur Province. Gisimba, Mukunzi, and Bakunda decide to stay at Obilo. I leave with Marcelline, Assumpta, Virginie, and Zuzu. The long trek through the equatorial forest begins.
4.1997	In the area of Boende, about five hundred kilometers from Mbandaka, our route once again crosses that of the rebels. Many of our companions on the road, among them Kabeza, are killed.
5.1997	I arrive exhausted and sick in Bombenga, about one hundred twenty kilometers from Mbandaka and am taken in by a Mongo peasant married to a woman from Bukavu. Virginie, Marcelline, and Zuzu are with me. We were separated from Assumpta a week earlier. After news that rebels are in the area, the family takes us to a hiding place in the forest, where we stay for a week. Zuzu dies. I leave for Mbandaka with Marcelline and Virginie. I arrive in the village of Batsina exhausted and unable to take another step. I am welcomed along with my little family by Ya Pepe, a catechist.
7.1997	Marcelline's health deteriorates. Ya Pepe accompanies her to the Red Cross Hospital in Mbandaka. A few days later she is repatriated to Rwanda. Virginie and I are thrown out of Batsina by Ya Pepe's family. We find a new host family in the village of Bonde.
10.1997	Frans, a Dutch friend, finds us in Bonde after a long search. We leave with him for Mbandaka.
11.1997	With the help of colleagues in the Zairian NGOs, we leave Mbandaka for Kinshasa, where we stay until the end of March 1998.
4.2.1998	We arrive in Belgium, four years after my departure from Kigali.

Chronology of Political Events in Rwanda

1959	Social revolution. The Hutu majority rebels against the Tutsi monarchy. Thousands of Tutsi flee the killings and take refuge in neighboring countries, particularly Uganda, Burundi, and the Belgian Congo.
1962	Rwanda becomes an independent republic with Grégoire Kayibanda as president.
1962–67	Tutsi rebels carry out armed attacks against Rwanda, attempting to assume power by force.
12.1963	Tutsi refugees launch a raid from Burundi.
1972	Widespread massacres of Hutu in Burundi, carried out by the Burundian army, the majority of whom are Tutsi. Rwandan Hutu take this attack personally and avenge themselves on the Rwandan Tutsi, in particular the intelligentsia. In 1973 hundreds of Tutsi flee to neighboring countries.
1973	Coup d'état installs Juvénal Habyarimana as head of state.
10.1.1990	Under the name of the Rwandan Patriotic Front (RPF), Tutsi rebels based in Uganda invade Rwanda.
3.1991	Beginning of multiparty system.
2.1993	Large-scale offensive by the RPF. More than nine hundred thousand people displaced.
8.4.1993	Signing of Arusha Accords between the Rwandan government and the RPF.
10.21.1993	Assassination of the democratically elected Burundian President Melchior Ndadaye. Many Rwandans begin to have doubts about the democratic process.
11.1.1993	Deployment of troops from UNAMIR.
12.28.1993	A battalion of RPF troops arrives in Kigali to protect RPF politicians.
4.6.1994	The presidential airplane is shot down. President Habyarimana is killed along with the head of the Rwandan army. Beginning

of the Tutsi genocide and massacres of those Hutu accused of being allies of the RPF.

4.7.1994	Prime Minister Agathe Uwilingiymana is assassinated along with ten soldiers from the UN. The battalion of RPF troops based in Kigali attacks FAR.
4.8.1994	Formation of an interim government. Jean Kambanda named Prime Minister.
4.21.1994	UN Security Council decides to reduce the number of UNAMIR troops from 2,500 to 278.
6.22.1994	UN Resolution 929 authorizes humanitarian aid under French auspices. The following day, Operation Turquoise begins. French soldiers enter Rwanda through Goma and Bukavu.
7.4.1997	Kigali falls to the RPF. Two days later a transitional government is announced.
7.15.1994	Massive exodus of Rwandan refugees to Zaire. In a few days more than 1.5 million people enter Kivu through Goma and Bukavu.
7.21–28.94	During this week between fifty thousand and eighty thousand refugees die of cholera in Goma.
8.1994	Deployment of UNAMIR II. Complete retreat of Operation Turquoise. New exodus of refugees. Installation of the refugees in camps in the regions of North and South Kivu.
11.8.1994	The UN Security Council decides to create the International Criminal Tribunal for Rwanda to prosecute those Hutu responsible for acts of genocide and other serious human rights violations.
4.11.1995	Attack on Birava camp in the area of Bukavu. This attack, which left thirty dead and around one hundred wounded, was attributed to the RPF.
8.16.1995	The UN lifts the embargo on arms deliveries to Rwanda. The Zairian government protests this decision and braces for an escalation of violence in the region.
8.19.1995	Operation aimed at forced repatriation of Rwandan and Burundian refugees. Thirteen thousand Rwandan refugees and two thousand Burundians are forced to return to their countries.
10.1995	Zairian government delivers ultimatum to the refugees. They must leave the country by December 31, 1995.
1.1996	Zairian authorities forbid any economic activity or youth organizations in the Rwandan refugee camps.

2.1996	Administrative closure of Nyangezi II camp near Bukavu and Kibumba camp near Goma. For two weeks the camps are surrounded by Zairian troops.
2.15.1996	The Zairian army arrests ten Rwandans suspected of being "intimidators" and transfers them to Kinshasa to be imprisoned.
3.8.1996	End of UNAMIR II mandate.
6.29.1996	Madame Sadako Ogata, UN High Commissioner for Refugees, appeals to the Rwandan government to send "signals" to convince the refugees that is safe to return home.
9.1996	Kinshasa accuses the armed bands of Banyamulenge of attacking Zaire from Burundian territory and accuses the UNHCR, the International Organization for Migration, and the Rwandan, Burundian, and Ugandan armies of giving them logistical support. Armed people cross the border between Rwanda and Zaire heading toward the Mulenge Plateau in the province of South Kivu. The Zairian border-crossing at Bunagana on the Ugandan frontier is attacked by people coming from Uganda.
9.22–24.96	Exchange of fire between Cyangugu and Bukavu.
10.1996	The hospital at Lemera is attacked by the Banyamulenge. Many patients are killed, medications are stolen, and vehicles are set on fire. The same night the priests in the Catholic parish of Kidote are murdered.
10.21.1996	Around 250,000 Rwandan and Burundian Hutu refugees flee the camps in the region of Uvira.
10.25–26.1996	Kibumba Camp near Goma is bombarded. Around 195,000 refugees and ten thousand neighboring Zairians go to the camp at Mugunga. Heavy artillery attacks on the camp at Katale.
10.28.1996	Bukavu falls to the Banyamulenge rebels.
11.1.1996	In the area of Bukavu, Kashusha, INERA, and ADI-Kivu camps are destroyed by the Banyamulenge rebels. More than 250,000 people leave for Kisangani through the equatorial forest.
11.15–17.1996	In the region of Goma, Mugunga camp is surrounded and bombarded by the Rwandan Patriotic Army (formerly the RPF). The refugees are forced to return to Rwanda. Five hundred thousand go to Rwanda and two hundred thousand leave for Kisangani.
12.1996	Between 100,000 and 150,000 Rwandan and Burundian refugees flee the fighting at Goma, Bukavu, and Uvira and regroup at Tingi-Tingi, four hundred kilometers northwest of Bukavu.

1.20.1997   The Zairian prime minister announces a counteroffensive to restore the territorial integrity of the country.

2.23.1997   Kalima falls to the Banyamulenge rebels. Eight priests and three Rwandan Hutu nuns are murdered.

2.28.1997   Destruction of the camp at Tingi-Tingi. More than one hundred thousand Rwandan and Burundian refugees leave for Kisangani. One hundred kilometers from the city, they are sent toward Obilo, a little village on the railroad line between Kisangani and Kindu where a new camp was supposed to be set up.

4.1997   Fall of Kisangani. Several thousand refugees leave Obilo and go toward Mbandaka by way of the equatorial forest. The large majority go toward Kisangani to put themselves under the protection of Kabila. About fifty-two kilometers from Kisangani many among them are massacred by the rebels.

5.1997   The rebels massacre more than 1,300 Rwandan refugees in the town of Ingende.

6-8.1997   UNHCR repatriates the survivors. 62,639 people are taken back to Rwanda from the Democratic Republic of the Congo (formerly Zaire), the Congo, and Gabon.

WOMEN IN AFRICA
AND THE DIASPORA

Series Editors

STANLIE JAMES

AILI MARI TRIPP

Tired of Weeping: Mother Love, Child Death, and Poverty in Guinea-Bissau
Jónína Einarsdóttir

Surviving the Slaughter: The Ordeal of a Rwandan Refugee in Zaire
Marie Béatrice Umutesi
Translated by Julia Emerson

About the Author

Marie Béatrice Umutesi was born in Byumba, Rwanda, in 1959. A sociologist by training, she worked in rural development. The genocide of the Tutsi and the massacre of the so-called moderate Hutu in 1994 forced her to flee to Kivu in Zaire, where she lived for two years in the camps for Rwandan refugees that were set up along the border. In October of 1996, the camps were attacked by the Rwandan Patriotic Front, aided by the Zairian "rebels" and destroyed. One group of refugees returned to Rwanda and another fled toward the western part of Zaire, relentlessly pursued by the armies under the control of the Rwandan Patriotic Front. They were abandoned by the international humanitarian organizations that should have protected them. They were hunted like animals and most perished in the forests of Zaire or were massacred far from the view of the international community, despite the fact that the international humanitarian organizations had been alerted from the beginning of these attempts at ethnic cleansing by the Rwandan Patriotic Front.

The author, in the company of these condemned refugees, crossed the entire immensity of Zaire from east to west on foot. This is the searing account of her experiences.